# Chicken Soup for the

## Indian Women Soul

# Chicken Soup for the Indian Women Soul

101 Stories to Open the Hearts and
Rekindle the Spirits of Women

**Jack Canfield
Mark Victor Hansen
Reema Moudgil**

*Westland Ltd*

We would like to acknowledge the following publishers and individuals for permission to reprint the following material. (Note: the stories that were penned anonymously or that are public domain are not included in this listing.)

The Red Bicycle. Reprinted by permission of Parul Sharma. © 2010 Parul Sharma.

Speaking Out Aloud. Reprinted by permission of Harini Prakash.© 2010 Harini Prakash.

Small Gestures, Big Picture. Reprinted by permission of Lalitha Menon. © 2010 Lalitha Menon.

(*Continued on page 352*)

**westland ltd**
61, 2nd Floor, Silverline Building, Alapakkam Main Road, Maduravoyal, Chennai 600 095
93, 1st Floor, Sham Lal Road, Daryaganj, New Delhi 110 002

10 9 8 7 6 5 4 3 2

ISBN: 978-93-80283-28-9

Cover design by design on u

Inside book formatting and typesetting by SÜRYA, New Delhi

Printed at Repro India Ltd.

# Contents

# Introduction

Is it coincidental that I am writing the introduction to the *Chicken Soup for the Indian Woman's Soul* on Women's Day? As I write, I recall the supreme triumph of a woman director, Kathryn Bigelow, many continents away at the Oscars and remember all the women who have triumphed on smaller platforms and changed lives and perceptions without ever being acknowledged.

Today is the birthday of the lady who was my first teacher in the world of journalism. She gave me my first story to write. Taught me the stringent rules of editing followed in the early Nineties by newspapers, drove me hard and pushed me to learn new things, open my first e-mail account, protected me from office politics and set me off on a journey that continues till date. In the interim, from then to now, she has adopted and raised two children, worked continuously, recovered from professional set-backs and kept her family and her sense of humour strong. When her daughter was about two years old, I remember her buying more books than clothes for her. We lost touch and yet when I recently had my first art show, she was there, to write me a cheque for the biggest painting on the wall. Her style of supporting others is no-nonsense. But it is true. And when she holds your hand, she never lets go.

That's true for most women. They don't bail out easily on relationships, marriages, life. I have friends I have seen just once in over twenty-five years, who call me when I'm in a crisis and tell me things I can't read between the lines of my life.

There is a friend in New Delhi who lost her husband to a terrorist attack and never uses that as an excuse to feel sorry for herself. She takes care of her parents, her child and her friends when they need her and even when she is tired or hurt or angry, her first response is to laugh. And never in bitterness.

Then there is a neighbour, a beautiful lady far older than me, who bakes for me, drops in often to admire my cat, my child, my home, the blue stars decorating my door and lifts my spirit and soothes my cares. Some day, I want to be her and have love enough for life at seventy, to decorate my home with fresh flowers everyday and float a tea light in a bowl of petals outside my door every morning.

So many women have helped build my career and my life, wiped my bloody knees, ranted at the world with me, gone out of their way to give me a chance to be new, broken their hearts for me when I have broken mine, laughed and cried with me at the movies, shared desserts and sorrows, watched me struggle and occasionally triumph with the purest sense of kinship, without expecting anything in return and I feel blessed that today I can thank them all.

And offer this book to them and to those who need such friends too but have not found them yet. You probably know by now that everything serves a purpose. Suffering, most of all, because it almost always births something new. As a woman, you go from one skin to another. You search. You find. You keep. You lose. You become. You cease to be.

Everything leads to something. To someone. And everyone comes or leaves or stays for a reason. To give something. To take something. To teach something. To learn something from you.

Everything that happens to you has one purpose. To show you your real strength.

So the boy who broke your heart at eighteen did it because you needed to learn that there was life beyond him. That you could be more than you. That you were more than the girl he crushed without noticing. A failed marriage enabled you perhaps to look beyond the formula that works most of the time and was supposed to work for you. The formula that sums you up as a little x in a mathematical equation made up of relatives, parents, extended families, neighbours, children—where everything depends upon whether you are an even or an odd number. Whether you add up. Or not. All this so you would figure out that you are more than a number. That you are you.

Still, sometimes the questions will return. Why? Why me? There will be no obvious answers. No signs chalked on the blackboard of the universe. But then, one day, the questions will cease to matter because you would have walked away from them. And you will look at yourself in the mirror and say, 'Is this me? Did I pick myself up and walk this far, to look like this? Feel like this? Who did this?'

So maybe that was the whole point. So you would know that nothing really can break a woman without her consent. And that a woman always has a choice to soar or to suffer. A woman lives out many stories. Stories of loss. Pain. Failures that jeopardise careers. Lives. Relationships. They can be about illnesses that she or her loved ones suffered through. Stories about the children she has. Or could not have.

And all those stories find their way in this book. But all stories have one thing in common. The woman in them chose to soar. And now it's your turn. Your story. Your choice. Your chance to soar. Because it's your life and no one runs it but you.

*Reema Moudgil*

# 1

# LIFE LESSONS

*I* make the most of all that comes and the least of all that goes.

—Sara Teasdale

# The Red Bicycle

I must have been about nine when I learnt how to ride a bicycle. I taught myself, taking the cycle out in a leafy, shaded gulley next to our house every afternoon and teaching myself the fine art of balancing on two wheels and not crying too much when I fell down. I was very proud of myself when I finally started to ride the cycle like a grown-up, and quickly became almost surgically attached to the red bicycle—a hand-me-down from my sister—taking it everywhere, to friends' houses or running small errands for my mother.

The following year my father, a doctor who worked for the government, was posted in a small town. There were no schools there and my parents decided that my mother would stay back with the three of us while he went away. Though they did not make a fuss about it, it could not have been an easy decision for them. After all, they had not lived apart in the fifteen years that they had been married.

There were other practical implications too. Left to her own devices, my mother would now need to assume all the responsibilities that had thus far firmly fallen in my father's domain. She would need to buy groceries and drop my younger sister, all of five, to school everyday. She would need to go to the bank and take us to the doctor when one (or as it happens in families with multiple children, all) of us fell

ill. She would have to take us to birthday parties and attend
family functions and weddings.

I will leave the scooter behind for you, said my father. The
scooter would be of much help, given that Dehradun had
practically no local public transport to speak of at the time.
Local taxis weren't plying then. There were hardly any buses
doing the local rounds. There were motorised three-wheelers
or auto-rickshaws and seven-seaters, inexplicably called
'vikrams', but these were not sustainable options. The scooter
it would have to be, but these were the Eighties and women
in small-town India were hardly ever seen riding two-
wheelers. She knew that she would stick out a mile on her
scooter, a lone warrior representing womanhood in a sea of
facial hair. She did not care, she said, she would do what
needed to be done.

Even accounting for her attitude, there was still one problem
in this solution.

My mother had never learnt how to ride a bicycle. Without
the ability to balance on two wheels, how would she ever
manage to ride a scooter?

I will learn, she declared, possibly surprising herself as
much as she did us with this return to first principles. At
thirty-five, like most women of her generation, she had worn
a sari since the day she got married—not the best gear to go
riding a bicycle in.

You help me, she said, and I agreed. Every evening, I
would hold the bicycle from behind as she strived for balance.
We drew many stares in the beginning, a tall, ungainly pre-
teen instructing her beautiful mother with a sari flapping
about her feet, both trying to conquer a moody bicycle. A
reversal of traditional roles, perhaps, but she did not cower
once. It was perhaps just as well that I was at an age where
embarrassment did not come easily. Day after day we went
at it, sometimes assisted by Pinky, the landlady's domestic

help, an older girl with ribbons in her hair and a desire to help in her heart. The two of us would shout encouragement at my mother as she tried to learn the unfamiliar drill of placing both her feet on the bicycle's pedals and not have it fall to one side, taking her with it.

It did not come easy, not by a long shot, but she did it. This however, as we know, was only step one. She still needed to master the scooter, a bigger foe. She did not have too much time. My days of teaching were over. My father was the only one who could teach her and he had only a few days before he left for his new assignment. Again, she gritted her teeth and set about conquering the two-wheeled horse. She learnt how to shift gears and to release the accelerator gently at the same time. Half the battle had been won, my father told her, because she had already learnt how to balance herself.

The scooter was hers. She was independent. At thirty-five, she took over a role that she had been unprepared for all her life, shielded from the world first by her father, then by an older brother and subsequently by a protective husband. She used the scooter extensively in the time that my father was away, using it to give her children the best lives that she could, drawing gawks and attention from people not used to seeing a woman on a two-wheeler wherever she went but seeming not to care a whit. Slowly, other women, mostly young girls, started to appear in the streets of our town on two-wheelers, getting their first taste of independence. Our landlady, a graceful lady in her forties, finally learnt how to drive her car.

I don't know if she realised it then, but she taught us, her three kids, many lessons with that scooter of hers.

She taught us that parents don't care how ridiculous they look if what they are doing is good for their children.

She taught us that if what you are doing is worthwhile, it does not matter what the world thinks of it.

She taught us that it is great to be able to do things first, before everyone does, to start a trend even.

She taught us that we could do anything that a man could.

She taught us that it's never too late to learn a new skill, that it may take longer but it will become yours with perseverance.

And it all started with my beloved red bicycle. I look back at it now and I am still very proud of how I taught myself how to ride it. But I am prouder of my mother for teaching herself.

*Parul Sharma*

# Speaking Out Aloud

I come from a typical south Indian family from Palakkad that left its verdant past in search of a brighter future.

My sisters and I were generally very well brought up, except when caught after a rather rough game of dice, eight corners or four corners! My mother would have a tough time separating us, hearing us out and settling our disputes in the fairest way possible. Unknown to her and to us, we were already soaking up lessons that would later establish standards for judging situations and differentiating right from wrong. One lesson from my mother that has stayed with me till date is to stand up for what is right, whether the matter involves me or anyone else. My father was more silent and reserved. He was not really expressive, except on rare occasions.

My father worked for the Defence Estates Service in a highly respected but rather low-paying government job in those times. One of the rewards of the job was the annual transfer to a new place, which we sisters looked forward to with a great deal of excitement and joy, and one that my mother dreaded! We changed more schools than most people I know. The lifestyle came with its fair share of pitfalls but to a greater extent we all stand benefited. It made us open, friendly and fairly independent.

The incident that remains seminal to my life and continues

to guide and inspire me to date happened when my father was stationed in Jabalpur, a small town in Madhya Pradesh. The place did not have many good schools then and the one we studied in was no exception. Often teachers would not attend school because there was an India–Pakistan cricket match being aired on television. We did not have regular teachers for most subjects, and the school would often bring in part-time or ad-hoc teachers who were not serious about the job and were only doing it for the money.

We had one such teacher who taught us chemistry. I was then in Class 11. He was a young man just out of college, handsome but arrogant. In the first few days of his initiation, he impressed students, both girls and boys, with his plans about how he intended to finish the allotted portion. Then gradual changes in his behaviour made us aware that he had a roving eye. Everything he taught us took on a subtle sexual note, something I found very difficult to tolerate. None of the girls or boys could muster the courage to report his activities to the principal as we were already lagging behind in our portions and the year was quickly drawing to an end.

Then one day he crossed the line. During one of these lectures, while explaining the process of electrolysis, he referred to a cathode as a female part and the anode as a male part. It became his favourite topic and many more examples came our way to clarify the 'process'. It was then that I decided to zone out of the proceedings and block him out of my mind. It was easy to do that sitting on the last bench—I read a comic or two while he went on and on.

One day, he noticed my non-participation in his class. After a poke or two from my friend Sunita, I stood up with a blank expression. He had just asked me a question and I had not even heard it. As always, it was regarding the movement of ions in electrolysis. When I said I did not know the answer he asked why I wasn't paying attention while he taught. This was just the opening I was looking for. I immediately replied, 'Because you were teaching sex while I was expecting chemistry. I did not want to confuse the two subjects so I thought it would be better to study at home rather than listen to you in the class.'

He was livid with rage, red with shame and the entire class was in total silence. For my part, I must admit, my knees were knocking and I was scared to death by this exhibition of my spunk and impudence. I had established myself as a heroine, of course, but I had to face the consequences alone.

What followed was worse. He complained to the principal who called me to his office and demanded that I apologise. I explained my version of the incident but the principal, despite his show of sympathy, expected me to blindly 'respect elders'. I would have none of it. The result was that my father was telephoned and told that his daughter had become a menace and a nuisance. I stood outside the office, sullen, angry and not knowing what to expect. Would I be suspended or would my father scold me for my foolishness? I did not know.

The minutes dragged slowly and half-an-hour later my father came. He seemed anxious and knew it had to be more serious than just another prank for he had never been summoned to the principal's office. A few minutes later I was called in. The principal narrated the whole incident to my father who listened and looked at me, with a faint curiosity and a smile lurking in his eyes though his face was grim.

He then calmly told the principal, 'Sir, I think that you should be careful about the teachers you employ. I don't see any reason why my daughter should apologise. In fact she has done the right thing.'

That moment established between us a new feeling of trust and in me a sense of self-belief that has only grown deep with time. I realised that he may not be the kind who would routinely put an arm around me, but he was a rock I could lean on in times of crisis.

I do not know what transpired next but the next day we learned that the teacher had been removed and very soon we were to have a new one, hopefully someone with better credentials!

If my father had not stood by me that day, perhaps I would not have become the person I am today. Someone who always stands up for what is right and is never afraid of stating cold facts in the light of truth.

*Harini Prakash*

# Small Gestures, Big Picture

I had just joined a company as a corporate trainer and was feeling quite lost in the crowd of strangers and unfamiliar surroundings.

At the end of a second desultory week, a colleague came up to me and said, 'Hello, I am Naveen. How are you? You seem to be very lonely! Why don't you join our group for lunch?' Hesitantly I joined him and his other colleagues.

One day, as I was creating a module for my training and working painstakingly on a Power Point presentation, Naveen came up to me and asked, 'What are doing? Can I look at it?'

After taking a look he remarked, 'This is good but can I help you to make it better?'

I was to discover in the days to come that Naveen was a wonderful, sincere, but strict teacher as he helped me to negotiate complex software and unleashed my creativity—for no reason other than that he just wanted to help. I discovered new ways of doing old things and the newfound confidence and joy reflected in my work.

Soon, I had to conduct a training programme in a school and Naveen as usual monitored if my Power Point presentation was working, if there were gaps in my module and what were the areas that I needed to fine-tune. My programme was a success and I got much appreciation from several people over the next few days, but I knew that Naveen deserved all the credit.

Then there came a time when I had the chance to be the MC for the Apex Realty Conclave 2008, which had many dignitaries and eminent architects congregating from all over the world. After the conference, I received a standing ovation for coordinating and conducting the programme and for the Power Point presentations and films that I'd made for it. I also received an email from a dignitary stating that, 'Your imprint was seen on the fine film screened during the conference'.

And then I remembered the lonely person I had been in the first few weeks of my new job and how a kind stranger had taken the time to speak to me and teach me something that empowered me and brought me appreciation that I had never imagined. Naveen soon left us for greener pastures, but he left an indelible impression on my life and it is because of him that I am now totally at home with my work in the office. More importantly, the 'fine imprint' seen in the films has been transferred to my life as well, and it never ceases to amaze me just how powerful the smallest gestures of kindness are.

I have understood now that we must never underestimate the power of our actions. With one small gesture, we can change a person's life.

*Lalitha Menon*

# A New Gaze, A New Life

Tiny flakes sat on the window beyond which was a landscape of barren trees and snow-topped peaks. Strangely enough, today's dark and cold evening offered her the warmth for which she had been looking for years. This was her second winter in Montreal. She remembered her first, when she had sat in the airport lobby and shivered in her thin coat. She had been fidgeting with the coattails looking for something. This was not the offshoot of jetlag or nervousness of a rookie traveller. Neither was it sorrow at having left behind loved ones. It was just an inexplicable niggle, even though she had no longing to go back.

Today, sitting on a pew by the window, she drew refreshing draughts from an innermost fount of joy. She had made up her mind to go back to where it had all begun. She had decided to go home. But it was not an easy decision to make after she had closed the doors of her heart and had resolved that nothing would ever change her mind to return to her roots.

She was about to meet François for one last time. She smiled recalling how she had met him first. She had stumbled into the dimness of a great hall that contrasted with the sunshine outside. A blind man had assisted her in climbing up the stairs and directed her to a dark corner where she could sit and eat. And then he had read out the menu to her. This blind man was François and only later did she realise that this was a restaurant run by blind people where food was eaten in complete darkness.

Today, sitting by the window, peering at the frozen life outside, her mind again drifts to the times when her family had virtually disowned her. It had happened because she had given birth to a 'special' child. No one wanted to be around disability and they despised the baby doubly so because she was born a girl and was diagnosed with cerebral palsy which would impair her ability to walk, see, and hear. The baby would hold her little finger and smile, as if trying to cheer her but the tears flowed relentlessly.

Shaan, her husband, filed for a divorce soon after as he found it difficult to handle the situation. She got sympathy but no one offered help of any kind. Her relatives refrained from coming anywhere near her so she took it upon herself to raise her child. She named the baby Antara. As years galloped by, she grew lonelier. For her, life had come to a grinding halt and threatened to remain like that forever. And one night, she mulled how she wanted to spend the rest of her life. Life forked out in two diverse directions. One was to continue living in a state of limbo and the other was to break free and start life anew. She decided to give up her six-year-old Antara to an institution. She resolved to go somewhere where people wouldn't know her. A place she could start living again.

She saw in Antara's eyes a minefield of questions ... questions she had no answers to. She quietly packed her bags and then led her daughter out of the house into a waiting car.

Montreal was the destination where she planned to spend the rest of her life, and where she would live strictly on her own terms. She was not tied to any responsibilities here. But something niggled and told her that she had not done the right thing. She would often think of Antara and her eyes would fill with tears. Thoughts of her baby plunged her heart in darkness. And that began to affect her life too. She began to avoid light and people. Once she was roaming on the quiet streets when she heard someone crying, 'Neela ... Neela'. She still does not know if she imagined that voice or if someone was really calling out to her, but she ran till the voice stopped following her and that is how fate brought her at the doorsteps of François.

Unexpectedly, a bond developed between both of them. She felt some peace in this strange world of dimness but slowly, on the insistence of François, she began to meet him in the world of sunshine unmarred by shadows. She became, for François, the gaze that saw the world on his behalf and translated it to him. He would ask her how lively the world looked on a sunny day. And she would fall short of words to describe the world and its beauty that till now had looked so lifeless to her. One day, she managed to venture out in the open all on her own where people milled around her. It felt strange. She felt like a blind person who had, for the first time, seen sunlight. Soon she began to feel lighter and better. And ironically, it was a blind man who had led her into seeing a world of light and happiness. She no longer wanted to run away from the world.

She called up Antara and spoke to her. Her cheery voice melted her frozen heart and brought a flood of tears to her eyes. Soon she was at home with the child who was the core of her existence. She knew she would never leave Antara among strangers again. The world of sunshine finally was theirs to claim, and it was all because of a wise friend and teacher who had a dark world but a sunny heart.

*Pooja Nair*

# A Birthday to Remember

It was on a fine Sunday that I had my first glimpse of Bangalore. I had imagined it to be sparkling with life but what I saw was a faint representation of the world I had dreamt about! I moved half-heartedly into the women's hostel and was informed that I would be sharing my room with a girl named Maya.

Inside the hostel, I was met with blank, unfamiliar faces. I was ushered into a tiny room by the hostel warden. The stuff inside the room was neatly arranged. I wondered how Maya would take to a stranger in her space and how I would take to her.

My mind drifted back to old friends left behind in Mumbai, and to my parents who had left Bangalore that morning after dropping me. There had been a few calls from my friends to enquire if I had reached safely, but since afternoon, there had been no more calls and there was no trace of my roommate either. It was my twenty-fourth birthday the next day and my heart plunged into deep gloom at the thought that I would be all alone tomorrow in a city that I was beginning to hate already.

I remembered wistfully all the birthdays when my room would be alive with non-stop chatter all day. My mother would replenish supplies of sweets and snacks every five minutes. But this time, there would be no revelry, no friends to celebrate the occasion with, and no family.

Tomorrow, I would be joining the office where I would meet another bunch of strangers. I then curled up on my solitary bed and snuggled under the sheets with a book and a teddy bear for company. I must have dozed off because I woke up with a start when a loud knock rattled the door. I bumped into the bedpost twice in a soporific trance as I struggled to unlatch the door. I spotted a bunch of girls outside, with huge grins on their faces and a lovely cake in their hands. The cake had a congratulatory message and my name inscribed in icing. The girls had also brought streamers and balloons of several colours. One of them threw confetti in the air while everyone sang in unison, 'Happy Birthday!'

Was I dreaming? 'Oh, I was just not expecting this,' I muttered.

'What is life, if not full of sweet surprises? Hi, I am Maya,' said a pretty girl, about my age. She clasped my hands in hers and hugged me, while the others smeared my face with cake crumbs. These girls were Maya's friends; some of them worked in her office. I learnt from one of the girls that my parents had mentioned, in passing, the date of my birthday to the hostel warden, who in turn had informed Maya. They had planned to get a birthday cake for me and wish me at twelve in the night.

I was surprised and touched beyond words by this act of kindness. It then struck me that I had formed an opinion about everything, from the city to the people living in it, even before I had got to know them. On the other hand, the girls who had never met me or known me had made extraordinary efforts to make my birthday special. From that day onwards, I decided never to prejudge anything or anyone. Needless to say, my roommate went on to become one of my good friends and Bangalore too befriended me with open arms.

*Pooja Nair*

# Living Beyond Death

They were wheeling her into the operating room and she couldn't manage to keep the tears from spilling over. Shuchita had heard about life being an irony, but she was now living the irony. It was the same time last year that she had actually distributed sweets for not having conceived, laughing at the bewildered looks she had attracted. She had explained to her mother that she was not ready for a child just yet; after all it had been only a year since she was married and she was not sure she could handle the responsibilities that came with a child.

But this year things had reversed totally. Two weeks earlier, she had been confirmed pregnant and had celebrated once again by distributing the same sweets. And they had laughed at her again! But Shuchita was now ready to have a baby. And she was ecstatic about it. Until the day things began to go wrong.

Shuchita was enjoying her daily siesta when she suddenly felt something inside her give way and something started oozing out of her. She reached for the phone, clutching her belly, and dialled her mother. In half an hour, Shuchita was in the hospital. Her water had broken prematurely and it probably meant that the baby was lost. And her worst fears were confirmed. The doctor said curetting would have to be done, but also that she could try again for a baby in just three months.

As Shuchita lay recuperating, she thought of how easy life was when she was a little girl; and how traumatic and complex it had become now. Her mother had gone home to get her fresh, homemade food. Her dear husband was sitting by her bedside, like a rock, although he was broken inside too. But where was her father? He had not come to see her and that was quite strange. Just then her father walked in, looking spent and uncharacteristically weak.

Shuchita asked him about it, but he evaded the issue and said he was absolutely fine. Too weak after the operation herself, Shuchita let it go at that and closed her eyes to rest. She fell asleep only to wake up after two hours to the smiling face of her mother.

Her mother was a strong lady, who had braved many battles with a stoic heart. Shuchita had forgotten about her worry for her father's health and the day passed in a haze. The next day Shuchita was discharged and her husband took her home. She had expected to see both her parents at home to receive her, but she saw no one. Something was wrong, she thought, and when confronted, her husband blurted out the truth. Her worst fears were confirmed. Her father was critical and in hospital, on his death bed. Shuchita demanded that her husband take her to the hospital immediately. When she reached there, she took charge of the situation and started caring for her father and her mother, who was shaken to the core.

The end was near, the doctor had said, and there was little hope. Every minute she wondered, 'Will Papa come out of it? Will he survive?' She could not bear to face the truth. A rare strength kept her going, and she stood calmly by her mother in her hour of need. After forty-five days of hospitalisation, her father was considered out-of-danger and allowed to go home. Shuchita couldn't believe her ears. The doctors said that it was a miracle that he had survived. Her baby had died, but her father had survived. There was a God somewhere, after all, to even it all out.

Her father gradually gathered enough strength to go out for a walk. Things were looking better now. Six months later, Shuchita discovered she was pregnant again. This time the doctor advised her complete bed-rest. Her poor mother had to look after two patients now: Shuchita and her frail father. On one hand, it was about strengthening a man who had hovered dangerously between life and death and on the other, it was about nurturing a life yet to be born. Her mother was doing a great job of walking the tightrope between life and death.

It was spring. A time to rejoice really, but Shuchita felt uneasy. The day dawned, hot and humid, without a leaf moving in the trees. Ominously enough, the birds too were nowhere to be seen nor heard. Sipping her morning tea, Shuchita had a sense of foreboding. All was not going to be well.

Just then she heard her mother scream, and she ran inside. Her father had collapsed. It all happened in a frenzy; the ambulance came and her mother and her husband took him to the hospital. She stayed home as she was not allowed to travel. In the evening, her husband came home to fetch her. The end was near; she could see it in his eyes, feel it in her bones. Her stomach rumbled, more from fear than hunger. And she went, just in time to see her father breathe his last. This time God had not heard her fervent pleas. A month later, she was again being wheeled into the operation theatre. This time too, her water had broken. But this time the doctor had said that the baby would possibly survive. They would have to get it out fast.

But as Shuchita had discovered earlier, life was not always

easy. The doctor told her that her baby had only forty per cent chances of survival. The odds were stacked against her. Drawing from her inner reservoir of faith and courage, she prayed to God to not take her baby away and to give her the strength to face what lay ahead. She went through the tough C-section with an inner calm. Then she heard her baby cry. Loudly, clearly, and triumphantly, announcing its arrival to the world. 'Welcome dear baby, welcome!' she said to herself but why weren't the doctors telling her, like they did in Hindi movies, whether it was boy or a girl? Then she asked, and they said, it was a boy. 'Is he normal?' she asked. After an excruciating few minutes, they said yes. They added, 'But he is tiny and will have to be kept in an incubator.'

Heavily sedated as she was, she closed her eyes. They took her baby away for two weeks. Then he was back with her. A tiny, frail boy weighing three pounds. But he had survived. And, would survive. She knew it. God had once again taken one life and spared another.

Her father was gone, and though it took her long to accept it, Shuchita finally began to believe in the idea of the imperishability of the soul. She had come to believe that the soul never dies, because in the eyes of her strapping young son, ready to take on the world, she can see her father's undying love for life.

*Sonali Brahma*

# Dear Diary

Like many other south Indian teenage girls of my generation in the mid-1990s, I too went into a paroxysm of panic at the sight of boys. Talking normally to them was out of question, especially if one's hands were given to trembling and legs to shivering, and the heart usually did double beats at the sight of the male species.

'What is wrong with me?' I would often ask myself. I was on the verge of entering my mid-teens, and talking to a boy seemed like a Himalayan task. Oh, I wanted to interact with them as normally and naturally as possible, but I simply did not have the confidence. I could sense that I lacked something to which I could not put my finger on. To talk to a boy known to my family was absolutely fine, but a stranger or a classmate was unknown and daunting territory. I tried hard to smile at my classmates, but my lips froze. I read books to improve my self-esteem, observed wistfully other girls when they talked to boys oblivious of their gender.

Writing was another matter altogether, and writing letters to pen-friends, even boys whom I had never met, was my forte. I shared my debilitating weakness with one of my pen friends who was the same age. He wrote back to say, 'You have to face this truth. In daily life, you will have to interact with several men. And above all, you will have to live with a man. Unless you get over your inhibitions, how are you going to manage your future?'

These words probably did make a little difference. Months rolled by. I was taking baby steps to overcome my shyness, but approaching a boy for the first time even for any kind of assistance was beyond me. I was determined to get over this.

And then, an idea struck me. One day, back from class, I decided to turn my fears over to a diary. I listed what I wanted to achieve in the years to come. I prepared a list of questions to figure out just what the root of this fear I had was. And what was the worst fate that could befall me if I spoke to a boy! I began writing down my inhibitions, fears, resolutions, ideas and soon the burden of unresolved conflicts lifted off my shoulders as my diary began to absorb them.

I started looking at this diary almost every day. Whenever I felt low or high, I would write my feelings down. And even my pep talks to myself found their way into the diary, 'You are doing better. Your confidence has improved a little. Keep going.' I kept writing and kept trying to live out the answers I wrote down in my real life interactions with the opposite sex. On some days, I would hold this diary in my hand like a talisman and recite something in front of the mirror to bolster my confidence.

Within a year, I was feeling comfortable, and in the second year, I was completely at ease with boys. I even noticed other girls staring at me and wondering how I could manage to interact so easily and naturally with boys and girls alike.

I smiled to myself, thinking of the days I had to struggle through to gain the confidence I had today. It was just the beginning of my journey to meet and interact with hundreds of men in my social and professional life. Finally I started a life with my husband, without any complexes.

I had used my diary as a great tool of change, of self-improvement and self-expression. I realised then that when we befriend ourselves we can befriend anyone.

*Resmi Jaimon*

# Many Helping Hands

It was 1990. I was a headstrong, self-willed, young, twenty-four-year-old woman in the last month of my first pregnancy. I had spent a good part of the previous year in bed 'resting' as the doctor had instructed, and my restless nature had made me quite difficult to live with.

My husband had lost his beloved mother recently after a prolonged illness, and I was too immature to give him space to grieve. When I found that he could not spend all of his time with me, I withdrew into a shell. I made myself believe that I could manage myself and my about-to-be-born baby and needed no help. Of course, outwardly, there was no sign of anything amiss, but I kept feeding this toxic feeling that I needed no one. I refused help from everyone and lived rather dangerously for a woman just twenty days away from giving birth.

And then, one day, my water broke and my mother, who I was staying with, asked me to speak to the doctor because I wasn't due as yet. I called the doctor and she wanted me to come over instantly. Ignorant as I was, I thought I would go for the check-up and then turn up at office after a half-day of casual leave!

My husband was about to leave town to attend an important function and only an emergency could have stopped it but I could foresee no emergency at all. Perhaps I chose not to foresee one, annoyed that he hadn't made a conscious decision to stay back to welcome his first-born into this world.

I helped pack his bags, saw him off and then got ready for hospital. By then I was feeling a bit uneasy. My father went out to look for a taxi and came back with the bad news. The taxis and autos were on a flash strike. I only wondered if my husband had made it in time to catch the train and not how I would reach the hospital. Soon I became more than uneasy and had to sit down. All my self-assurance was dissipating fast, and I lay on the sofa watching my mother make call after call to ask people if a car was available. Most of our neighbours and friends had left for office by then. It was the era before cell phones, so we couldn't call anyone directly. A good twenty minutes later, our neighbour, Mr Ramachandran Nair, came rushing in to offer his car but the fuel, he rued, may not be enough. We would have to stop for a fuel refill before we reached the hospital.

We bundled into the car and sped off to the nearest fuel station, which was just a kilometre from our home. And there was a group of miscreants picketing on the road! We tried another station, but since we lived in an area of political decision-makers, picketing crowds had blocked most of the roads. We managed to make our way out and just a kilometre or so from the hospital, the car stopped! It was finally out of fuel. Mr Nair now hopped out in desperation and, borrowing a stranger's cycle, he rode to a fuel station. By the time he came back, after about twenty minutes, my contractions had started.

The petrol was put in the tank but it still wouldn't budge. Some people standing nearby offered to push the car and they did push for some yards, but the car would still not start.

'Saar, take the car to a workshop, it isn't going to start,' one of them joked, but then happened to look into the car, and caught sight of my face contorted in pain after a spasm had hit me. He shouted, 'Hey this is a hospital case!' Then he and his friends pushed the car, inch by inch, yard by yard till we reached the hospital!

I reached in the nick of time, and delivered a baby boy barely two hours after reaching the hospital. Perhaps it was life's way of showing me something that I would never again forget—that we all need each other and that we can never get anywhere without each other's help. I knew that day that our purpose as human beings is to graciously accept help when it is offered and extend it generously when it is asked for. God has put us on this earth for this purpose alone, and I shudder to think what would have happened that day if I had been left alone to help myself.

*Suneetha B.*

# The Unspoken

It was 6.30 p.m. My husband and I were enjoying our weekly drive to my in-laws' home. It was a pleasant evening ... not even a single cloud in the rain-washed, blue sky. As usual, I was hanging out of the car window, enjoying the wind on my face. The familiar landscape changed from the bustle of the city to green fields and tall rubber plantations. My mobile rang with the sharpness of a whiplash, jolting me out of my reverie. Wishing heartily that I had kept it on silent mode, I checked the number. It was my mother. 'Hello,' I said and waited. 'Hi dear, Achu Ammavan died half an hour ago.'

Uh-oh, I thought, there goes a treasured Sunday. 'He had been deteriorating in the last couple of days,' my mother went on.

She seemed tired, a little sad. 'How is grandma?' I asked. 'She is okay ... seems to be taking it quite well.' 'We will come tomorrow for the last rites,' I replied.

Achu Ammavan was my grandmother's younger brother. I had always called him 'ammavan' (uncle), like my mother. He had been ill for a long time with liver trouble. My knowledge of him was limited to the perception that he had always been old, and bald and wore spectacles. That he drank copiously and seemed drunk whenever he called me. Rumours of his son's negligence had been hotly discussed for some time now. He had lived not too far from my husband's home. So, we could definitely go for the funeral. But for my parents and grandparents, the journey would be long and tiring.

My parents had never believed in exposing their children to such sombre sights as funerals. Even after my marriage, this would be the first one I had ever attended. So when the morning dawned indecently bright and clear for a monsoon day, I felt oddly curious about a very grown-up event, a gathering of mourners that had come together to say goodbye to someone they had known and loved. I checked my wardrobe for something suitable to wear. It was a solemn occasion and my usual deep reds and violets wouldn't do. One hour of rummaging yielded results—a black and white churidar set; perfect.

The ceremony was scheduled to take place that afternoon. We started soon after lunch by car. The last time I had travelled this way was nearly one year back, soon after my marriage, when we had gone to visit him. His family lived in a big and comfortable house in the middle of a sprawling rubber plantation, and I remember envying them their acres. This time too, the journey was very enjoyable—the road snaking between tall trees on either side while sunlight battled fiercely and filtered through them with great difficulty. Only one thought niggled me. Ammavan used to call me regularly. At least once a week. And I had made a mental note to call him, but never did. Even when I knew he was in the hospital, I hadn't called him. But when nature was weaving her seductive charms all around, it was quite easy to shake away the cobwebs of guilt and shame.

Outside the house, my father was waiting for us. He took my hand and led us both in. On the way, I met my grandmother's youngest brother. He looked extremely tired. I went up to him. He smiled the familiar smile and asked, 'There has been no news of you since you married and went away, little one. How are you doing?' His words transported me back to my grandmother's home, where even in old age and from far distances her brothers and sisters had always gathered together. I had spent my college days with my grandparents, and so, had often been a reluctant participant in many such gatherings.

He looked at me for some time and then added, 'Keep in touch, little one, just one phone call would do,' he said softly before getting up and going away.

My grandparents hadn't come after all. My grandfather was too old and grandmother too sad. I met my mother and my aunts and a whole host of other people. After an hour of talking in respectfully low tones, the last rites started. He lay on the floor on a white cloth and looked as though he was sleeping. Outside, the skies darkened ominously. 'A storm's coming,' someone said quietly behind me. 'Hope it holds till the body is burned completely.'

I didn't wait to see the fire engulf the wasted body; my head ached and I was feeling feverish. Thunder was rolling in the distance, but there was not even a single drop of rain. 'The last time grandma talked to him, he had said he wanted to come home to her. Through the phone you could hear him ordering his servant to pack all his clothes. He said, "There is not much time. Just pack them all; I will wash the worn ones later, when I reach home,"' my mother was saying in a thick voice to my aunt. Sometime later, on the way back home, a resounding crack announced the opening of the heavens, and a cool, quiet rain fell.

I wondered if Ammavan had finally reached home. The one he would never have to leave. I wondered if it was too late to say something to him. Maybe, it wasn't. Only the living have communication gaps. He would understand. And forgive.

*Parvathy Mohan*

# My Aptitude Test

Lately, my younger son—studying in Class 9—had not been doing well in his exams, especially in languages. So I spent much time yelling, screaming and assuming that all this will solve the problem and he would somehow get more serious about his studies. Yes, I prayed too, but the stress was overwhelming.

I arranged tuitions for him, monitored him religiously and yet was called often to the principal's office and warned that he would be chucked out of the school if he didn't get above seventy-five per cent! He often came home with red remarks in his diary and books and it was tough for me to reconcile all this with a boy who I know is talented, intelligent and articulate, and is well-informed about many diverse topics.

I attributed his 'failure' to his lack of interest or application and the stress began to tell on him as well. Once after being called to the vice-principal's office, he broke down and cried uncontrollably, but didn't answer the repeated query as to why he was not studying seriously. I continued talking down to him and sermonising and lecturing, but to no avail. And, then his principal suggested that I take him to a child care centre for assessment. After going through a full day's assessment, I found out that my son is dyslexic. It was one thing to sit in a movie hall and watch a movie about dyslexia and another to know that your own son is dyslexic. Though I had adequate knowledge about the topic and was also aware that some of the most famous and successful people have been dyslexic, yet, as a mother, my first reaction was panic and the eternal question, 'Why me?' And yet, after a day or two of moping, I wiped my tears, switched off my self-pity and decided that I had to overcome this problem. I had no choice but to fight this situation with my son and for him.

I repeated to myself what the special educator had said at the assessment centre, 'Who knows? You may have an Einstein in the making or perhaps an Edison!'

I began to glean as much information as possible from the internet and found out that I had to learn new techniques of educating my son and to some extent his educators to sensitise them to his problem. I prayed that they would show him compassion and not give up on him. Thankfully, they did not.

On a roller coaster ride, shuttling between doubt and faith and hoping that we would make it through this phase if we persevered as a team, I utilised every opportunity that could help me to help my son and from the bottom of my being, wished that I could transform my pain into something others could gain from.

As a soft-skills trainer, I often refer to my life experiences, and one day, I happened to mention this incident in one of my talks. At the end of the programme, one of my trainees came to me to talk about her son who she now suspected to be dyslexic after listening to me. I gave her all the necessary information and she kept thanking me profusely. I realised at that very moment that my dream, to make my pain useful in some way for someone else, had been realised. I also understood the answer to the question, 'Why me?'

I guess, we are all given parts to play in life that show us our real potential. Adversity empowers us to help ourselves and show the way to someone else if we can. Like an eagle, I have to soar above my limitations to view the world from a different vantage point. God strategically places us in positions that we would otherwise not be in on our own, to bring out a wealth of courage within.

I have always rooted for the merits of a positive attitude in my talks, but am now practicing it. In the school of life, I, and not my son, was being put through the test and I intend to pass this challenge with flying colours, because as my favourite quote goes, 'Life is not about waiting for the storms to pass but about learning how to dance in the rain'.

*Lalitha Menon*

# Time Out

When I came back from the US to India after completing a magazine internship, I had utterly lost the urge to write. Reverse culture shock and myriad family issues had zapped my creative juices. Thankfully, I had a portfolio of published books so I had enough assignments to keep myself afloat. For nearly five months after returning, I was busy freelancing and kicking myself for coming back, when an MNC approached me for the post of a copy editor. It dangled a very attractive pay package, along with a great team to work with. The only snag was the hours—night shift.

I took the job anyway. For the first time in my life, I was part of a young and vibrant team where every person was equal, irrespective of the job hierarchy. As a freelance writer, I often had to battle loneliness, and here I had intelligent colleagues who made me laugh. Our offices were right above the biggest mall in our city, which made chats over meals and impromptu shopping a daily affair. Meals were free, the company cab picked and dropped me at my place, and every month, a fat pay cheque was deposited into my bank account. Life became positively a bed of roses.

Now, about the thorns. Everyday, you race against time to finish a project. Nerves are frayed, tempers run hot, and till the deadline is safely met, no one dares to even move away from the desk. And if a deadline is missed ... there are enquiries and paperwork and phone calls to be faced with, in addition to keeping up with the new work that crops up every day. So people are generally very careful about not missing a deadline ... which meant, yes, non-stop work and tension.

I won't say that I disliked my job. Copyediting was fine, it kept me on my toes and took care of my bills, but my muse, that child of creativity that made me a writer, was starved. And the night-shift hours were not easy to adapt to. I left home when my mom started preparing dinner and came back when the milk man deposited two milk cartons outside my gate. I was always aware of that niggling voice inside my tired mind. 'You need some rest,' it would whisper. 'Make some time for it. Or else ... it will be too late.'

I was terrified about the 'or else' factor ... and anybody who has worked in a cubicle more than ten hours a day will understand the urge to relax in a place where the colours of the earth soothe your mind. And that's why, in August 2006, I chose to go to a place in Pondicherry that was near Auroville—that universally favoured retreat, bathed in mystic tranquillity. And I decided to make it a writers' retreat, because it was time to find my lost muse.

Of course I didn't know anything about planning a retreat. With encouragement from three writers from my online writing group, I managed to book the rooms and finalise the schedule. My three companions were also busy homemakers and needed a retreat more than me! A thousand emails and phone calls later, we were finally off to a guest house in the tranquil depths of Auroville.

Only during the retreat did I fully understand how important it is to have a few days to yourself. We lazed around the guesthouse garden, just talking and writing and experiencing the peace. We explored our gingerbread cottages with their neat little patios and small ponds. One of us, who had left her two kids with her hubby, squealed at the sight of the bed at our cottage, 'I can finally sleep on a bed myself, without having four legs on my tummy!' I too fell asleep the minute I hit the bed. It was a sound, restful slumber—not only because I was sleeping in the night after a long, long time.

The retreat was a great rejuvenator. Healthy, organic food at the visitor's centre purified our body, while the serene greenery of Pondicherry flushed away our fatigue. We attempted writing exercises every day and came away with finished pieces. We walked a mile on the red earth of Auroville, looked at the sky and composed funny poems. We laughed and giggled and sang and shared secrets. In short, we forgot our worries and lived an ideal life for a short time, not unlike a second childhood.

That weekend gave me the perfect chance to think about life choices. I was so comfortable in the 'I'm-working-in-an-MNC-and-I-don't-have-time-to-write' rut that I had almost given up writing. I was in danger of forgetting who I was—a writer—and slowly turning into what I never wanted to be—a corporate workhorse, but those two days amidst lush greenery woke my muse and made me figure out my main purpose. Words and ideas, which would not even make a cursory appearance before, now poured out of my spirit.

And the most important revelation was that it's never too late to get your life back on track. We can have a hundred pressing engagements, but nothing is more crucial than recharging yourself now and then. A yoga retreat, a beach retreat with the family, or just a few days at home in meditation will work wonders in the long run. Thanks to that retreat, I found the courage to quit my soul-less MNC job and pursue a creative career. And these days I get to sleep when it's dark and write in sunlight!

*Radhika Meganathan*

# Metamorphosis

It was the last day of 2008 and I felt really old. It had been a bad day. I had entered my forties a few months back and today, for the first time, a cute young thing had called me 'aunty'. I had been shocked at first and even turned back to make sure that there was no lady behind me who was female, fat and forty. There was no one else but me. I blinked twice and realised that I was the 'aunty' in question.

Driving back home, I tried to analyse if the title I had just acquired would have wounded less had it come from a child. That a girl in her twenties had called me 'aunty' was an acid reminder that I was over the hill. The minute I reached home, I made a beeline for the mirror. Why hadn't I seen it before? The first strands of grey hair peeping out near my temples. How could I have missed it? 'Come, come,' I chided myself. 'This is the age of botox and skin clinics which can make you look twenty when you are forty. Not to mention yoga and meditation.'

But I found my shoulders drooping. The events of the morning had driven home something that I had been in denial about. I was in a state of shock and felt a bit like a female Methuselah.

I was rustling up lunch and trying to psyche myself into a cheerful mood but secretly thinking that things could not get worse. 'It's a new beginning tomorrow after all,' I told myself, 'I need to find time to colour my hair. Of course I shall have to add yoga to my list of resolutions . . .' Slowly a warm glow crept in and took over my despondency.

I did love this holiday season, especially New Year's eve. Invariably my spouse would turn up late, but for the past sixteen years, my son had been with me to ring in the new year. Each time we tried out new methods to celebrate. I smiled as I remembered how, when he had been five, we had run and thrown open the back door to let the old year out and then run back to open the door to the new year. Then when he had been twelve, we had put together a play with one of his friends dressed as the old year hobbling away and my spiky head impersonating the new year had burst into the proceedings with a shower of glitter and balloons.

I decided that I must get more innovative as my son was getting older. And then suddenly, my son poked his head through his doorway to say, 'Mom, where are my jeans? I have been searching all morning for them. I'm getting late. I must be off to Kiran's now. We are going to ring in the new year together.'

I did a double take and halted, saucepan in the air. 'You mean you won't be spending New Year's eve with us?'

'Not to worry,' he said blithely. 'I am only going to the next block, you know.'

'But we always ring in the new year together,' I said, visibly upset.

'Mom, come on. You surely don't expect me to sit here at home while my friends are all next door having a blast, do you? You can't be serious.'

Ten minutes later, the front door slammed shut. I suddenly felt like a parent who goes through the empty nest syndrome. I heard the television blaring in his room. Scatterbrained as usual, I thought, and sighed as I went into his room to switch it off. A smile flitted across my face as I saw it was Cartoon Network. Somehow it helped me cling on to the idea that my son had not left his childhood behind. It was becoming difficult these days to hold on to his childhood. I kept trying in vain now to find my boy in the long-haired, dreamy-eyed youth who spent his days locked up in his room strumming his guitar to the tune of Opeth or Nevermore.

I discovered a lump in my throat as my eyes fell on a photograph of him carrying his pet tortoise. I remembered that summery evening when my son had rushed into the house with a tortoise he had traded for some rare stamps. I saw again the tears in his eyes as days later he set it free in a nearby lake, torn between his attachment and his insistence to do the right thing always. I heard myself telling him, 'True love lets go. If you hold on to it, you will only stunt its growth. If you really love it, you will allow it to experience life in its own way.'

But the questions remained. Was he drifting away too fast now? How could any child change so much? Why do children have to grow up and go away? I felt a pang as I realised that I would be seeing him only the next year! I walked out into my garden, hoping the fresh air would bring some healing. I slumped into the rickety old swing. We had set it up for our son because he had never got a chance to get his hands on the swing in school—the girls always got to it first! The more he had grown, the less the swing had been used until it had become an antique piece in the garden. I myself had never taken time off to sit in the garden. I had always been busy, doing all the usual things a woman has to do to run a family. 'I shall find time one day to sit here with myself,' I'd tell myself. Now that I found myself in that moment, I really wondered how I could have longed to be alone. But a little while after the rusty swing had groaned under my weight, I found it really was a good place to sit when you wanted to be alone with your thoughts. You could just drift along here and there just as your thoughts did. I had just got through the hundredth reason why my New Year's eve would not be picture perfect and how both my son and my husband were heartless to leave me alone on such a day, when my eyes fell on the little cocoon growing on the plant which bloomed beside the swing.

Something fascinating was happening. A little creature was struggling to come out of the cocoon. A new life was beginning! The scene was enthralling enough to jolt me out of the same stale thoughts that had been running like a stuck record in my mind the whole of the afternoon. A new life? Rather it was a new stage in a life that had already blossomed in the garden of life. It was Life which was experimenting with a new chapter. I watched in rapt attention as the tiny little creature struggled to come out.

'Why does it need to struggle so.' I clenched my fists. Maybe I should be giving it a nudge in the right direction. I slid off the swing and went to the cocoon. I would just open the cocoon a teeny weeny bit and help the little fellow emerge, I decided heroically; sort of assist it in those last few steps to freedom from a cocooned existence. I rose and bent over the cocoon when a sharp, 'Mom, what are you doing?' made me freeze.

'What are you doing here?' I whispered as I saw my son standing at the kitchen window.

'I was wondering where you were. I came to pick up some clothes. We all decided to drive down to the beach. Kiran's mom has a farm house there. She said we could have our party there. We are going to jam a bit and then sing in the new year. No alcohol or cigarettes or any such stuff. Trust me, Mom. Just some music and my good old friends.'

Oddly enough, that did not worry me. I was the one who had nurtured his roots and I had a mother's gut feeling that they were very strong. It was the thought of him flying away that was so upsetting. I straightened up, trying to hide my hurt.

'By the way Mom, were you really trying to break the cocoon open? Didn't you know that it is the struggle the butterfly goes through to worm its way out of the cocoon that gives power to its feeble wings? Leave it alone and it will test its wings in its own time and soar.' And I thought, 'Why is it our children who sometimes bring us life's greatest lessons?'

'Hey, how come you are here, son? I saw all your friends at Kiran's.' My husband had burst into the kitchen. He continued, 'I thought you would be there.' I was surprised by his calm acceptance of the fact that our child was growing up. Maybe that is why they say that men are from Mars and women from Venus! 'Yup, I came back to pick up some clothes and also because Mom was alone. I thought I would stick around till you came to give her company.' The long-haired boy had the same bright, compassionate eyes of the spiky head who had loved a tortoise unconditionally.

The familiar, stinging lump in my throat returned as I saw the wistfulness in his eyes, the longing to be off to begin life in his own little way.

'Run along now and have fun with your friends. Hurry up. You shouldn't be missing all the fun. And as for being alone, I really don't think I'm so intolerable that I can't bear to put up with myself a few hours each day! By the way, do you want me to help you put together a few things for your night out with your friends?' My smile widened as I saw the relief in his eyes reflected in my husband's. Why did the image of a small boy valiantly swallowing back tears and releasing a tortoise in a lake, come to my mind now?

It suddenly became easy to let go. Intuitively I knew that wherever he swam across the seven seas or wherever in the big wide world he flew, he would always come back to the warm sanctuary of home. He was flapping his wings, ready to take off, and allowing him to test his wings was the greatest gift I could give him.

Later that evening, my eyes fell on the old swing and I remembered the worm's struggle and ran out. I searched high and low. There were two or three white butterflies flitting about, wrapping up their day as evening took over. How could I tell if my little worm had made it? Suddenly it became important for me to know.

Then I saw her—a beautiful orange glory resting her wings on the leaf next to an open cocoon. A new phase of her life had begun! How awful it would have been if I had meddled with and messed with the coming out of this wonderful being.

The much awaited new year's eve proved to be a quiet one. My husband was watching cricket and I was curled up with a book I had never found the time to read till then. As I rose to get us some coffee, I caught sight of my face in the mirror. The strand of grey caught my eye tauntingly, but this time I just smiled. I felt free and light, now that the fear had evaporated. It actually felt great to be forty and wiser. A whole new year, a whole new world stretched before me. No more running from pillar to post searching for a suitable crèche to keep my son while I was away at work. No more rushing back home from work on days the school bus did not drop him. All the time in the world to take up Tai chi and catch up with my writing. All the freedom to soar and let my loved ones soar.

I was not growing older. I too was just growing up.

*K. Gitanjali*

# The Goddess with the Buck Teeth

This story begins four decades ago. Like most little schoolgirls, I too loved playing the teacher, and at times, I would wrap myself in my mother's old sari to play the part. I would write on the walls in my room to her dismay! With a stick in my hand, I would pretend to hit my imaginary students. I wished to have a student in flesh and blood, who would be ever obedient and learn something from me. We humans rejoice in authority even before knowing how to spell the word, I suppose!

Before long, my prayers were answered. My mother hired a new domestic help, Hanumi. Her story was no different from any other maid in Bangalore. She had a husband who would drink and beat her up till she was black and blue or till he would collapse. She had five children—four daughters and a son. The eldest of her daughters was Laxmi. She was about eight years old, dark and with four of her front teeth protruding, lice-infested hair and bright eyes. She came to our house every day with her mother to look after her little brother who was not even a year old.

Laxmi was a responsible little mother and spent the whole day looking after him. In the evening, when I would return from school, her little ward would be sleeping and she would be bouncing around the house, touching things, gazing at newspapers, opening books and generally exploring her new surroundings. Her favourite place was my room. She would hang around while I finished my homework, always warning me not to study lest I go mad!

I recognised a potential student in Laxmi—someone who would fulfil my dream of being a teacher. So my wall became the blackboard and Laxmi, my first student! Everyday I would tempt her with my share of snacks and torture her with my teaching. Whatever I had learnt at school that particular day would be enacted, mimicking my teachers! It was fun. To my surprise I found her really 'learning', and soon she became literate! Her word power increased at an amazing pace. Our classes got more focused on language and arithmetic. She loved numbers. So did I. Soon we were more companions than tormentor and prey.

She now looked forward to my return from school and was ever ready to learn. To break the monotony, we had our share of dancing and singing and she would tell me stories of who fought with whom in her neighborhood!

All good things must come to an end, and so one fine day Hanumi and Laxmi just disappeared from my life. All our efforts to learn about their whereabouts went waste and I lost my student and companion. Later we learnt that Hanumi had left Laxmi with someone as a bonded labourer.

After a few months of sadness, I forgot all about Laxmi and got on with my studies, completed my graduation, got married and settled in distant Gujarat. Another three decades passed.

In one of my annual visits to Bangalore, I was at the bank and I spotted a sari-clad, serious, dark lady with four of her teeth protruding out. Yes, unmistakably, this was my Laxmi! She waited for me to complete my transactions in the bank, and then, with tearful eyes, she narrated her story.

When the days of her bonded labour ended, Laxmi's mother got her married to a man who was physically challenged, ill and four times older than her. Laxmi was barely fifteen years old and grew up to inherit her own quota of beatings every day. Eventually he died, leaving Laxmi to manage all his financial liabilities.

Laxmi then decided to run her own life. She began to cook simple meals for daily wage workers, auto drivers and labourers. Every afternoon, she would sell lunch portions and slowly built up her business. Today she had come to deposit her savings in the bank! Wiping her tears, she looked at me gratefully and said whatever I taught her for fun had helped her to bring her life on track! No one could cheat her now, as she could read and write, count money, keep accounts—just enough to avoid exploitation. She was 'empowered' she said.

I realised that day that any good that we do, whether consciously or unconsciously, never goes waste. That sometimes even a Laxmi needs a Mukta to set her free.

*Mukta Srinivas*

# Hello Dolly

My first job was in an American medical transcription company where I was appointed as a trainer, which is perhaps equivalent to the job of a lecturer in a college in India. Most of my students were graduates and postgraduates, but I also had a sprinkling of professionals, like pharmacists, dentists and medical language specialists. I taught them American English and found that since they were chosen due to their aptitude and command of the English language, it was not really difficult to teach them. They were keen and earnest in their approach.

Among my students—trainees, as they were called—I had one favourite student whose name was Dolly Pricilla. I say 'favourite' because she was a mischievous teenager, but underneath the froth and bubble was a serious, introspective and deep, young girl. She was petite and slender, and carried herself well. Her features were small but sharp and just a hint of make-up was enough to accentuate her subtle charm.

Well, if Dolly was just another student, maybe I wouldn't have remembered her so vividly. No, Dolly was special. She was a face in the crowd, unique and hard to ignore. And she had that one quality which I always admire in human beings, a sparkling sense of humour, which spilled over in her everyday encounters with students and trainers.

She would often make her friends—Padmaja, Parvathy and Renu—burst into peals of hearty laughter which would cease only when the trainer made her entry, at which time Dolly would switch the funny face for a serious one and say in all earnestness, 'Why are you girls laughing so much? Don't you know that you must be quiet and attentive in class?'

Dolly had that streak of mischief which fortunately was not a cunning and conniving kind. Her banter was usually innocent and harmless. It was this quaint impishness that made Dolly all the more lovable and irresistible. Once, visibly perplexed by her arduous test paper, she came up to me and said with a perfectly straight face, 'Ma'am, help me with this work. I will give you a chocolate.'

Being a strict disciplinarian, I said harshly, 'No, Dolly, this work is meant to be done independently. If I were to help you, who would be getting the grades—you or me?'

As the academic year progressed, Dolly's joie de vivre won her many fans.

But I was destined to be her biggest one, yet. On one cold, balmy day on 23 December 1998, I was at work when suddenly I got a message from the front office saying that I was required to report immediately. In this particular company, the staff is not called to the front office unless there is an emergency. Therefore, with my pulse racing and my heart pounding, I rushed to the front office. Bracing myself for a shock, I met my sister who told me that my father had suddenly suffered from a heart attack, was dying and wanted to meet me. In tears, I rushed back to the classroom to inform my students that I would be leaving and ran into Dolly who immediately asked, 'Ma'am, why are you crying?' And I was touched immeasurably because her eyes had welled up too.

Quickly, I told her what the matter was. What she said next, I will never forget. 'Ma'am, don't cry. I will pray for your father. Please pray with me and remember this prayer

aid. "The Lord attends when people
...e can hear/ He knows not only what we
...at we wish or fear/ He sees us when we are
...nough no one else can see/ And all our thoughts to
...n are known/ Wherever we may be." Take courage and
be strong, Ma'am.'

I was overwhelmed and forgot my fear and panic for a moment. I had been trying to teach Dolly things which in retrospect were insignificant. What she had taught me was profound. She had taught me to keep faith and to believe that in our darkest hours, we are watched and cared for. I was forever touched and marked gently by the wing of an angel that day.

*Heera Nawaz*

# The Craft of Life

It was a chilly November morning, and I woke up with a start. I had just remembered that I was supposed to submit my craft project to the strictest teacher of my school. I was about nine then, and of all the subjects I feared craft the most. Sometimes my friends wondered how I could solve the toughest math problems so easily and get so terrified at the thought of craft! It so happened that Ms Beena was my craft teacher, and although this was only her second class in the new semester, stories had begin to float around about how cruel and strict she was with students who disobeyed her.

I had no idea how I was to deal with her since I hadn't completed the craft assignment of the previous class. I was so terrified that my knees started shaking and I started to howl at the top of my voice that I did not want to go to school. My mother assured me that by lunch break she would get my craft assignment ready and then I had no choice but to go to school!

I waited eagerly for the day to pass fast, even cried a little in the prayer meeting in the assembly hall, hoping that I wouldn't have to stand out of the class in the craft session. Finally the lunch break arrived and I jumped out of the classroom to search for my mother, only to find her near the dreaded teacher's cabin! What on earth was she doing there instead of giving me the craft assignment! And there was Ms Beena too, laughing away merrily! They saw me peeking from a distance and called me to join them. My heart was pounding so loud that I felt the children around me could hear it too!

Ms Beena asked me, 'So Kavita, you think I am a tiger or something? You think I am going to swallow you up?'

Tears rolled down my cheeks!

In the craft class subsequently, Ms Beena could not help flashing smiles of amusement in my direction. She stopped by often and tried to make small talk and my fear began to turn into trust. Soon, I began to flower in her presence and my creativity blossomed. She became my favourite teacher and I her favourite student. In the next semester, she taught history to my class, and even though I wasn't too fond of the subject, I took to it because she made extraordinary efforts to engage me. She would come an hour earlier than usual to give me extra lessons.

Then one day, I won the best craft exhibit award of the year and went to thank her and all she did was to smile at me, the same way she had when she had watched me from a distance, crouching in fear.

Years later, when I was passing by my school building, I decided to go and meet my old teachers, and the first one to spot me was her. In her usual quiet way, she made me feel that I had made her proud. I could sense that she was thinking of the little, fearful girl of the past and was happy that she had gone out into the world and done something worthwhile with her life.

I wondered what would have become of me if she had not taken the pains to change my fear into self-assurance, if she had not helped me with the love and compassion that all great teachers in and outside our schools have for us. Teachers are often judged for being strict or being ineffective, but when they care enough to impact a student's life, miracles happen. My miracle was that the veil of fear had been removed from my life forever by a teacher who had cared enough to smile at me.

*B. Kavita Chandrashekhar*

# The Small Stuff

Every once in a while, a stranger walks into your life and
touches your world in the most unusual way. What happens
is nothing short of a miracle—a reaffirmation that God sat
with you and patted your head! And so it happened with me
too last year.

Life had always been a dream playing out for me in real
time ... from making it to a coveted degree college, to
marrying my college sweetheart, from starting a software
firm at twenty-two, to a taste of fame—there was very little
that my husband and I had not experienced in our twenties.
In fact, I secretly dreaded that something would give, for the
picture was getting eerily perfect!

The day came all right! It crept into my life stealthily and
left my family reeling in the after-effects of a tornado. All it
took was one year—of shattered dreams as we lost our
business, of broken hearts as we saw relationships disintegrate,
of loss and fear as we fought for the lives of loved ones, and
of heartaches as we struggled for financial comfort and a roof
over our heads.

Nothing was the same again, certainly not within. Jaded by
our loss, we forgot how to live, to aspire, or dream. As our
lives changed gears, we went back to corporate jobs, struggling
to put together the broken fragments of what we had. Material

side-effects aside, that one year made us lose perspective of
everything that was important to us—relationships took a
backseat, the community project my husband and I had
nurtured seemed irrelevant, and 'living life' was replaced by
surviving it.

In the meantime I had started working at a firm. Although
it did provide respite in the form of challenging and enjoyable
work, there was nothing that really filled the void of loss
deep within me—whether it was accolades at work, high-
visibility initiatives, a climb up the ladder, strategic events or
more. My life was in a premature mid-life crisis that had
come in unannounced and decided to stay! Until one office
event that changed the way I think forever!

While sipping my drink in a corner that evening, a petite
young project manager came and sat beside me. Beautifully
dressed in a salwar-kameez, she had delicate jewellry caressing
her neck and ears. I had always admired the graceful way in
which she carried herself, talking softly and smiling gently as
she spoke. The two of us had got acquainted recently and
there seemed to be mutual affinity between us. So when there
was a lull in the evening, I was glad that she came and took
a seat beside me.

She spoke, 'I want to tell you something ... it's not
something I share with everyone, but I feel like sharing it
with you.'

I was a bit surprised at the abrupt declaration but was
already all ears. I felt privileged that she had felt a connection
with me and wanted to share a part of her life with me.

'I want to tell you about my life with Ramesh.'

'Oh! Your fiancé?' I had heard her refer to him as her fiancé
once.

'Yes,' and her eyes lit up with a smile. 'Ramesh and I met
pretty much like you and your husband,' she added. 'We
were college sweethearts.'

'Oh, so you're marrying your college friend too! Wonderful! How does it feel?' I added, trying to make small talk.

'Well, he was always the most important person in my life but somehow marriage was not a concept I was ready for,' she laughed.

'What about him?' I probed.

'Oh, he was always ready! He wanted to be married to me the day we graduated!' she laughed again.

'And so, you two got engaged?'

'No, as a matter of fact, we did not get engaged for nine years after college.'

'Oh my God! You've made him wait that long!' I was truly surprised.

'Yes!' she nodded, 'He waited nine years for me to give the final nod! And all along, though I was so sure I wanted to be with him, I didn't want to marry him just then.'

'So what made you decide finally?'

'It was a simple walk in the park! Some things just cause your thinking to shift a whole paradigm, you know. He and I were walking in the park one evening, when we saw a child fall. Both of us rushed forward to save the child in an instant. That little dash to save a life completely changed my view. It was as if a dormant maternal instinct suddenly pierced my heart. And in that moment, I wanted nothing more than to be his wife, to have his children, and set up home with him! Just like that.' She finished by snapping her fingers.

'And so the two of you got engaged?'

'Not immediately. We booked a home together, met each others' families for another six months, planned an elaborate ceremony with all the rituals and a well-known priest, and finally fixed a date for the engagement!

'You know Tina, I have never been happier in my life. My engagement was the happiest day—I could literally see my dream come true before my eyes. I was going to be Ramesh's wife—the architect of our life together, the creator of our home. Both sides of the family were pampering me . . . it was all so magical!'

'Awww!' I said in affirmation. 'Your wedding's going to be even more special! Wait and watch.'

'No,' she said. 'Ramesh left the engagement ceremony after lunch to get to work. On the way to the airport, his cab collided head-on with a goods carrier and Ramesh died, Tina . . . and I didn't want anything more than to be his wife.' She was staring at the carpet before her, tearless eyes, heart clearly laden with sorrow, but speaking so matter-of-factly that I was numbed into silence.

There are times when you know what to say but don't want to express it for fear of sounding improper. This wasn't one of those times. This was a dark hole of a moment, when I could not have spoken anything for the life of me, even if I went back seven lifetimes to find the right words.

I gently put my arm around her and squeezed her shoulders.

That one moment transformed my life. How shallow I had been in my grief, how selfish, how ungrateful for crying about material comforts . . . when I had a family still intact. How weak I had been in judging the important things in life . . . how wrong!

I have little memory of how the rest of the evening went. But I distinctly remember feeling that I would give anything to heal my friend and also that, in her own way, she had repaired my life forever.

*Tina Mansukhani Garg*

# Unschooled Wisdom

After completing his engineering, Kartik was pursuing his MBA at a business school in Pune. 'What am I doing in life and why am I doing it?' he used to wonder. He had never planned anything. He just happened to go wherever life took him. His roommate was a guy called Kumar from Delhi, who was the class topper. He had a poor family to look after, that included a younger sister to marry off. So he had no choice but to score great marks and to try his best to get a well-paid job.

Kartik and Kumar were to go to Aurangabad, one of the industrial towns of Maharashtra, for their presentations. The town harbours some big names in the automobile, manufacturing and agricultural sector. Kartik was an excellent presenter, while Kumar was a genius with facts and numbers. They made an excellent team and were confident of their presentations.

They reached the Aurangabad bus station at 11 a.m., dressed in deep blue trousers and blazers, odd men out in a crowd of villagers and farmers in grimy dhoti-kurtas and turbans or Gandhi-topis. Kartik and Kumar's destination for the day was a town called Jalna, about seventy kilometres from Aurangabad. The red bus with the plate 'Aurangabad–Jalna' arrived on platform three, and the two of them boarded it.

They consulted their laptop to confirm the sequence and PPTs of their presentations. Curious onlookers were bending their necks to look at the 'small TV' these two people were tinkering with. Both Kumar and Kartik were enjoying the respectful admiration they were getting from the people around.

In some time, the bus left for Jalna. It travelled through tiny hamlets, with no apparent hurry. The bus stopped at every other village it passed to pick up some passengers, smelling of coconut oil and cheap talcum powder. The heat and sweat around wasn't making things easier. Most of the passengers were chewing tobacco and spitting the remains of the same, either straight out of the window or below the window, under the seat or in the front. One person had put on a hand-held transistor at full blast. It compounded the chaos of the rattling bus. Kartik, who hardly travelled by bus, was getting irked by the shabbiness around. He came from a blue-blooded family, and hardly ever travelled the countryside in local transport.

After about an hour's travelling, the bus stopped at a dilapidated bus-stop on the dusty road, bringing in gusts of dust. Kartik already had a handkerchief on his nose, and Ray-Bans shielding his eyes.

A family got in the bus. The matriarch was a skinny woman, perhaps forty, but looked older. Accompanying her were five children—three boys, two girls. They apparently had no father. It was one of those families left to fend for themselves with the head of the family either perpetually drunk, or absent or absconding or dead. The woman's jowls moved rhythmically as she chewed tobacco.

The family had boarded the bus with what looked like their entire belongings—a couple of quilts, torn at the edges, three knotted, stuffy bundles which probably carried their clothes, some utensils and a transistor. It was clear that the family was living a hand-to-mouth existence. The five kids were enthusiastic and rushed to the last seat of the bus which was vacant, and huddled together. They looked as if they had been deprived of a bath for a week at least, and their clothes perhaps hadn't been washed for quite some time. But the grime on their faces couldn't diminish the twinkle in their eyes. The lady, without any place to sit, stood near the bus door.

'See?' muttered Karthik. 'She cannot possibly feed those children, but she gave birth to so many! How can we say we're the next superpower? Do you even think that woman has ever seen what a school looks like? Or her kids have for that matter?'

All Kumar could do was nod in response to his friend's mounting frustration. 'They need to be educated, man!' Kartik was eyeing the woman and her children with a mix of sympathy and anger. He wasn't sure whether he should pity them for their penury, or loathe them for their ignorance.

By this time, the conductor approached the family for tickets. The woman pulled out some crumpled notes tucked away in her blouse. Kartik wondered if this was all the money she had in the world.

'Four full, two half, Jalna,' said the woman, after spitting her mouthful of tobacco juice out of the window.

The conductor looked at her, and then at the children. Of the five, the two girls were old enough to need a full ticket, but the three boys looked young enough to travel on a half-ticket.

'But why four full tickets, chachi? I think it's just the three of you who need to get a full ticket. The boys are small.'

Without changing the expression on her face, the woman said, 'You see my boy near the window? He looks small, but is well past his age for a half-ticket. So give me four full, and two half-tickets.'

The conductor was dumb-struck by the poor woman's unassuming honesty. She handed him the money. The children continued to jostle in their seats. The conductor shrugged and gave the woman the tickets she wanted—four full, two half.

Kartik and Kumar looked at each other—surprised, amazed and ashamed.

*Sagar Haveli*

# Merry Christmas

'Sunny, get the eggs for the cake,' my mother implored. She was baking the family's favourite chocolate cake for Christmas. When my father was still with us, both of us would get together and help her bake the cake. Today she was doing it all by herself.

My conscience niggled at me to get up and help her out but I remained sprawled before the television. 'Get the eggs please,' she said again. Half-heartedly, I was about to get up to fetch the eggs when the phone rang. I got up to answer it. By that time my mother probably understood that I was in no mood to help, so she got the eggs herself.

It was Jenny, my girlfriend, on the phone and she chirped, 'Hey! It's Christmas eve! So what is the plan for tonight?' For the next fifteen minutes we made plans for the evening, deciding that we would meet up at a friend's place and continue the party from there.

'Who was it, Sunny?' asked my mother as I kept the phone down.

'No one,' I lied. She asked me if I could get some dry fruits from the market but I shrugged off the request. 'Mom come on, make it with whatever we have; only two of us are going to eat it anyway!' I could see the flash of disappointment on her face, but she said nothing and instead, with a sweet smile, said, 'Okay, as long as you are happy.'

Strange thing that. No matter how much you hurt your mother, she will still love you back with the same die-hard devotion. No matter how much you neglect them or drift away from mothers, they keep coming back into your lives to bless and guide, help and soothe. In retrospect, we all take our mothers' love and affection for granted. I feel they are to be blamed too, because we tend to take for granted the very things which are abundantly available.

In the evening, as I got dressed in a black dinner jacket and black trousers, my mother smiled at me and exclaimed, 'My, you look so handsome! God save the girls!' Then she asked me where I was going and if I would be late. I said I would be going out with my friends. And yes, I might be late. Suddenly her cheerful expression faded away into bleak disappointment. In a soft voice she asked me to come home by ten so that we could start our Christmas celebrations. Though my father wasn't there anymore, my mother had never let me feel his absence. She kept up with all the family rituals, and bought me new clothes even as she continued to wear the same dress she had got six years ago on her birthday from her brother. She'd bake me chocolate cake as always, make biscuits and all sorts of delicious desserts tirelessly, but tonight, I just wanted to have a night out.

So off I went, met Jenny, partied and had a nice time. We went to the most popular disco in town and the place was packed with the rich and the glamorous. I spent all the money I had got as a Christmas present from my mother. It was quarter past one when I realised how late it was and that my mother had asked me to come home by ten so that we could celebrate Christmas together.

I reached home at about two in the morning. I tip-toed across the hall. When I switched on the lights, I saw the brightly decorated Christmas tree standing alone in the dark corner, and next to it were all the untouched gifts. My mother's Bible was open on the couch, which was very unusual, because she always reads the Bible, prays and then keeps it away in the shelf neatly. As I took the Bible to put it away, I saw that it was open at Psalm 23, which reads, 'The Lord is my shepherd I shall not want . . .' In the dining hall, a table for two was nicely laid out but the food was untouched. The chocolate cake was standing pretty in the middle of the table, waiting for me to come home. I was about to turn and leave, when I saw a note on the table. It said, 'Dearest son, I am sorry I couldn't wait any longer. I am going to sleep. I made your favourite dish. Please eat it before you go to bed. Merry Christmas! Love you always! Ma.'

I learnt much later that she had waited for me, sung Christmas carols to herself and had prayed for me, for my dad and then some more for me. And then she had cried herself to sleep.

Next morning I got up but didn't know how to face her, for I was feeling guilty and was hoping that I wouldn't run into her on my way to the toilet. But she appeared at the doorway and looked at me. I thought to myself, 'Here it comes, the shouting.'

But she didn't say anything, she just came close, hugged me and said 'Merry Christmas, son!' I held onto her. I hugged her for a very long time, probably because I couldn't face her. I was scared I might break into tears. She probably understood that as well, for she let go of me, turned around without looking back and walked out of the room. Then I did something for the first time in my life, something I hadn't even done when my father was taken away from me in a cruel accident.

I cried.

*Shoumik De*

# A Cake for Mom

It was 8 p.m. already and our mother hadn't come home from work yet. 'When will she come?' moaned my twelve-year-old brother. 'I cannot wait any longer,' he sighed grumpily. 'Besides,' he said, a tiny smile appearing on his impish face, 'she has to bake the cake today!' A dreamy look came on my brother's face as he pictured himself devouring the hot, freshly-baked cake. Just then, we heard the sound of her car and my brother rushed to open the door.

Now our mother was obviously very tired after a long day's work, so she was expecting a slightly different welcome than the one my brother gave her. 'Helloooo mummy!' he said (she had barely entered the room). 'We are finally baking the cake, aren't we!' Uh oh! You must never, ever try to get a tired, disgruntled woman to cook anything—she'll probably burn whatever's in the pot. Anyway, you should have seen the cold look on my mother's otherwise cheerful face. My poor brother was bamboozled.

She stormed into the house, headed straight for the bed to lie down, but there was someone there already! My examinations were just a week away and my books and I had taken over my favourite place—her bed! I was curled up inside her blanket with one book in my hand and dozens scattered all over when she snarled, 'Can't you study at your table?' I was taken aback and a bit upset. For one thing, that was not how she behaved normally and for another, I hated it when somebody tried to dislocate me when I was studying. So ignoring the fact that she was frightfully tired, I sighed and sprawled dramatically on the bed she was aching to park herself on.

My mother had had it and she swept my books out of the way to make place for herself on the bed. Now my brother had realised that something was definitely wrong with her. 'Err, you want coffee, Mummy?' he asked timidly. 'No!' retorted my mother, though I'm sure coffee was the very thing she had wanted then, along with some peace and quiet. My brother left the room.

Then entered my father. 'What happened?' he mumbled, gazing at her. She got up, glaring at nothing in particular. 'I . . . ,' she began in a huff, but then suddenly her tone changed. She sighed and, gesturing towards me she said, 'I just scolded the poor thing for nothing. She was studying so hard.' Then my brother entered majestically into the room, with a cup of coffee in his hand. He had decided to make it anyway. 'Ah!' exclaimed she, taking the delicious cup of coffee in her hands at once, forgetting that minutes ago she had said she didn't want it. 'Oh, the cake!' she remembered suddenly. 'I hope all the ingredients are there . . . I must get to work at once!' By this time, I was shaking with laughter.

She was funny, this woman. What had happened to her anger? Oh yes, she was feeling bad about scolding everybody I guess. How typical of most women! And yes, she had decided to bake the cake! Hadn't she just returned home from office? So I decided to speak. I popped up from inside the warm blanket, taking everyone by surprise and declaring, 'Today, I shall bake the cake!' My mother happily agreed but she was a bit wary. All the while I was in the kitchen, baking the cake, she would keep popping in, handing me some stuff, giving tips. When the cake (which was lip-smacking) was baked finally, she exclaimed happily, 'Good girl, you did everything yourself!' even though she had been the one guiding me every step of the way.

And that's a mother for you in a nutshell—very warm, a happy workaholic, multi-tasking and unselfish. No wonder they say we women (I am a 'little woman' after all) enhance any environment. I just hope when I grow up that, like my mother, I too will have the strength left over after a hard day to bake a cake for my family or at least to pass on wisdom and ingredients as they bake it for me!

*Aparna Srivastava*

# Tough Calls

Simi and I bonded instantly. She had moved in next door and we very quickly became more than just good neighbours. As we began spending time in each other's homes, she told me how happy she was when she got engaged to Rajiv, a few years ago. As a couple they complemented each other well. He was lean and handsome, she was tall and striking. They had everything going for them. Both had secure jobs in their chosen fields, were saving up for their first home and had the backing of loving families. What more could Simi ask for?

One day Rajiv's friends came for a visit from New Zealand. They told him about the good life over there, complete with fantastic salary packages, big independent villas, fancy cars and a life time's security. They managed to convince Rajiv that New Zealand was the place to be and conveyed that the massive influx of migrants would kill his chances to move abroad if he did not act immediately.

'I wasn't so easily convinced. After all, India is my home with my near and dear ones here, a stable job and familiarity. How could I just turn my back on everything?' recounts Simi as she sips freshly brewed coffee. But Rajiv became adamant. It was as though he underwent a transformation overnight and became obsessed with the idea of settling abroad. Nothing seemed to be good enough for him—his lifestyle in India suddenly became inadequate.

He issued an ultimatum to Simi to either get married to him and move to New Zealand with him or go her separate way. 'At first, I was numb with shock. This was my fiancé talking. The man I wanted to have a future with. How did he become so cold, so indifferent and selfish?' After several sleepless nights, with a heavy heart she decided to go ahead with the move, consoling herself with the idea that if things didn't work out they could always come back home to their family. She married Rajiv in a simple ceremony. Her entire wardrobe underwent a change as she now needed practical western outfits rather than the more traditional trousseau she had previously saved up for.

Rajiv's visa was approved without a hitch and he left to set up things and Simi followed two months later. It was only when she was aboard the flight that the finality of her alienation from all that she knew struck her. 'I had given up everything to be with the man I loved. The prospect of a new life in a new country was exciting, but at the same time extremely scary. Doubts plagued my mind—what if I didn't find a decent job, what if I wasn't able to settle in? With a silent prayer and a brave face I set out to face what God had in store for me in an unknown land,' recounts Simi.

'Nina, we only slogged in New Zealand. The rent was exorbitant. I couldn't identify with the local ways, I had no spare time juggling between my work and managing home. On weekends I did my household chores, on weekdays I dealt with a boss who thrived on racial discrimination.' After three years of a life without roots, it was time for Simi to issue an ultimatum. She says with a smile, 'I had a straight talk with Rajiv. He would either move back to India with me or I would return without him. I was jittery about his answer. He seemed to like the way we were killing ourselves for nothing, but he relented. Simi ensured that all three of them came back home—she, Rajiv and their as yet unborn child.

As I watched her enjoy the companionable silence, I realised that a woman like Simi can follow her man to the end of the earth, but she also knows exactly when to make him follow her back to her heart and home. It is all about knowing when to give in and when to claim what is rightfully hers.

*Nina Irani*

# Pause and Twist

Life is like a merry-go-round. I have lived a pretty diverse, and to some people, disconnected, life. Some people need to see and understand the pattern before they make the next move, and while I swear by logic, I am quite prepared to watch it evolve. I have studied in ten different schools during my pre K–12 years and have lived in Zambia, Japan, US and am now again in India. However, in life, one tends to follow certain paths only to find that one is back where one started. For most, this may be a cause for dismay, for me it was time to pause and ponder.

My first pause came soon enough. I am a computer engineer and have since picked up a few more degrees, diplomas, certifications and designations along a restless, fifteen-year career path. I became a general manager five years into my career and received a Special Achievement award from Wipro for the first year of my entrepreneurial venture, SMS, a technology-based company. Thereafter, destiny started to play its role and I became severely ill. My doctor asked me to choose between my business or my baby. No brainer that one, so I shut shop and accepted God's gift to me instead— a son.

Now onto my second pause. Families have a way of creating ties that bond but also bind. Like women all over the world,

I too had to make the choices that demanded just a little more of myself than I probably had bargained for in life. I used to consult but then I gave up my career completely and travelled the world with my husband. Exciting stuff actually, until I attended a session at the Cleveland Community College, US, called 'Women in Transition'. It is of course well known that Americans are very good at therapy and I realised that day that I was in denial and that I had never got over the loss of my first baby—my first business. I had to stop and learn to deal with what my life was and take a call on my future.

My first pause had made me realise the transient nature of life as well the futile belief that you can be in total control of your fortunes. I had of course gone off the deep end and decided not to even bother; things would happen and we would manage. Wrong again. My second pause taught me that life is about balance. Balance is integral to a fulfilling life and has to permeate every decision you take and everything you do. Caring for, sharing with and giving to those less privileged was one such decision I took to find a sense of balance. Thanks to the volunteering spirit and the concept of stewardship so dominant in the American ethos, I got involved in a number of Volunteer Service Organizations (VSOs) and charitable institutes. The experiences opened up a whole new dimension of professional options with social responsibilities. Though I kept very busy intellectually and socially through projects and volunteering, I also took up a job with a bank, albeit on a freelance basis.

My third pause came when we returned from the US to settle for good in India. It had been some time since the days of my career and I had lost touch with most of my peers. I got online and started to search out communities. All the reconnecting with familiar turf made me feel like I was on a home run, and maybe I was! However, instead of leveraging my US work experience, I found myself facing my third pause. I caught myself wondering if I really wanted to have a corporate career or whether I wanted to pursue my social inclination and find a space for myself in the development sector.

Soon, I was offered a position as operations director at KSWA-Yuva Parivartan, an NGO that works with underprivileged school dropouts. I took up the challenge. I also became a visiting faculty at a premier B-school. Incidentally, most of my life I have earned, learned, lectured and laughed simultaneously. I do not know if that can be construed as a lack of focus, but I think multi-anything is critical for personal growth and yes it's stimulating, if exhausting! My life's inspirational quote by Gandhi is, 'The difference between what we do and what we are capable of doing would suffice to solve most of the world's problems'.

After a year, I knew that I wanted my life to have more impact and I also wanted to do something that I could be passionate about. Another NGO was not a solution. I needed to marry my personal passion for social contribution with my professional capabilities that demanded performance and accountability. I charted a course of action. I went back to the corporate world one last time, as head of business development for India in an MNC. Sometimes you need to prove as much to yourself as to others what you stand for and what you are made of.

And then came the twist after all the pauses. This year, I finally took the plunge and started my second business. Most NGOs, women, senior citizens, rural and green producers and service providers find it difficult if not daunting to reach out to organised markets and consumers. We fill this gap that supports their viability and hopefully ensure the sustainability of a better world and a greener planet. I do not know if I have the requisite sterling credentials (I have made my share of personal and professional errors of judgement, and rode the waves of success and failure) but with God's grace, I do know that I will make the most of the pauses and the twists life throws at me.

The future? I am grateful for my life. And the paths that may not have always been what I asked for but which the Almighty decided I needed to walk on. I do have a few grey hairs and more than a few extra pounds to show for it, but with a spouse who is my spine and a son who is my heartbeat I look forward to the next pause and the next twist!

*Karon Miranda Shaiva*

# My Mother's Shoes

Juggling life and balancing relationships has become my forte. My friends praise me for having fantastic PR skills and for being protocol savvy. Besides these two assets, I believe I am extremely skilled when it comes to planning. Because of this 'compulsive disorder' (like my best friend tags it) I am the butt of umpteen jokes too.

I have no qualms in declaring that I am extremely methodical when it comes to maintaining relationships. Well, it's because, ever since my childhood, I have seen my mother (a single parent for most of my adolescent life) battle with relationships to maintain them, whether it was the estranged relationship with my father, dealing with an overbearing sister or her mother who left her demoralised and alone to pick up the pieces of her life.

My mother tirelessly, without any ulterior motive, went on giving her all to relationships that were long gone, had no future and were not worth wasting her life on. I would often tell her, 'Ma, why do you do this to yourself? Just let go, you will be happier.' And she would always tell me, 'Baby, it takes a fraction of a second to break a relationship, but years and years of effort to maintain it.'

At that time, I felt that my mother was being foolish. At this rate she would never learn to let go and she was making

these statements which only appear in fables or books, but
are impossible to follow in real life. Yet, because I had seen
her struggle and do her best to make things work selflessly,
I guess this aspect became a part of me and I did not realise
it until very recently, when I faced the biggest battle of my
life with relationships.

I am married and today, by the grace of God, all is well.
But when it all began, it was far from being so. My world, my
values, my thinking, my way of functioning—everything was
crippled before my eyes. I had married my childhood
sweetheart, who I dearly loved and who loved me
unconditionally too. But we belonged to two very different
sects. I call them sects as we were not different in status or
religion or education. If we differed, it was only in our 'mind
set'.

My family was not superior but we had a much more
unconventional approach to things. We don't follow traditions
per se, and we all have a very strong sense of individuality.
But my marital home had some fixed beliefs about how their
daughter-in-law should be or behave. I know this is the story
of every house, but when I fell in love at the young age of
nineteen, I did not realise how such things affect everyday
life. Even if I had known this, I would have plunged into
matrimony anyway, as I love my husband, not
unconditionally, but to an unfathomable extent for sure.

Twenty days into my marriage, a few situations had already
cropped up between my in-laws and me. Even before I could
process what was happening, fate played saviour and my
husband got transferred to my hometown. I was now officially
the 'nasty daughter-in-law' who had manipulated her husband
and taken him away—not by in-laws, but most people around
who just loved to wag their tongues anyway. Unfortunately
at that point, no one, including my husband, saw the good in
the situation. In the days before the transfer (which were the

early days of marriage), I was not spoken to or shown any affection in a way that I wished, although perhaps everyone did their best in that situation. I did not feel welcomed in the family. I was afraid, upset, longing for love, but to no avail. All a newly-married girl wants is to be respected and loved for her own identity in her new home. I wish more Indian households understood that and did not try to change a girl's identity, way of thinking, dressing and being overnight.

I felt shattered, depressed, angry and wanted to give up. That's when my mother's words rang in my ears. I remembered why she never let go of all those dying relationships for all these years. I also realised that losing out on my husband's affection and all these relationships to satisfy my anger was a heavy price to pay. That is when I decided that I will not break my new relationships and would do everything to make them work. I made it a point to call my in-laws every morning for months tirelessly, without ever receiving a call from them in return (even sometimes till date). It took a lot of patience and immense will for me to be able to portray my real self to them and show them that I am content with myself and don't wish to change or change them.

Initially there was too much hurt on both sides, but slowly the ice broke and today I see deep respect in their eyes for me, my thoughts, my values, my thinking, my way of functioning and my world and vice versa. And I can only thank my mother for that, who instilled in me values of being confident, loving myself and, above all, balancing relationships that matter most.

*Roma Kapadia*

# Three Mothers and a Bond

There is nothing as healing as going back to the place where you were born, where old, pleasant memories come rushing back, where you remember happy childhood days spent with family and friends. As these cherished memories come alive, your life seems to flow with ease and grows more joyful.

In the Christmas break of 2009, I went to Chennai to my mother's house and this was a time meant not only for relaxing and reading but also for keeping my date with three mothers I have there waiting for me always—my own mother, Mother Mary and the Sea Goddess.

I love Elliot's Beach in Besant Nagar and have been a regular visitor ever since my family shifted to Adyar nineteen years back. My equation with the sea has changed over the years and keeps changing, but underlying it all is a great love and connection to the ocean. In my youth, I loved running on the yellow sand. Then as I haunted the Vellankanni church close by, the sea became a place I would stop at, after my regular visit to the Divine Mother, Mother Mary. I would always be filled with the positive energy I got from surrendering my cares to Mother Mary. These visits to the two mothers became quite regular as I would take my little son to the beach to play with his father while I would join them after visiting the church. There was always a feeling of carefree abandon on the way home, because I knew my mother would have a cup of tea ready. Later, I often left the burden of rustling up breakfast to my mother as I stole visits to the sea to welcome the sunrise. For it is only with your own mother that you can count on the pleasure of coming back home, warm after a morning at the beach, to delicious idlis and sambar and no judgments whatsoever on how late you are and how lunch needs to be made.

All of this just became a memory after I shifted to Bangalore.

But one memory that lingers with me more than the rest happened two years ago. I had come back home for the summer break and I went to Elliot's Beach to see the sunrise—something I had really missed in Bangalore. I was in a bad mood and rather cross with life. I plonked myself by the sea without the usual excitement. As I just sat there in a black cloud of negativity, I felt the ocean reach out to me. It was almost as though she was saying, 'Chin up now. Remember you always tell me you and I are one? Take that part of me which is healed and heal yourself.'

As I felt the warm, loving presence of the ocean, healing did take place. A deep calm filled me, and as I got up and walked at the edge of the sea, I felt the salty water take away all the negativity. I just let go, wondering if this was what the Buddha felt under the Bodhi tree when he dropped all effort and strife and simply let go. I came to such a level of peace and healing that I felt there was nothing to worry and that, 'God is in heaven, All's right with the world'.

Life went on, and though I got caught up in the hustle and bustle in Bangalore, I never forgot that beautiful May morning when the summer sun shone down at me, the waves accepted me unconditionally, the beach dogs came and lay down near me—a morning that reminded me that there was nothing I need to strive for. A morning that taught me to be.

Last Christmas I was back with my mother, and on Christmas morning, as I prepared to go to the beach and to the Vellankanni church after a gap of more than a year, it felt like coming home. This time I did not leave the burden of rustling up breakfast to my mother. My equation with my mother too had changed. I was the caregiver now as she was aging. I saw to it that the food was cooked and ready before I dashed off to the beach and church.

I felt once again the peace that passes all understanding as I sat before the altar. Peace turned to joy and oneness as I saw another Hindu girl like me carrying a book about Swami Vivekananda; a devotee of Lord Aiyappa with his forehead smeared with holy ash; another Hindu family, devotees of Shakti, flowers in their hair and kumkum in their foreheads praying earnestly along with Christian families. It gave me hope to see how they all saw in Mother Mary what I was seeing, the Divine Mother of all beyond religious divides.

This time as I prayed, I didn't burden the Divine Mother with my problems. There was a sense of knowingness that all would be well with the world and me, and all I needed to do was to send up thanks for the blessings received and for those which would be received. As with the sea and my mother, my equation with Mother Mary too had changed.

I walked over to the beach feeling connected to the sea, sand and sun. As I felt connected to the Divine feminine in all her forms, I felt connected to all the people who had come to the beach—the family playing near the waves, the fishing boats out at sea, the child searching for shells. I felt connected to life in all its various forms, God in His/Her many guises.

Then a shadow crossed my mind. When would I come back here next? When would I be able to bask in the warm love of Mother Nature as she expressed herself in the form of this ocean? When could I go to the secular Vellankanni temple again? Who would give me the space to explore life like this, apart from my own mother?

As I gazed a bit sadly at the waves, the sea seemed to laugh. 'What are you laughing at,' I demanded crossly.

The answer came loud and clear. 'If we are all connected as you just felt, why do you have to come all the way here to connect with me or to anyone else? I am in you. Whenever you want to connect with me, go deep within yourself. Dig out the memory of this day and I shall be with you.'

As I walked back home, I was happy. I would love to visit the sea physically whenever I could, but if I could not, all I had to do was to go within and connect to the ocean which is alive in me through my memories and through the essence of peace and healing it had brought me. All I needed to do is bring that energy alive again in me. I could do the same whenever I missed anyone else in this world or out of it. Just know that a part of them lived in me and I was not separated from anyone at all.

What better gift could any mother have given her child? My equation with life had changed—for the better.

K. *Geethanjali Balakrishnan*

# The Child of God

I am no hero. Truth be told, I'm quite a coward, fearful of consequences, and afraid to rock the boat. But with my mother's words ringing in my head, I had to stand my ground, come what may. She always said we should stand by our principles, especially when it was challenging to do so. And challenges there have been many when I've tried to hold fast to my principles, and today was one of them.

Two weeks ago my mother died, literally in my arms as I was trying to make her sip a warm drink. She'd suffered a massive brain haemorrhage and I didn't realise she'd gone just like that. Now, shaken by shock, disbelief and grief, I sat in the temple hall waiting to be served the ceremonial meal by the holy priests of the temple. I was three months pregnant and the morning sickness didn't help. My nine-month baby was beside me, held tightly in the arms of young Padma, the daughter of my mother's life-long house-help.

Eleven-year-old Padma had been with me the night my mother died, keening as bitterly as anyone because she felt the pain almost as sharply. She and her mother Lakshmi had loved my mother and they were family too for my mother. My mother's had been a small world of just a few who were close to her. Lakshmi and Padma were part of this circle. She had almost adopted Padma.

Today was a special day when a puja or a prayer ceremony was being done at the temple in my mother's memory. Family and friends were present and my mother's face smiled down on us from her picture that was decked with garlands and vermillion. I tried to come to terms during the prayers that my mother now existed in framed and decorated pictures and I'd never hear her warm voice or feel her soft touch again. We were called from within to take our places for the meal. This was a special meal for the occasion, cooked and served by the priests. Long tables were set along the four walls and I settled down with Padma by my side. As we waited for the food to be brought in, I sensed whispered comments from my rather traditional and conservative aunts and other relatives.

My sense of foreboding gripped me when an older cousin approached me and, with some awkwardness, said that Padma could not eat with us. I needed to send her out.

Perhaps having lived away from India for years, the concept of caste and class had lost its significance for me. And then there was *madi* or fastidious decorum which I had all but forgotten. Try as I might, I found it difficult to translate or explain this to my Western husband: cleanliness, auspiciousness, fastidiousness, holiness or all of these rolled into one? Padma was clean and resplendent in the new clothes I'd bought for the occasion. But clothes could not a Brahmin make. Her appearance gave her away as being from the 'lower' caste. She came from a caste that would not even be allowed inside some Brahmin houses, let alone in their kitchens. They were certainly not allowed to cook, or even touch food articles of the very traditional, conservative Brahmin families as that would destroy their madi. When I'd newly moved into my present apartment in Bangalore, a neighbour had dropped in to see the new kitchen I was getting built. We talked about maids and I asked her if she had a good maid and what chores she did; how about helping with cooking, I asked naively. She looked surprised and said, 'But my maid is not a Brahmin'. That explained everything.

I was brought up by a mother who not only allowed her maid into the kitchen, but even cooked for her. Lakshmi and Padma were given breakfast and tea every morning prepared by my mother, who in fact went so far as to seat herself in front of the two to make sure they ate a hearty breakfast. This was also to make sure none of the food was packed and taken back to feed the useless lout of a husband who drank away most of his wife's hard-earned money. My mother had no way of preventing Lakshmi from giving her alcoholic husband her earnings, but she would be damned if she let Lakshmi take any of the food she had cooked for the family, which included the maid and her daughter.

Years ago, I had been amused at the horrified reaction of my husband when I told him my great aunt did not eat in my house as there was no madi in my mother's lifestyle. The old lady was nearing eighty and was fiercely protective of her madi. She brought her own food when she came to spend the day with us and would only eat fruit that my mother bought for her. My husband's understandable reaction was, 'How rude!' He asked whether my mum wasn't offended. He was even more astonished when I laughed and said, 'Not a bit!' The fact was my great aunt loved my mum and had accepted the fact that she had married outside her community, that her husband and children ate meat, and that the maid was allowed into the kitchen! My mother loved her aunt and respected her traditional and deeply conservative Brahmin outlook even if she herself did not share it. Their relationship worked. The old lady wished to see my mother and spend time with her when she could and my mother was delighted to see her aunt, who travelled miles in the busy crowded city to spend a day with her niece, even if she had to carry her own food or survive on fruit! Each accepted the other's ways and it was a wonderful example of the 'live and let live' idiom.

One of the things I learnt from my mother was that some traditional laws at least had perfectly good reasons and were not just there to punish us. So many of our superstitions, she'd pointed out, were based on reason and scientific fact. It is up to us to retain the ones that help in our hurry to discard those that harm.

And here I was facing one of the latter. 'Please send Padma out,' I was instructed. Taken aback at first, I asked where she would eat.

'Out on the steps.'

'But why?'

'She's not a Brahmin. You know the rules.'

My back went up. I'm sorry, I said, I could not ask her to leave now that she is sitting with me and my baby. She was only a child herself. Yes, but she was not a Brahmin! I tried a weak argument saying, neither was my baby as her father wasn't even an Indian. I was told to stop being difficult and contrary. At this point, I could feel the eyes of the elders upon me and mutterings about why I should be so awkward. I panicked. Had I known this would happen, had it occurred to me that Padma did not belong to the elite caste that was allowed to partake of this ceremony and eat with us, I would never have brought her here. But then the reason why we were all here dawned clearly. We were all here to honour my mother. And she would have wanted Padma here. She probably cared more for Padma than some of the relatives present, who had not shown through words or deeds that my mother had mattered to them in her lifetime. I heard again in my head Padma's wails when she realised her beloved amma had left us forever.

No, I decided. There was no way I could ask the child to get up and leave the room. Padma, by this time, knew she was the reason for the exchange. She asked me if she should go. I asked her to sit tight and simply told my cousin if Padma had to leave, then so should my daughter, which meant that I would leave too.

The priests would be insulted and would take offence, I was told. I could only reply that if they refused to serve a child, then they were not men of God. If they discriminated against human beings based on man-made castes, then I had no respect for such holy men and would gladly leave. My cousin went back to her seat looking visibly annoyed.

It was time for the meal to be served and the priests, clad in their white traditional priestly garb, brought out the dishes to serve us. As they came closer, I grew more nervous. I kept looking at my mother's picture for strength. In spite of all the bravado, I was terrified of the unpleasantness, and so was Padma as she sat shivering next to me. Only my little baby was gurgling happily, blissfully unaware as yet of caste or creed or religion.

The priests served me and then Padma, and carried on. I heaved a massive sigh of relief and smiled reassuringly at Padma. She barely touched the rich food she was not used to, while we quickly ate up the first serving. The priests came around a second time. This time the head priest stopped in front of Padma, bent closer to her and said in the gentlest voice, 'Eat up my child, you are so thin. You need feeding. Don't be shy.' I sat there with tears pricking my eyes, thinking, yes these were men of God. I hoped the others who were worried about offending the priests had overheard. I know my mother had and that she was nodding in approval.

*Rani Rao Innes*

# Double Take

When you are pretty, smart and fifteen, you are always right. You've seen the world and you know how to deal with everything. The school sash hasn't just made its way down from the waist to the hip. Life's taught you a few things.

It was a Thursday night, my father was travelling on work and my mother and I were home alone. Dinner conversation over the last week had revolved, quite literally, over why I shouldn't be allowed to go for a particular bash at a lounge bar. Reasons ranging from safety, to sex and drugs, to spaghetti straps, to it being a waste of time and money had all been countered by me. Unfortunately, I ran into a wall with the 'just because we say so' argument.

I was in the 'NO' phase.

Five p.m. My mother peeked into my room and caught me studying. 'No TV today?' 'No,' I replied without looking up. 'After all, it's a waste of time.'

Seven p.m. 'You want to go for that movie we were planning on tonight?' asks a reconciliatory mother. 'Nope,' went the reply. 'It's Hollywood—I'm sure it will have sex and drugs.' Shoulders sag and the rotund figure makes its way out.

Eight p.m. 'There's yesterday's leftovers for dinner. Your favourite corn and mushroom bhaji is still there. You want some papad along with it?' asks the placating voice again. 'No,' replies the skinny sarcasm queen. 'Haven't you read, it's not safe to eat leftovers?' 'Order pizza then?' asks the congenial one, but the answer is again, 'No, it's a waste of money.'

'So shall we skip dinner then?' Skinny knows Rotund's patience is being tested and that's exactly what she wants. 'No, let's go out and eat healthy, fresh vegetarian fare and live up to our Indian values,' I demand. Mom softens and gives in to my teenage tantrum.

I change into a skimpy top. Eyebrows are raised. 'It's safe when I'm with you parents, right?' I shrug.

'Yes, just out of place,' she retorts.

'Well, since I have nowhere else to wear it, an Udipi it is,' I dismiss.

We leave and head over to our favourite neighbourhood restaurant. I've been here since I was a chubby five-year-old, so I'm a local celebrity anyway. Tonight, a few extra heads turn. I preen. Mom fumes silently. We wait to be seated. Our favourite table near the window is not yet cleared but there is another one empty. Mom is willing to take it but my petulance prevails.

'Why not?' she demands, finally irritated.

'Just,' I respond, relishing my revenge, 'because I say so.'

Table in demand clears and we eat our meal, more or less in silence. We are on our way out.

'Zenobbbeeeeeeeeeeee,' a screech pierces through the ambient commotion. 'Pushpeeeeeeee,' someone screeches back. Oops, that was my mother. I thought I'd heard all the voice modulations she ever had. I was wrong.

'Zenobbbeeee. I can't believe it's you! After all these years! You look exactly the same.' (Yeah right aunty, your glasses are obviously missing the point that I look exactly like her when she was fifteen!)

'You too, Pushpee. Where have you been? And here? Now? Suddenly? Why? I heard you guys had migrated.'

'Yes, to Australia, after Ronin. And? You have always been here? Married? Kids? Career? We have a motel down there. Business is great—of course, there are ups and downs. Remember how we as kids thought that "life is a roller coaster" meant that it would have to be a fun ride all the way?'

'Yeah. And how I never believed in the "live and let live" formula?'

'Haahaaa. Well, you always thought that life was just black and white, without any greys.'

'And you always believed that everything can be made right with a kiss and a chocolate cone. I hope Ajit still works on that formula,' says mom, eyes sparkling.

'Yes, yes, he does. I'm so glad I married him. I wouldn't have been able to go through Ronin with anyone else.'

'Hmmm. So, what brings you to Mumbai?'

'It's Ronin's twenty-first birthday and his grandparents wanted to be there. Besides, Sneha has never been to India. Anyway, you tell me about you. What's my rebellious classmate up to these days? Any more joints at Juhu beach? Or double-seat bicycle rides to Lonavla along those treacherous curves? My god, what a dare-devil you were!'

My mom? Dare-devil? She doesn't even cross the road without waiting for the lights to turn green!

'Well, it's just different being young. You just believe that nothing will ever go wrong with you—only with someone else.'

'Yeah true. But I still remember you went off to live in some farm in the outskirts of Maharashtra, without electricity or a loo, right?'

My mom living without electricity? Darkness freaks her out so much she even keeps a torch by her pillow, just for that one day in a year when Mumbai may have a power outage! As for no loos, well lady, you must be totally mistaken. This mother here is a hygiene fanatic. She not only needs a loo but a spotless one at that.

They went on for half an hour to speak of dandy dances, boys crashing in on girlie parties and picnics in the wilderness. Topics spanned from boyfriends to beer; never being seen without stilettos; trendy tie-up tops and short skirts. Mom reminisced about how dad and she used to save up through the week simply for a cola on the weekend. About days when not having cash simply wasn't a deterrent because 'the fun, waves, laughter, youth, everything comes free'.

And then, a pause. Two minutes of silence. Mom remembered me. 'Oh, meet my daughter. This is Pushpa aunty, we were in school together.' We smile. The childish chatter ceases. Goodbyes are said and tight hugs exchanged along with phone numbers.

'So are we going to catch up with her again? I mean, it would be fun to meet Ronin and Sneha,' I say, hoping that the Australian freedom they enjoy will make my mother realise that I live in bondage.

'Ronin died when he was fifteen. And Sneha is just six,' says mom.

'Oh! What happened?'

'In a road accident after his school farewell party. Their driver was not drunk. The other car's was. Sneha was born a year later.'

We are home and say our good-nights and head off to our rooms. As I lie down, my head is abuzz. Is the accident what is freaking my mother out? How could these two boring parents ever have been adventurous? My grandparents are both rich: how come these two didn't have money for chips and chocolate? What was my mom doing on a farm anyway? Did she and dad run away from home?

Mom walks in, thinks I'm asleep and quietly puts 500 rupees in my wallet. As the round shadow recedes from the room, I'm left thinking of a pretty young girl with a spark, with dreams of tomorrow, with a vision for a better world. A girl at fifteen who believed that she was always right. We were not that different after all. I was my mother with all her vulnerability and her strengths, and she was me.

*Ashishwang Godha*

# An Angel on Crutches

February is a very cold month in Michigan. It was the beginning of a challenging work project and my first trip to the US. I had lived in India most of my life and the idea of adjusting to this new place was taking a toll on me. The freezing weather in Michigan was quite a contrast to the warm tropical climate of Mumbai. I had left my city on a warm sunny day and had arrived in the US to find ice everywhere and temperatures that sank well below zero.

After settling in the hotel, I looked outside my window at the snow fall. The whole environment looked very beautiful but at the same time was quite depressing too. Life in Mumbai and Michigan was as different as it could get. Questions swirled in my mind—Can I get through this project successfully? How am I supposed to make friends all over again? When will I feel comfortable in this new place? Starting afresh in this new country was like learning to live all over again.

I decided to walk down to the lobby to clear my mind and to clarify some questions about the hotel accommodation. Hoping to catch a familiar Indian face, I noticed a car drive up slowly towards the hotel. A woman in her late twenties stepped out of the car on a pair of crutches. She walked to the back of the car and slowly started removing her luggage. It was obvious that the snow wasn't helping her situation as her crutches seemed to slip at times.

I walked upto her and asked, 'Hi, can I help you with that?'

'Sure!' she smiled. 'Usually I have no problems doing this by myself but today the snow is really bad. I must be cutting quite a sorry figure here in the snow with these crutches,' she said without a hint of self-pity.

Once we were inside the hotel, we both brushed off the snow and took a moment to catch our breath. 'Are you Indian?' she suddenly asked me.

'Yes. I just came here today,' I answered.

'Oh! I have some Indian friends too. You will love it here, the people are really nice,' she assured me.

I smiled, trying not to notice her disability too obviously. I was trying to figure out why she was travelling around in this bad weather all by herself. She got her room key and I offered to cart the trolley of bags to the room. En route I noticed that several packages contained clothes and elaborate costumes for some kind of dancing event. It can't be, I thought. She has a missing leg ... would she be doing something related to dance in this condition? The incessant chatter went on in my head.

'Are these related to dancing?' I blurted out.

'Oh yes, they are! Those are my costumes,' she answered happily and went on, 'Dancing is the only thing that has always made me happy ever since I was a kid. I started dancing when I was in school and the love affair still continues.'

I wanted to ask if it wasn't difficult but I just couldn't frame the question properly. I think she understood my thoughts because she added, 'I never stopped dancing even after the accident.'

I must have looked embarrassed because she added, 'Don't worry. I really don't mind talking about it. I was petrified of dancing again after the accident but it was my mother who gave me courage. She told me that whenever she saw me dance, she was amazed at my transformation. I would have the biggest smile on my face and it looked like I was in a world of my own. That's one memory that she always had of me. She told me specifically to never abandon my love for the one thing that I cherished so much. She wanted me to continue being a dancing star, no matter what.'

She continued, 'It was difficult at first to learn it all over again, but my mom was right. Nothing is impossible even if life gets in the way sometimes. Sure it's painful at times with the artificial leg, but I never feel inadequate in any way. I stopped doubting my abilities a long time ago and I am very happy. Today my husband says that many people are inspired by what I do.'

I smiled listening to her story and felt a new courage and warmth seeping into my chilled self-confidence. The abundance of energy radiated by this brave and independent woman had taught me that tough circumstances are created to toughen our spirits, to make us realise just what we can do when the odds are stacked against us. The positive energy of her spirit was staggering and I could not but marvel at the courage that had helped her to relearn her craft and excel at it despite her disability.

As I left, she thanked me for my help and smiled, 'Come and see me dance sometime . . . we perform at a place not far from here. By the way I am Michelle.' We both had a good laugh about the late introduction.

Somehow perfunctory introductions seemed redundant. The truth was that, though I had helped her with her luggage, she had helped me leave my baggage behind and to start my journey afresh, without fear, without misgivings. On a cold winter day, the chill had suddenly thawed.

As I walked back to my room, I realised that sometimes in

life, God really takes our problems personally and sends us people or guides just when we are in the dire need of some inspiration. A random encounter with a stranger and her life experiences had possibly altered me forever and taught me a wonderful lesson.

I had begun the day with an anxiety about my capability to do things from scratch in life. And Michelle's beautiful story had shown me clearly that, despite being able-bodied, I had foolishly demanded too little from myself in the face of a new challenge. I had been depressed because I had to get adjusted to a new place! My spirits soared, because a stranger had become a friend in this distant country and also renewed my faith in myself. The snow was still falling outside and India was still a million miles away, but for some reason I didn't feel lost and lonely any more.

— *Beryl Kunjavu*

# The Edge of the World

High up on a concrete wall
220 metres to freefall
No crowds screaming into your ear
No need to drive in fourth gear
No buses, no trams, no trains, no cars
Not a sign of pollution's unsightly scars
No ringing phones, no alarms, no horns, no chores
Not even a salesman to ignore
No breaking news or whispers of dread
Travelling companions fade into a fog of arabesques
At the edge of the world
It's just you and the voices inside your head
People jump before your eye
Some with an ecstatic war-cry
Others with an athletic discipline
Makes clumsiness look like a sin
You're planning to do it with swan-like grace
One glance downwards, freezes your plotting brain
                                  in its place
White, black, gray—cloaked in funeral hues
The reservoir of jagged rock puffs up mist as if on cue
Step back from the edge
Cautions self-preservation, an inbuilt reflex

The ordinary world is two steps behind
Reasons the coward in your mind
Why do this? What have you to prove?
In a world which is bound, by habit, to disapprove
But you're here now, too proud to walk away
The stage is set; it's your turn to play
Eyes clouded with doubt and fear, off the ledge you fly
No graceful swan dive, no war-cry
Just a deep, sharp breath, and eyes wide shut
Let the elements do as they must
Gravity doesn't skip a beat
You plunge to the bottom, head before feet
The walls of the dam rush to meet you
The world's a blur of kaleidoscopic hues
A sharp wrench at your ankles, a sign of hope

You've hit the end of your rope
Now yo-yoing out of control
You tell yourself, 'Be still my soul'
But patient you shall have to be
Till the bungee cord bounces out of potential energy
And there you hang, toes over tête
At peace with yourself, a song in your head
Wondering if the world has an umbilical cord
That won't let you crash against the rocks
One that nourishes, whether you know it or not
One that knows every dream and every thought
One that won't let you give up or give in
No matter how impossible things might seem
A world that thrives on people of strong will
Where each new idea is grist for the mill
A world that feeds off every shot in the dark,
That has a stake in every gamble, and watches each turn
                                        of the card

At the edge of the world, there's nothing to prove
So much to win, nothing to lose
Step up to the edge of the world with faith
Leap off, my dear, your destiny awaits.

*Averil Nunes*

# What I Learnt from Cancer

One day I woke up in the morning without any hair. It is only then that I realised that my hair was an extension of who I was—it framed my face and it did not matter whether it was frizzy or oily. I had hair, like everyone else. When all you can do is run your hand over a bald pate, does it do something to your self esteem? You bet it does. But this came much later. First I learnt that I had cancer cells. My response had been, 'You're joking, right?' 'No,' said the doctors who removed my ovaries and a cyst. A pathology report is not something you can refute. Not when it classifies those abnormal cells as second stage and gives them a name you do not want to hear but cannot run away from.

Cancer is associated with mortality. I went through denial, then a stage of 'Why me?' and finally acceptance, when I told myself, 'I will deal with this.' Sure, it's tough, but the doctors told me an angel had been watching over me, and therefore my ovarian cancer had been detected at an early stage.

My magazine editor was supportive when I told her what I was scheduled to do. Take six cycles of chemotherapy. I would lose my hair, would have side effects (nausea, stomach upsets, constipation) but whenever I felt fine, I would come to work. Sounds easy, but it wasn't.

Because when my friends, not all, heard that I had to go

through chemo, they got spooked. The responses varied from, 'Oh, I don't want to meet her now', to 'Perhaps she asked for it?' and 'Why didn't she get a check-up done?'. Somehow the tenor of all conversations focused on some sort of lapse or fault, made by me, naturally!

But what if you don't have any signs? How will you know that the cyst sitting in your ovary for some time has turned malignant? By the same logic, how will you know that the pain in your breast is a cause for worry?

The answer is simple. You just do your medical checks. I know a lot of women who haven't done their mammograms every year, but hey, it takes just ten minutes, and it could save your life. Because anything that is detected early can be fully cured.

Coping with cancer wasn't easy. More so when, after the first cycle itself, my hair fell out in clumps. I laughed about it, telling myself, 'It's only hair, it will grow back.' But try telling that to yourself for eight or nine months, when you have to go around wearing a scarf or avoiding social events. *Chin up!* I told myself every morning, when I looked at my face in the mirror, but I looked different. I looked as if I was sixty and not forty, and I told my dad, 'So this is what I am going to look like when I get older. Remove some teeth, and that completes the picture.'

My husband bought me a couple of books which made my days and nights not so long. I got drawn into meditation. Almost daily I stared long at the gulmohar tree and its flowers outside my house. I waited for sunsets, I sat under the morning sun, I worshipped the rain. I continued to read my emails and do a few assignments when I was well enough. But some nights I was scared. My mother had died of cancer. What if I did too? I didn't want to die so soon—I wanted to see my daughter all grown up, I had to live. So, when I couldn't sleep, I didn't let those negative thoughts prevail. I just popped a sleeping pill!

Life stopped for me, but went on everywhere else. My daughter got dropped and picked up from school, my mother-in-law fussed over her trips to the market like she always did, my husband went for work, wishing me best of luck, the maids came and went. My cats missed me though, I know, as they sat alone waiting for a cuddle on my parapet, while I went out for long walks alone. I connected with my mother, who was no more, and spoke to her while I walked; I looked at the clouds above and imagined shapes, and often found myself talking to them. I listened to the birds as they flew home in flocks every evening at exactly 6 p.m., and I walked every day, and ate well, as well as I could tolerate, of course.

I stopped being scared. I learnt that when you are this sick, you need people around you to support/care for you. My father, a nutritionist and dietician, made sure I ate green, and I ate stuff like ragi which would hoist my haemoglobin to respectable levels so that I could take my next chemo and not have to take a blood transfusion. So did I survive it all? Sure, of course I did, with flying colours too! And what can I share with you after this?

The fact that I needed a spank like this one for taking my health for granted all these years. For delaying my meals, not eating enough greens, ignoring low haemoglobin counts, living with low immunity levels, carrying work home, and then carrying guilt back at work when I wasn't home enough for my child, and basically accumulating a lot of emotional garbage, which I could happily live without. Cancer breeds when you carry emotional luggage, and like Joel Osteen says, 'An airline allows you to carry two bags, but I say you need to walk through life with no bags at all. Throw away the past, forgive yourself, and others, as God has already forgiven you long ago.'

I learnt that anything eaten in excess is wrong for you, as is not drinking enough water and not finding time to exercise or even walk or giving up the leisure to unwind and enjoy the quieter moments. Sure, look after your family, but do that little bit extra for yourself as well.

I also learnt that I wasn't the boss. I think God upstairs is the boss and we need to be alert, careful and live life with hope, charity, forgiveness and love.

The other great learning is to hang in there. And try telling yourself that if you can accept both pain and pleasure (in your mind, that is) equally, then the battle is not so hard, and the journey is not so tough.

*Madhuri Velegar K.*

# Change with Change

I spent the first twenty years of my life in Calcutta, the city where I was born. I lived in the same house, went to the same school, grew up with the same set of friends, went on holiday once a year, packed two days in advance, couldn't figure out gadgets beyond the on/off switch . . . life was good and I was happy.

Then my father decided it was time for me to get married. Mr Right was identified, except that he lived in Delhi. That was a major problem for me as I didn't want to move out of my comfort zone and live away from my family and friends. I was brainwashed into at least meeting him. Surprisingly, we hit it off instantly. I set aside my reservations, got married, moved to Delhi and thought that I would live there happily ever after.

Twenty years later today—my husband and I live in London, I have moved home at least half a dozen times in the last few years, I have a multi-locational family with children in a residential school in Dehradun, in-laws in India, parents in Singapore and friends all over the world. To me, holidays mean getting a break from travelling because I am constantly packing and unpacking. I am completely dependant on the internet, my laptop and Blackberry in that order . . . life is better and I am happier.

te: I used to be a complete perfectionist, ...u to be planned well in advance and executed ...ay according to plan even if it meant going on a holiday. So god forbid if anything happened to disrupt my plans, I would become completely hyper as it involved reworking everything again to perfection. I soon realised that no one but me cared two hoots whether things were perfect or not so long as they were having a good time. So over the years, I have learned to chill and let my hair down, make the most of the existing situation and enjoy myself equally. It made me feel young and carefree.

Moving to London from India brought about a sea change in my life. Along with learning to say 'Please' and 'Thank You' before and after every sentence, being on time, standing patiently in a queue, obeying traffic rules, and of course learning how to cook, I have—most importantly—become self-dependant and independent. Work is also much more challenging in the global environment and consequently much more exciting. Life may be gruelling at times but never boring or monotonous.

Though the transition has not been easy, it has been more than rewarding. My horizons have broadened and today I encourage my children to spread their wings. The catalyst of the change in my life has been my husband who thrives on challenges and change. I had a choice between adapting to the changes in my life and helping him to realise his dreams or digging my feet into the sand and refusing to accept change. I opted for the former and I know I made the right choice.

*Vibha Chowdhary*

# Spice Girls

'Hi Nani. Guess what? Today I made yellow dal, paneer, and matar-aloo pulao with jeera tadka. And it was surprisingly good. You'll be shocked to hear that I actually know vegetable and fruit prices! I am learning how to bargain. But these shopkeepers are smart; they know a potential victim from a kilometre away, even though I pick up the fruit and smell it and everything.'

Silence on the other end and then comes the barrage.

'That is nothing to be happy about. Why are you in Mumbai? You should be in Delhi with your parents and family. You are sitting there alone doing everything yourself. You should be pampered, like your married sisters. We should never have sent you to America. You think you are too smart, too intelligent for everyone else. You just don't listen to us anymore.'

Wow! And I had thought my culinary and bargaining skills would be celebrated by my grandmother. I should have known better. I had not conformed to any of the standard behaviour patterns expected from an almost-thirty-year-old woman. My grandmother, not surprisingly, christened me a 'rebel without a cause or clue'. I was nevertheless proud of myself. I had moved to Mumbai—a city that represented excitement, a warm spirit, a promise, wanting to inhale it all.

My rented flat in the charming, hip suburb of Bandra felt like home. I had a new job that I loved but others found difficult to connect with. 'You work with an NGO that advises other NGOs?' they often asked incredulously.

I didn't know a soul when I got to the Maximum City, but now had a truckload of friends. I had, however, failed to find *the* 'connection' that would allow Nani a restful sleep.

I couldn't help the fact that I was single. I considered my life to be a hot-air balloon and I was floating in the clouds with abandon. I'd never been happier. I felt free. I felt relieved. I felt like myself. But there were times, like the one I just described, where my large colourful balloon developed a tiny hole. Did I mind? Not really, because the person who brought me down to earth was unique and very dear to me. The idea that she was upset upset me.

After all, she was my seventy-eight-year-old, English-speaking, self-driven, Vedanta-studying, pearl-string-wearing, super Nani.

As her eldest unwed grandchild, I was the centre of her universe. Our thoughts are intricately interwoven and our personalities fiercely similar. I have often told my grandmother that if she were born in my generation, and had the choices I did, she would be like me: independent, strong-willed and a drama queen. She laughed and disagreed with me. She is a conventional grandmother in many ways. Like others born in the 1930s, she has an ability to infuse flavours of food into any conversation; keep her legs un-waxed but her eyebrows shaped; express unnecessary concern about each family member's health, spending habits, appearance and lifestyle.

I like to call her Nani-plus because she comes with an extra helping of wisdom, sympathy and an I-don't-care attitude that is worth emulating. She and I have a unique relationship; we argue, pamper, lecture and trouble each other, causing friction and evoking attachment in equal measure. Our conversations are melodramatic, intellectual, inspired by culinary adventures and yoga insights, instructive and life-changing. We discuss Vedanta philosophy, politics and life. We agree that there is a certain thrill in stretching one's mind, enjoying solitary time with books and tackling loneliness through discipline.

Among her other endearing qualities, I admire her for her relentless zest for life. Every year she explores different parts of India with her like-minded friends. While she values quiet moments, she is always ready to watch a new-age Hindi movie.

Predictably, Nani is full of surprises. She once rejected a marriage proposal on my behalf by saying, 'My granddaughter should want to sleep with the man. This one is not for her!'

Over the years, my relationship with my grandmother has hit its highs and lows alongside the waxing and waning of my prospective matrimonial graph. Even if I disagreed with her, I tried to internalise the key messages of her heartfelt sermons. I had to remember that she was half-a-decade ahead (and not behind) me. There were many moments where she became my contemporary, my trusted friend, my confidante.

One Saturday afternoon, in 2008, Nani and I were having a laughter–filled chat over countless paranthas made by her. Our conversation then steered in a direction I could not have imagined. She suddenly looked straight at me, and said with utmost seriousness: 'Can I ask you a personal question?'

Before I had a chance to respond with 'Depends,' she continued, 'Don't you miss sex?'

I would not have been shocked into silence if that question came from my not-so-subtle brother or my worldly-wise sister. I couldn't have imagined, however, that my grandmother would be the first to touch the subject of my celibacy. Before I could pretend I did not understand the question, there was more, 'It's a very natural impulse, child.

Don't you want to be with a man? How do you cope without one? Tell me!'

'Nani, I eat chocolate!' is what I was about to say, when she simply turned towards me and smiled. I still don't know what she believed then or does now. But each time I recall that day, I laugh. In a society where the mere mention of sex creates discomfort and gynaecologist visits are only recommended after marriage, my Nani had the guts to say it all out aloud.

This wasn't the first time she has displayed boldness. She has a certain sensibility and sensitivity that transcends socially-constructed barriers in the mind. My paternal grandparents (as incredible as they are) longed for a boy for their only son. When I was born, the second girl, the disappointment on their faces was clear. Such a sullen environment had dampened my parents' obvious excitement. But then Nani brought boxes of mithai to the hospital and exchanged kind words with my grandparents. She supported my very existence.

And even though today she may not always approve of what I do, I know she celebrates my existence, my journey and my choices as a woman. And through her engaging words and precious advice, she spices up my life—leaving a smile and a thought in her wake.

*Shweta Bagai*

# 2

# ON DREAMS

*The future belongs to those who believe in the beauty of their dreams.*

—Eleanor Roosevelt

# My Best Friend for Life

This is the story of a woman whose life took a hundred-and-eighty-degree turn just because of a computer! I am that woman.

When I was at the peak of my career as a freelance journalist and author, circumstances forced me to migrate from Mumbai, a city I had lived and worked in for twenty-five years, to Kolkata. The shift in 1995 changed the entire course of my career. When we shifted, I had to leave behind my trusted electronic typewriter. Writing, therefore, came to a complete standstill. My husband hired a manual typewriter for me to get on with my work.

But where were the assignments from local papers? Knocking on the doors of Kolkata dailies did not yield much. 'We are overstaffed already,' said one editor. 'We have stopped taking submissions from freelancers now,' said another. Meanwhile, the manual typewriter was getting to be a pain in the neck. The 'r' was broken and the 't' did not function at all. Conditioned to the cartridge of the electronic typewriter, I hated changing the black ribbon. The reels did not move properly. I decided that perhaps it would be best to 'retire' and concentrate on being a housewife. After fifteen years of full-time writing, it was not a happy thought.

Then, a family friend mentioned the magic word 'computer',

and my life changed forever. My husband ventured to shell out the cash, provided I did my own market survey. Taking elementary notes on the configurations I would need for my kind of work, I set off, scouting the market for a PC that would suit my needs and my husband's pocket. I ultimately landed the kind of machine I was looking for. Every day, I would spend two hours teaching myself the basics through the online tutorials—from how to move the mouse, to editing files on my word programme; I learnt to cut and paste from one article to another, how to install and use the printer and a hundred more different things I once thought were beyond me. The 'learning process' was a continuous journey of discovering oneself. But it did little to fatten my empty bank balance—I was still without work.

Then, my husband voiced an idea that was already there at the back of my mind. 'Why don't you write that book on cinema you had promised yourself years ago?' The idea took root. There wasn't much work around anyway. So, I dug up all the paper and magazine clippings I had collected as raw material for the proposed book over the past ten years. I joined a film library and made extensive notes from books I could not afford to buy. Then, I sat myself down with a determination I never knew I was capable of.

It took much heartbreak, hours of frustration, as chapter after chapter was returned by publishers who were not interested in 'stuff' they had never heard of—film criticism with a feminist slant. I made a file of the rejection letters from publishers. It reminded me that these letters were the only obstacles in my race to the finishing post. It was only a matter of time before I reached my goal. I finished one chapter and got on to the next. I always gave in to the temptation to go back and revise. I ended up revising, editing, brushing up, polishing, re-drafting every single chapter so many times that I finally lost count. I realised that this fine-tuning, this desperation for that Utopia called perfection, would never have been possible without my computer. I updated facts and broadened my database all the time as the book got written.

My book was an analytical study of the portrayal of women in Indian cinema from the 1920s to 1998 from a feminist's standpoint. It was something no one in the country—journalist, film scholar, film critic or filmmaker—had even attempted before. I wanted my work to live beyond me. I wanted to carve my name into the history of writing on cinema. The computer became much more than a machine. It evolved over time into a friend, philosopher and guide. I should have dedicated the book to my computer!

Three years later, after god alone knows how many revisions, I finally pulled myself away from the computer, from all the .doc files I had saved up as chapters—I had still not learnt to function from a 'master document'—and declared that the book was complete. No publisher still. The subject was new. I could only write, I did not know the first thing about how to print, publish and market it. My husband stepped in once more—he offered to print and publish it. He is no publisher. He did not know where to begin. With a little help from my brother, an art director in a publishing concern, who did the cover, the book finally rolled out of the press on 21 December 1998.

Soon after the book was released in the Indian market, writing assignments began to pour in. I went back to being a freelance journalist and film critic, writing for newspapers, magazines, e-zines, all over the place. My computer is my partner in this wonderful enterprise of creating and re-creating myself through my writing. By January 2000, my next book, *Indian Women: From Darkness To Light*, was released at the Kolkata Book Fair. The imprint was the same—my husband's firm Parumita Publications. My computer, albeit in an indirect way, had given my semi-retired engineer husband a brand new occupation at sixty! The next book, *Paroma and other Outsiders—The Cinema of Aparna Sen*, won the National Award for the Best Book on Cinema in 2003. My husband won a National Award too, for publishing the book that bagged the National Award! Today, at sixty-six years and counting, I have a doctorate in history (Indian cinema), sixteen published books under noted imprints, two National Awards, one state award, three national research fellowships and one commissioned book to be completed by March 2010. I have travelled across twenty-odd countries across the globe on invitations over the past twenty-three years. I have an average output of twenty published feature articles a month in five print media publications and three e-zines spread across the Internet. The computer is now my closest friend and ally. And even though I step into the kitchen every day to nourish my family, I return to my computer to nourish my soul.

*Shoma A. Chatterji*

## Spelling Success

From the time I was a little girl I knew I was special. While most girls my age wanted to be doctors, models or pilots, I would proudly exclaim to them, 'I want to be a writer!' This statement of mine would often evoke a sniggering laugh from my audience, and more so from my sibling (the academic genius). He would often tell me, 'Roma, do you know what you're saying? You can't even spell "where" correctly!'

The worst part was, he was right, like always! I could not spell correctly. I had a great vocabulary and would flaunt it too, but I couldn't spell the words I used and it would frustrate me endlessly. I would often question myself, 'Why can't I spell correctly? What's wrong with me?'

You know what? There *was* something wrong. I was a borderline victim of dyslexia!

My mother (I call her my spinal cord) tried everything to help me. She would make me write a word a thousand times. She arranged for me to take special tuitions (which cost her more than she could afford at the time) in my second grade, where I would sit and spell words while everybody else my age would play. She also made colourful word charts for me where words I would often spell wrong were broken up in different colours and pasted on my cupboard, so that I could see them all the time. A lot of effort was put into nipping my disability in the bud, but that did not happen.

There were small dividends though. I would still make mistakes, but not as many as before, and I erred only when it came to big words that I had never written before or words that sounded similar but were spelt differently.

Slowly time, the healer that it is, made me feel less humiliated and more confident. But then my confidence was shattered once again and how! I clearly remember this incident, which I call my 'wake up Roma' moment'. It changed me forever. I was in Class 9 and had missed school for two weeks, due to an ailment. My English teacher did not give me grace marks and failed me in English, which was unfair because if you fail in English you fail the term. That was a day I will not forget as long as I am alive. I saw my world crumble in front of my eyes. The pain, the humiliation, the demeaning remarks that I had safely buried in my memory came back to haunt me with a vengeance. I had yet again been stripped of my self-respect and I wept like it was the end of the world. I did not know how I would tell my mother, how she would react. Would I have to hear more hurtful remarks?

I sobbed as I told my mother the bad news. She tried to calm me down, but I was inconsolable. With all the crying, I had got really tired, so I put my head in her lap and, between sobs, kept saying, 'Sorry Ma! I disgraced you yet again.'

She sat there calmly, with confidence and no shame in her eyes. She put her hand on my head and said, 'No baby, I know you can never fail in English. I am sure there is a mistake. You just put this behind you and move on. I know you will make me so proud one day that all this will not matter at all.' Though my sense of pride had snapped and had been crippled that day, my mother had yet again stood by me, rock solid, confident and determined to see her child bloom to success!

I truly believe that this moment was the turning point of

my life. In front of me was a woman who believed in my
capability completely and would fight the world for me. If
she had the faith, what was stopping me from believing in
myself? I pulled myself up. The fighter in me sprang up as
well. From that day, I have never looked back. I went on to
top my school in English and top my college in BA in English
Honours. I also joined one of the most reputed women's
magazines in India with no prior experience.

The day I got my first byline, I remember how I stood,
numb, holding a copy of the magazine in front of me with my
name printed in the credits. I could not believe it! I had
finally had my first taste of success. I was so happy! I came
back and proudly showed the copy to my mother, who said,
'See beta, you have done it and this is just the beginning.' Yet
again she was right. It indeed was just the beginning, because
since then I have worked with more than twenty-five
publications in India and internationally.

Today when I look at my mother and see how proud she
is of me, I get a high! Each time I see her, I feel there is so
much more I can do and I will. I do give the credit of all my
success to my mother who inspired me with her faith, but
there is one special mention without which I cannot complete
this story. My disability: dyslexia! It was in college whilst
studying psychology that I realised that I was dyslexic. Even
today, if it were not for computers that spell-check on their
own, I would be making a lot of mistakes. Every day is still
a struggle for me and I have accepted it as a challenge. I am
not ashamed of being dyslexic. On the contrary, I am proud
that I can overcome my disability each day to write, satisfy
myself creatively and also earn my livelihood through what
was believed to be my biggest weakness.

My disability turned out to be my biggest treasure and I
owe my success to it because it drove me so much to prove
my worth to myself and make my mother proud that I had

no time to waste on lesser things. I never drank, never lit a cigarette. I had bigger things in life to do and I allowed nothing to come between me and my goal.

*Roma Kapadia*

# The Flight of a Butterfly

The wrinkles on her face told of the years gone by since she had first narrated to me the story of the butterfly. She was retelling the story now, a story I'd first heard when I was six, but this was not the only story my sixty-five-year-old grandmother has told me. She often comes up with little tales of profound wisdom peppered with thoughts like, 'Every stage of life is like a cricket match. A new ball is bowled to the batsman each time. And the batsman's aim is to make the runs. We're all always running after something at every stage of our lives. Some batsmen make centuries while some get out on duck. And then we play a new match. It's only just a matter of time,' she said.

My grandmother is a power house of knowledge accumulated over years of reading—from the *Mahabharat* and *Bhagwad Gita* to her current favourite, a Marathi translation of Sudha Murty's *How I Taught My Grandmother to Read and Other Stories*. It's difficult to believe she dropped out of school at thirteen, when you hear her read out some of the most beautifully-crafted Marathi words. That was the age when she married my grandfather, who was studying to be a doctor. Her whole life thereafter revolved around her husband, in-laws and children. Coming from a small village in Karnataka, she didn't have much exposure to anything else.

Whatever she learnt was in the school of life.

Her initial years were lessons on 'how to make chapatis for fifty guests or more' and 'how to keep her in-laws and husband happy'. But her love for the written word didn't die. She continued to read. 'I could have been an Ayurvedic doctor,' she sometimes said. She read a lot of books on Ayurveda when she was younger and then went on to devour religious scriptures. She began to write a lot more once her children grew up and it became clearer with time that she could have been many things—an orator, a spiritual guide, an Ayurvedic doctor, and more than anything else, a writer. But in the Fifties, child-marriages were a norm rather than an exception, and a woman's life revolved around her husband even before she stepped into puberty.

My mother too got married when she was only nineteen, but managed to complete her graduation after her marriage. Where was the opportunity to even think about what she wanted from life? With my father's great support though, my mother tried her hand at taking tuitions before she became the independent and successful businesswoman that she is today.

Like my grandmother, my mother too loved writing. I remember reading some stories that she wrote for local Marathi magazines. It was a side to her I saw only in my teens. Even today, she yearns to write. She scribbles some notes whenever she gets the time. Like her mother, she too sacrificed her own ambitions to a certain extent for her family and is proud of it. Now she has the time to write, yet a large part of her mind remains preoccupied with her children and their lives.

I was their first child and my parents decided to bring me up like they would a boy. Yes, at that time it was acceptable that a man pursue his career while a woman must find a suitable match and start a family. But my mother gave me the freedom of choice and the wings to explore myself. I chose to write. I started when I was twelve, and each time I brought a piece of writing to my mother, I could see her joy. She cried when she sent me away to pursue my career. Perhaps tears of joy more than of separation. She had succeeded in providing her girl with what many generations of women have been deprived of—the freedom of thought and action.

Indian women of their generation couldn't even dream of this kind of freedom to follow their heart. It was impossible for them to even imagine shifting to a big city, living alone, being independent and single at the age of twenty-seven. In a way, I am the butterfly in the story that my grandmother told me when I was six. I am the butterfly that was allowed to find her truth and the glory of free flight by the two women who love me enough to let me go. Sometimes I feel I am living out their dreams—the dreams they couldn't realise. And I am blessed to have learnt how to write from such amazing storytellers.

*Suparna Thombare*

# Sweet Success

She stood staring at the garlands placed outside the sweetmeat shop unmindful of the crowds rushing past her, oblivious to the people who pushed her in their hurry to run their daily errands and complete their shopping for the festival of Makar Sankranti. The petite-in-body but strong-in-mind Vidya stared at the garlands for a while longer before she tentatively ventured inside. 'Excuse me, these sugar garlands are very pretty. Are they for sale? How much for them?' she enquired. A casual conversation with the shopkeeper revealed that the demand for such jewellery was immense—in fact, he told her that if she could make some for him, he would welcome the extra supply. And that was how Vidya became fascinated with the art of halva jewellery. With her children in college and plenty of time to kill, she took it up as a challenge in January 1970.

Today the drawing room in her home is filled with around six women, mostly domestic workers. All of them come to Vidya for training and raw material to hone their creativity and become economically independent as she did almost thirty-nine years ago.

What started out as an effort to while away time has become so much more now and all because a determined woman refused to cow down to society's perception of what an ideal housewife was supposed to be like during that time. She was only supposed to look after the house, raise kids, support her husband and have no individual identity of her own.

Coming from a well-to-do family, Vidya's determination to go commercial with her craft was strongly opposed by her family. 'I was told that I was bringing shame upon my family. Neighbours and friends would debate about my husband's financial situation and snigger behind my back. But he supported me in my endeavour. For us, it was also a way to provide women, who were earning paltry incomes, with hope to fulfil some of their dreams,' recalls Vidya proudly. Vidya's dedication even managed to win over her greatest critic—her mother. 'When I turned fifty, my mother used to urge me to devote time to religious pursuits instead of the halva business,' she recalls with a chuckle. But her mother came around when she realised how much her daughter was helping others. 'Once, when my mother was visiting, one of my workers came and told me that she had bought a year's supply of wheat for her family from the money she had made under my guidance. My mother was touched to hear this, and told me she now realised that I was already doing God's work,' recounts Vidya.

I walked away from my meeting with Vidya thinking that she exemplified the tenet that when you create something with a smile and a prayer, miracles happen and lives are changed forever. For the better.

*Khursheed Dinshaw*

# A Story Comes Full Circle

When I was a girl, I had no ambitions at all, except to be free and untrammelled. Left free to do what I wanted. And yet, when an astrologer, after seeing my horoscope, predicted that I would never earn money in my life, I was furious. But it seemed that he was right, because when I got married, I had neither a job nor any serious thought of a career. Our first son was born just a year after marriage and the other one followed within three years. Now, of course, the idea of my working outside the home seemed impossibly distant. Caught up in the relentless routine of the needs of two infants, I had no time even to think of such a possibility. But soon I began to feel an emptiness in my life. A huge empty space, not in my emotional life, which was fuller than it ever had been, but in the thinking part of my life, which had always been very important to me. And in time, something which had been lying dormant in me through these years of looking after my little boys, began to quicken. Thoughts. Ideas. Words. People and their lives. Using the little spare time I could get, I began writing short stories. Some time later I gave three of my stories to the editor of a national women's magazine, hoping she would publish at least one of them. She took all three. The day I saw my first story in the magazine, I was filled with joy. But I had no idea what I was letting myself in for!

I found myself craving for more and more time for myself, more and more time to write—time which seemed to be always outside my grasp, always slipping out of my hands. The routine of wailing babies, sleepless nights, sterilising bottles and changing nappies changed to one of ironing school clothes, packing school bags, lunch and snack boxes and coping with teachers' demands. All the while an anguished voice within me was crying, 'Let me out, let me out'. But how could I do that, specially since I was determined not to let my writing come in the way of my children, my household routine? I didn't give up entirely.

I struggled, scraped minutes from my routine; but it was never enough. I thought: how did other mothers, working mothers, manage? How did they combine work with children? But this was not like any other work, was it? Writing was like mothering itself, it was something that never let go. I could not allot a little time for it and say, 'Now it's done!' I tried to be stern with this craving, to compartmentalise my life by writing only when the children were at school, never during weekends, never during holidays, never in vacations.

Rushing through my housework and going to my table, knowing all the while that the precious minutes were ticking by. Getting up from the table the moment the children came back home. Never letting them see my occasional moments of resentment, of frustration. It was as if I was rope-walking, afraid each moment that I would lose my balance, that I would fall.

Then came the time when I knew I wanted to write a novel, that I had to write a novel. Things got worse; it was harder to put the work away, harder to pick up later. I found myself doodling, writing words, sentences in the flour when I was making chapattis, framing sentences in my mind and fiercely willing myself not to forget them. And I was constantly fighting demons within myself as well. Why was I taking precious time away from my family for something which seemed to be going nowhere? What kind of woman was I that my heart fell at the thought of interrupting my writing for my family, for guests, visitors? And how could I justify this work when I was not earning any money? When nobody was waiting to read what I wrote? I was constantly nagged by guilt, I called myself selfish, self-indulgent. Even worse, there were days of depression and frustration when the rejection slips came. When I knew I was being ignored, undermined and subjected to put-downers of all kinds. A 'twit of a housewife' I savagely called myself in a little piece I wrote.

Nevertheless, I knew I took myself seriously as a writer, I took my work seriously—never mind if no one else did. And so, despite the fact that the first two novels seemed to have dropped into an abyss, I began a third one in what even I could see was a most unpropitious time. My father was very ill, both the boys were in crucial years in college, my husband, after years of being in a cushioned job, was struggling with the exigencies of private practice, and we changed four houses in three years. I remember scribbling, 'I can't go on, I can't go on,' over and over again when I sat to write.

At some time the novel came alive. I completed it, sent it to a publisher and waited patiently for nearly a year-and-a-half for an answer, which, when it came, was enthusiastic and positive. This novel gave me, finally, a modicum of recognition, something which had escaped me for years. I also began earning money, very little, but enough for me to thumb my nose at the astrologer, to say to him, 'There! I've proved you wrong.'

Things were better after this. The boys went off to hostels, and then to their own homes. There were less demands on my time. I was able to write with less guilt, with more confidence, knowing that this was my work. That it was something I had to do. And that, not to have done it would have been a betrayal of whatever it was that had instilled this urge, this ability in me. Tight-rope walking it may have been, but nothing else was possible.

This year I received a National Award. I was flooded with congratulations and good wishes. But the best ones came from my sons. The older one said, 'This is something you deserve. Something you've got entirely on your own.' The younger, less articulate son, home for just a few days, received the news on his arrival and immediately took us out to celebrate. And I thought—It's been tough, I've tried hard to balance myself and despite the pole in my hands, I've often been in danger of losing my grip on the pole, of falling off the rope. But finally, I've got to the other end, I've got home, safe and erect.

*Shashi Deshpande*

# The Universe and I

When I was all of seventeen, I left the relative comforts of my home in Mumbai to go and live with my grandmother in Birmingham, UK. I was desperate to do only one thing—become an actress. Being half Kashmiri and half German and having been born in the UK, I felt that perhaps my future lay in the West rather than in the Hindi film industry.

My sweet German grandma was delighted to have me live with her whilst I studied for my A levels and looked around at how I could get into an acting school. I started off with evening classes at the Birmingham Theatre School, where I also left some of my latest portfolio pictures one day, simply at the request of one of the teachers there who 'had friends in London'. Eventually, I auditioned for the Guildhall School of Music and Drama in London and won a place despite the fact that they only take nine girls and twenty-one boys in a year, out of some hundreds of applicants!

I was over the moon with joy, but did not have the kind of money required to pay the fees. We had a middle-class background but not huge sums of money in the bank. I tried all avenues open to me. I am a British citizen so I wrote off to a hundred charitable organisations to fund my course. No one wanted to fund an actress, it seemed. I was not eligible for those government grants that students in the UK avail of as I had not lived there for three years prior to my course. Deep down, I knew that chances like this did not come every day, so I ended up working all my holidays to earn and save money to pay the fees. I worked in a hospital as an auxiliary nurse. This basically meant that I cleaned floors and toilets and brought in the tea trolley and the lunch trolley and so on. After a few months I had the money for the first term's fee.

A call from my father, who is directly related to the Nehru family, to the then Indian High Commissioner in London, the late B.K. Nehru, resulted in a room for me at the Indian Students Hostel in the heart of London in Russell Square. So I packed my bags and drove down to London and then drove up to every single hospital, looking for an opening for an auxiliary nurse on Saturdays and Sundays. Not one did! It was a Sunday evening and there was just one hospital left to try. I almost didn't but well ... I did and that was the one that had a vacancy!

I joined the following weekend, as my course at Guildhall was starting on the Monday. Whilst I was there, cleaning away, I happened to pick up the *Evening Standard* newspaper. There on the front page was a picture of an actress I admired very much, Olivia Hussey. She had starred in Franco Zeffirelli's film *Romeo and Juliet* and was now going to play Mary in a three-part serial, *Jesus of Nazareth*. I sighed to myself and thought, 'Lucky girl', and went on with my work.

I started school on Monday, and loved every minute of it. But the Indian Students Hostel was quite another story. Although it was housed in a series of lovely old buildings, the hostel was the saddest place a student could hope to stay in. One look at the old, dirty curtains, sofas that looked like they had been picked up at a junk yard, and peeling walls, and my heart sank deep into the depths of my being. Thoughts of struggling actresses starving in garrets flashed through my mind, appealing to my sense of romantic struggle. Later I would find out about the rats the size of cats too. But the place was cheap!

The cook, Pati, would dish out very bad slushy Indian vegetarian food and passable chicken and mutton curry. So I managed not to starve. But the fact that I was in a little mini-India in the heart of London helped me to get through many a dark patch. The comfort I got from just being in an environment which felt a bit like home, even if it did not look like home, was an immense support. I also started to realise then how Indian I actually was inside of me when I started missing the sound of Hindi film songs and the smell of masala dosa.

On my third day in school, we were called in for an assembly at around eleven in the morning. As the programme came to a close, one of the senior students spoke into the mike. 'Will Soni Razdan from first-year drama please contact the office immediately? Regarding something that could make her into a star of television and screen!' I nearly fell off my chair and rushed to the office. I was told that Franco Zeffirelli (yes the same!) had asked to see me! How did he even know I existed, I wanted to know. Well, Mrs Knight from the Birmingham Theatre School had given my pictures to her agent friend in London who had passed them on to Dyson Lovell, the casting director for *Jesus*. When was that? Nine months ago! And nothing had happened after that. But a few days ago Franco had chanced upon them and had apparently gone ballistic wanting to meet me immediately! So there it was!

Well, off I went of course. I met Zeffirelli, who kept looking at me and saying 'Maria, Maria' in a very Italian accent. He was a darling. He asked me if I could come to Italy for a screen test. I said, 'Sure, as long as you pay for it 'cause I don't have a dime.' They all laughed and after a few more 'Marias' he told me that he wanted me to test for the part of Mother Mary. Olivia had been signed up so that was the only hitch. The *Evening Standard* flashed through my mind. I thought things like this only happened in films! They told me to come back in the evening to find out. Well, I just couldn't go back to school that day. I walked around London feverishly all day, my mind in a total tizzy. I think I even went back to the hostel and wept. Out of relief, excitement, gratitude and fear too maybe. Finally I went back in the evening. They told me that they could not get Olivia out of her contract without paying a lot of money. But they wanted me to be a part of the series, as part of the 'rep' group of actors, and shoot for two months in Morocco. I would be paid seven hundred pounds a week! That was like seven thousand pounds today.

For a poor student who was struggling the way I was, this was enough to make me believe in God all over again. I grabbed the opportunity and a week later I was off to Morocco. My school even let me go for the whole first term, saying that it would be a good experience and I think they knew how hard I was working to put money together. I had a wonderful time shooting in Morocco, and played different parts. I was something of a glorified extra if you like. But it really didn't matter to me. I earned enough to pay for the rest of the year's fees and even a ticket back home to see my family. And more . . .

But most of all, I learnt that anything that you get out of life is in proportion to what you put into it. I had struggled so hard and somehow, somewhere, the universe was giving me something back in return. And this truth has stayed with me all my life and I have always lived by this tenet. You do not get anything out of life by sitting at home and thinking about it. You only get by doing, doing, doing. And putting yourself out there to play the game of life.

Other really amazing things happened to me after this too. Equally serendipitous. But then, that is a whole other story!

*Soni Razdan*

# Dreams Unlimited

Little drops make an ocean. I could only think of that proverb as I chatted casually with Newbery Award winner Linda Sue Park at the Golf Club. Next to me, bestselling authors Juanita Havill and Eileen Spinelli were talking shop, while Mr Kent Brown, editor-in-chief of *Highlights for Children* magazine, looked at our table and smiled.

For a minute, I thought it was all a dream. I dug into the smoked salmon on my plate. Delicious! It seemed surreal that I, a twenty-four-year old middle-class woman from south India, one who had never been inside a star hotel or a designer boutique, was exchanging email IDs with the literary who's who in America.

The occasion was the 20th Annual Children's Writers' & Illustrators' Conference, hosted annually by *Highlights for Children* magazine. Every year a small number of writers from around the world are sponsored to attend this weeklong conference, and in 2004, I was the lucky winner from India.

It all began when children's writer Santhini Govinden, the first Indian writer to be sponsored for the conference in 2001, posted details about the 2004 contest on my online writing group. Entries needed to be submitted in the next ten days. I was really excited and wanted to enter the contest, but I had a problem—my MA exams were only a week away. It was a tough call but I opted for the fellowship, as I figured I could always write the exams in the next semester.

Such a decision might horrify most people, but my near and dear ones know that it is exactly the kind of choice that a risk-taker like me would take. After all, I had already ditched an expensive architecture degree to become a (gasp!) freelance writer! I applied on the very last day of the deadline and promptly forgot about it. I was busy placating my furious parents about my postponed exams, even though they had almost given up on their wild child who would never listen to them.

On 30 May 2004, I received a call that would change my life. It was the Indian co-ordinator of the contest, calling to tell me that I had won and was invited to an all-expenses paid trip to the US. Wow! Talk about dreams coming true. On 16 June I received the official invitation and on 13 July I was kissing my stunned parents an enthusiastic goodbye. The next day, it was Hello, America!

From my arrival at Newark International Airport, to the four-hour trip to Honesdale, to the bangle-sized onion rings at a diner, everything was a happy blur. The days sped by in a blur of hectic but exciting activities.

Winning the fellowship was the most exciting incident in my life. Apart from a great travelling experience, it paved the way to a wonderful writing career for me. I had networked so well at the conference that I went back again the next year to do a well-paid internship with *Highlights* magazine! Since returning to India in August 2004, I have written several books for children, edited a famous children's website and organised the first women's writing retreat in India.

So ... what did I do to deserve such happiness?

That's what I ask myself often as well. I am not famous. I am not perfect, and I certainly am not financially blessed. What did I do that elevated my status from a confused professional to a successful writer?

The answer is quite simple. I think I deserved it all because I took small steps to the big miracle. I didn't leap without looking; neither did I stay at the same place, afraid to venture out. I progressed from one phase to another in slow, steady steps.

If I had given up hope when people berated me for choosing writing as a full-time profession, I'd have remained an unhappy architect all my life.

If I hadn't maintained constant touch with my writer friends, if I hadn't persuaded myself to join a writer's group, I wouldn't have been at the right place at the right time.

If I hadn't believed in myself and that I had a good chance to win the contest, I'd never have experienced the most incredible moments in my life.

So there it is, the answer to the question—perseverance and consistent work is all it takes to realise your dreams. The key is to do what you want to do, and keep doing it, irrespective of the curveballs that life and others may throw at you. There were times when I was incredibly depressed because all my friends were in a secure job and I was struggling to pay the phone bill. But I never let my inner fire go out. If you are passionate enough about what you do and willing enough to reach for the sky, you leave no choice for success but to reach for you. I was an underachieving introvert in school and college, and if I can be a success story in life, so can anyone! Choose your path, stay on it through thick and thin, and inevitably, you *will* reach your destination.

*Radhika Meganathan*

# Gift Shop on Call

I believe that our subconscious has a hotline connection with the power that listens intently to its whispers, its purest surges, its deepest longings and then answers from a place we did not know existed. What we want most fervently always comes to life. Oh, that penthouse or that corner office may not materialise, but something more important will. Something that will make us believe in the power of our dreams. Something that will connect us however fleetingly with the source of abundance in the world and beyond it.

What adds most meaning to our existence always finds its way to us and I know this because I was once a young girl, living in a small town where my TV set was my only conduit to the world I loved—the world of art, writing, films, theatre, music. From the time I could make sense of the world, I had a deep and abiding love for beauty, and for creative opportunities. I longed to meet people whose world was bigger than mine, whose minds could open doors to riches I had not yet discovered.

I read about Professor A.R. Jaisim who, inspired by the idol of my teenage years, Ayn Rand's Howard Roark, had started his radically experimental architectural firm, Jaisim Fountainhead. I wished I could see his projects and meet him. I watched Merchant Ivory productions like *The Bostonians* and *A Room with a View* late into the night, smiled through actor and director Shankar Nag's inspired take on R.K. Narayan's *Malgudi Days*, drowned in the voice of Jagjit Singh, longed to go to a really great art school to learn to paint, to converse with the likes of Imtiaz Dharkar and Shabana Azmi whose lives I had read about in magazines, and to watch Naseeruddin Shah polishing his craft because his portrayal of Mirza Ghalib had brought the bard alive for me. I wanted to attend glittering pageants, to be at concerts, plays, buy as much music as I wanted to. It did not happen. Nor did I ever expect it to. Such dreams were impossible to come true—or were they?

A few years later, in Bangalore, on the basis of my freelance writing, I became a cub reporter for a national daily and later joined another as a feature writer. And it was almost as if someone up there started ticking off my wish list for me. As a rookie reporter, I got to cover the Miss World pageant where educated, opinionated girls from all over the world broke for me the myth that beauty queens have little substance. Over the years, I got to interview singers like Hariharan, Shankar Mahadevan, Shubha Mudgal and the legendary Manna Dey who sang a few lines at my request of a favourite song, *Har taraf ab yahi afsane hai*. And poet Javed Akhtar, who shared his faith that India's secular spirit could never be torn apart. And Shabana Azmi who told me about the inspiring social work her father, the great poet Kaifi Azmi, had done in his village Mizwan in his last years. I saw Naseeruddin Shah on stage performing *Antigone* and also Ismat Chughtai's stories and got to interview him. I remember walking into Waheeda Rehaman's Hacienda to interview her with *Aaj phir jeene ki tamanna hai* playing in my head! Yes, I got to attend many Jagjit Singh concerts too and to interview the man himself. When I became a design writer, I also got to meet A.R. Jaisim in his cavernous office and to profile his work.

And to talk to musician Richard Clayderman whose cassette I had bought years ago. I was even blessed to receive the best art education anyone can hope for when, for over ten years, as an art critic, I got to review the works of painters and sculptors from all over the world. On one charmed evening, I remember sitting next to M.F. Husain, being taught a thing or two about art and life. And it was a surreal, magical moment when I found myself interviewing Ismail Merchant and Madeleine Potter who I had admired all those years back in *The Bostonians*. Though Shankar Nag had passed away, I saw his dream theatre space Ranga Shankara coming to life in my neighbourhood thanks to the tireless efforts of his wife, Arundhati Nag. As a music reviewer, I began to receive more music than I knew what to do with and remembered how I had never been able to buy enough music as a teenager. Many more lesser known but equally inspiring people were put in my way as lessons or gifts for me to learn from and to make more of my life.

No, that dream home of my own has not materialised yet. Nor has the Tuscan vacation where I will paint flower-strewn slopes, but I know today that my dreams, like yours, are dreamt for a reason. And that we must never stop dreaming them even if there is no reason for us to believe that they will ever come true.

*Reema Moudgil*

# One Life to Live

*There is great beauty in going through life without anxiety or fear.*
*Half our fears are baseless and other half discreditable.*

–Christian Nestell Bovee

My passion for travel is such that sometimes I wonder why I wasn't carrying a cap, camera and a carry bag when I was born! Of course, God offered me ample opportunities to use them once I grew up and had what I thought was the noose of being single. Thence began my struggle as a single woman desirous of exploring the world, regardless of the dangers inherent in all adventurous ideas.

'No risk … no game. Take calculated risks and fulfil your dream,' I told myself every time paranoia gripped me in a new place. So I decided to start travelling in a group with strangers. An exhilarating adventurous trip in the Himalayas paved the way for more trips down the untrodden path.

I planned my second trip to Rajasthan. I wondered if I should take off alone but the thought of spending the night in the desert with a camel and a bunch of strangers was unnerving. Yet I continued making my itinerary undaunted. Just in the nick of time I found a partner in a friend's sister who wished to 'do' Rajasthan before settling down in

Canada. I will never forget the sense of fulfilment I felt as my body did a tango with the camel's trot in the two-night desert safari where I also learnt a very important life lesson. Far away from civilisation, under the moonlit sky, I had peeped out of my sleeping bag to ask a lone Swiss girl, 'Emma, aren't you afraid, travelling on your own in a new country?'

She replied, 'Just use your sixth sense and you will be fine.'

After observing her over the next two days, I bid goodbye to fear even though I had wanted to ask her, 'But how do you develop a sixth sense, Emma?'

Through exposure and insights, I finally did develop a sixth sense along with confidence. Of course, I was lucky to have got my basic lessons in travelling from my parents. Thanks to them, I had visited Uganda, Nairobi and Tanzania as a child; Amritsar, Kashmir and Delhi as a student; and the Far East, Dubai and Muscat as a grown-up woman of the world. So armed with travel-happy genes, a sixth-sense, soaring spirits, raging curiosity, zesty disposition and youth by my side, I travelled to Madhya Pradesh and Garhwal to hobnob with the tigers in the wildlife sanctuaries, lolled in the houseboats in the backwaters of Kerala, chirped with the birds in Kabini resort in Tamil Nadu and in Dandeli and relived history in Karnataka. I even took an organised tour to Europe and the Far East but discovered that that fast-food-style of travel was not for me.

Time took wings. Body got older and the spirit turned jaded. The lust for life dulled and confidence got a beating from hormones. But the list of the countries to be visited got longer and my belief in angels who would be travel guides or just watchful caretakers remained unchanged. Then in 2008, I decided to do four of my favourite countries at one go, all by myself. My zeal to make it happen was so great that I was determined to get the visas and worked hard at it, and enthusiastically researched on the Internet to make the itineraries.

In the US, as I moved from the East Coast to Florida to Chicago, my anxieties about losing my passport or missing planes disappeared. I encountered angels in London and Germany in the form of people who helped me lug suitcases, gave me directions and chatted me up smilingly to ask, 'Are you from Puerto Rico?' Staying alone in hotels and even a youth hostel at one instance was not as unnerving as I had thought. My belief in the goodness of people and the abundance of life was reinforced, and as I sipped hot chocolate in an elegant boat cafeteria in Switzerland, I had wondered, 'Why do a few bad incidents make headlines in the newspapers and why do people stop living because of fears when there is so much to love and so many lives in one life to live?' The uplifting and stimulating experiences of each adventurous day did not leave me any time to ponder over the answers to that question.

After having been on my own and exploring the countries the way I wanted, when I returned in two months, I felt an overwhelming sense of victory. I am glad I listened to my heart and did not let fear overcome me when I was warned about things like mugging in the metro in Manhattan, racism, crimes against lone women and more by well-meaning friends and family. By letting go of the fears, I have let go of the noose too and have reaped big rewards in terms of enriching life experiences. My being single is no longer a liability but a passport to new vistas and, armed with it, I'm ready to explore the rest of the world.

*Darshana Doshi*

@LAVANYA KARTHIK

*Reprinted by permission of Lavanya Karthik*

# 3

# A LIFE OF PURPOSE

*A bird doesn't sing because it has an answer, it sings because it has a song.*

–Maya Angelou

# Anjali

I had accompanied my friend Vandana to Palassar village, which is about a hundred kilometers from Ahmedabad. Their NGO, Manav Sadhna, had organised a medical camp in the village. Along with the camp, the volunteers were carrying out a 'green drive' by planting trees and had even taken up cleanliness and hygiene projects of sorts. Each group consisted of four to five volunteers conducting the specific task assigned to them. It is there that I met Anjali again. I have known Anjali over five years; apart from documenting the NGO's projects, she fills in wherever it is required. Over the years she has accompanied me on various occasions in my sporadic social service ventures.

Here she was in Palaasar, carrying two jholas on both her shoulders. One seemed empty, while the other, full and heavy. I could see small saplings peeping out from this bag. Her face had random mud marks, her hands were dark with dirt.

'Hey Anjali, you cleaning or dirtying the village?' I joked, wiping the mud stains as best as I could with her dupatta. 'And what are you doing with that empty jhola?' I asked.

She invited me to join her in her cleansing drive; 'An inner one,' she said and winked.

I followed Anjali as she patiently made her way to individual homes with her signature bright smile and Americanised

Gujarati (Anjali is a second generation Indian American). She would ask for the man of the house; once he appeared, she would extend her empty jhola, telling him to donate to her their *vyasan* (bad addiction). In time the family too would gather, and she would speak of the ills of chewing or smoking tobacco, and would even show them pictures or read literature related to this. By the time she was done with the family, every single pouch of tobacco (both chewing and smoking) would be neatly packed away in her empty jhola. In exchange, she would give them a sapling to plant and nurture. I followed her to about ten homes. In some, men were difficult and took longer to get convinced, in others she took no more than a few minutes to seal the 'exchange programme', as she termed it! In every home though, she earned heaps of blessings from all the womenfolk, right from the seventy-year-old majis to the four-year-old children! I saw her empty jhola slowly fill up with all brands and types of tobacco while the stuffed jhola gradually emptied out as small plants found new homes.

As I made my way to the car to leave, she accompanied me to dispose of the tobacco and refill the plants bag. We got chatting. I know that Anjali is an engineer and was in the highest income bracket in the US before she came to India on a service vacation for a three-month period. It had already been five years and she was still around!

'Anjali I know that since the last five years you have been completely committed to social service, but does it never get too much, doing this day in and day out, and that too as voluntary work?' She had been staying with the founders of the organisation and I knew that she took up commercial projects when she needed money for some specific personal reason—but these were few and far between. Honestly speaking, I considered it a little impractical and naïve, almost as if being young she had no idea of what she was forgoing!

She smiled at me, the same smile she had been showering all along to the residents of the homes we had visited. 'It's a kind of power, Raksha. The power to change lives. The power to make a difference, the power to bring a smile, ease an aching heart, support a stumbling life and in return get what we crave for most: love.'

As I struggled to understand, she continued.

'Tell me, have not men through the centuries done everything they could, foul or fair, to gain power? Men have fought wars, killed each other, indulged in dirty politics, have lied, laboured day and night—for what? Power? Don't you think what I am doing is just a simpler shortcut, an easier way where there has to be no loser or defeated? We can all win together. Do you know an easier way?' she asked me in return. Before I could answer I saw about forty women and young girls making their way to us—no, to her, Anjali.

They knew Anjali didi was the one running the exchange programme and carried two jholas on her frail shoulders. They walked straight up to her and said, 'Didi, come to our house also please!'

*Raksha Bharadia*

# Dejunking Life

I was just thirty-two years old, but even sitting on the floor was a dream, because I knew I wouldn't be able to get up. My knees and back hurt all the time. Breathing was a difficulty, my chest felt constantly constricted and I would often break into an incessant cough. I lived on tablets and pain killers that I took at least six times a day. All this was just because I was grossly overweight. I weighed 160 kilos! Was I born fat? No. I did not have a thyroid or hormonal problem. I was born skinny and had weighed just six pounds. Like a normal child, I had played games actively, and swimming had been my greatest passion. I was fussy about food and took ages to eat. I liked simple food; three meals were more than enough, and I was petite and tiny, which worried my family.

In my growing-up years, after my evening play time, I would feel famished and exhausted, and would start eating quick and easy snacks like French fries, wafers, milkshakes and buttered cheese sandwiches or fried cheese toast. My addiction to packaged junk food, full of preservatives and chemicals, had begun.

My parents would want me to eat my dinner too, so that I wouldn't miss out on my vegetables, salads and roti. So I began to eat those meals as well and this kicked off a habit of over-eating. I would eat one roti and then fall asleep at the table. My family grew concerned about my poor intake, not realising that the evening snack had been far too heavy for me to have had a full meal at dinner.

These habits ingrained in childhood became a part of my lifestyle. Just as a drug addict craves his daily fix, a junk-food eater craves junk. I needed a fix of sugar and white flour loaded with fat, and so would gobble milkshakes, sandwiches and fried Gujarati snacks like puris, chakris, sev and ganthias. School timings became longer, lunch breaks became shorter, and food had to be eaten faster. I steered clear of vegetables and salads and ate only daal and rice, which I could gobble fast and then run out to play. Not satiated still, I would then savor wafers, batata vadas, samosas, sandwiches, aerated drinks, ice creams and chocolates in the canteen. My weight slowly and steadily crept up as school hours became longer and exercise became negligible. This crazy food routine took me from skinny to plump to fat to obese. My concerned mother took me to a naturopath when I was in Class 7. He tried hard to wean me off these foods but I could not stick to a fruit and vegetable diet, or bear those steam boxes and massages.

I was too hassled with it all and went to him on the sly and asked him to tell my mother that this is not for me. Then she took me to another dietician. He used to make me march through his clinic and I hated it and so I gave up on myself! In Class 9, I was eighty-five kilos.

I was even hospitalised in Breach Candy Hospital to lose weight. Those were ten days of sheer torture, and I had had to lie to my friends that I was on a holiday because I did not want them to know I was in hospital. I was popping pills, and battling starvation and enemas. The result was a ten-kilo weight loss in ten days, which was not to last for too long. I regained double the amount of weight soon after, and was gifted with constipation for life.

In Class 12, at ninety-six kilos, I was sent to a health farm. Being a city girl, I went completely crazy there and ran away in twelve days with fourteen kilos off.

On a holiday in Europe, I landed on the surgery table with a cyst in my rectum. I refused to do anymore dieting for a few years. I went back to my old ways of eating and touched 145 kilos, and then swung back and forth between protein powders and a high-protein diet. Ridiculously expensive, these potions left me with no energy and so I gave them up. Then came my trips to gyms and other assorted dieticians. The gym instructors expected me to work out for a whole hour not realising that I could barely walk! The diets were all fad diets I could not stick to.

At thirty-two, I crossed 150 kilos and it was then that I realised that I had a choice between life and death. I went on a sensible weight loss and exercise programme, and in two years, I was down to sixty kilos! I had a lot of loose skin and I had slipped into anorexia. Constipation was my companion still and I had to undergo a surgery for an abscess. I realised that I needed to study nutrition to get out of anorexia as well as various other health-related problems. I started studying with a passion and qualified as a nutritionist.

My experience has made me a completely different person, and today I am obsessed with the cause and effect of food on our lives. I think of food, dream of food and write about food. I have only one mission: I do not want anybody to go through what I have. I know today what junk food can do to our system. The chemicals, the preservatives, the addictives, and the growth hormones are the ones that are causing complete imbalance in our bodies. Psychological disorders, mood swings, constipation, humongous sizes, eating disorders, elevated blood pressure, lipids and even cancer are some of the after-effects of thoughtless eating.

I run a health centre today which guides people on how to

loose weight sensibly and healthily. I conduct workshops for companies and educational institutions on healthy living and nutrition. I plan health food menus for hotels and institutes. I advise shops about healthy products. I write articles for leading newspapers and magazines on health-related topics.

In today's high-stressed lifestyle and fast-changing world, the one person with whom you spend the longest time is yourself. Do you not think then that you owe it to yourself to be careful with your health? Do you not owe it to your children? Do you not deserve a better life and a healthy body protected from dieting fads and eating disorders?

I have been there. I have walked the path. I know the pain and the pitfalls. I know there are days when temptation rules, but then they cannot match the days when I have experienced the joy and the triumph of resistance! I have only this to say to you—I understand that it is hard but I know for sure that it is possible! And I am a living proof of that.

*Naini Setalvad*

# Waking Into the Sunset

She stood looking at the city. From this height, roads looked like blue snakes and buildings like matchboxes. A friendly breeze cooled her hot cheeks and ruffled her hair. She watched the evening bus leave the office premises. The next one was at 11 p.m. If she was lucky she could get out then. Otherwise, it would be another long night at the office.

The roof-top cafeteria was deserted. She liked it. It made her forget the world inside the walls. It was too early for sunset, but she waited. Her coffee cooled rapidly as cobwebby thoughts enveloped her.

'You need leave?', they had asked. 'You are single. No boyfriend. No one to wait for you back home. No sick child longing for you. Why do you want leave?'

She had replied, 'I want to watch the sunset.' They had laughed at her and ridiculed her. 'We don't encourage idleness here. Surely only married women need free time.'

Like Azkaban, this office too was a prison without walls, sucking all happiness out of people, making them remember only depressing thoughts. No chains were required to keep the prisoners in; they remained trapped in their own depression. She had always loved fairy tales, but nineteen months into her first job, she had seen the wrong end of the rainbow.

She had seen it all. Cinderellas trying to fit themselves into glass slippers too tight for them. Red Riding Hoods walking straight into the big, bad wolf's mouth. Steadfast Tin Soldiers with their noses in computers. Beauties turning into Beasts and Peter Pans who never grew up. Never Neverland at its worst.

As if on cue, the sky turned a brilliant orange. One good thing about tall buildings, she thought. They make you feel you can touch the sky. 'There you are,' someone said from behind. 'The PM wants you. Some clarifications required on the new code.'

'I am coming,' she said. Night was falling.

The next afternoon found her at the PM's office. 'Congrats,' he said, 'you did it again. They like your code.'

He looked like Santa Claus with an early Christmas gift. 'For all the overtime you put in, a US visit is on the cards.'

She replied, 'Thank you sir,' and gave him her resignation letter.

No goodbye was said. As she walked off into the sunset and the breeze ruffled her untied hair, she smiled. Time to write a new fairy tale. Time to claim her happy ending.

*Parvathy Mohan*

# The Cake Does Not Have to Crumble

It isn't unusual for people to look at my mother's special, all white, oval cake laced in baby-pink icing with widening eyes and sigh, 'It's so pretty! I can't cut it!' What a story this cake with its warm, rum sides and fruit and spice spirit could tell you! If it could, it would say, 'Actually, I'm not even as symmetrical as I ought to be. The flooring in the home I was baked in tilts southwards and so does the oven. This translates into cakes with one shoulder slightly higher than the other. But you'd never have known that if I hadn't been on a truth-telling spree. Hmm ... perhaps all those tiny flaws we fret ourselves into a fury over are inconsequential in the big scheme of things after all. Not that this is going to stop Mrs Nunes from practicing till her fondant is as smooth as silk, and sans a single wrinkle.

'I'm just one of the many practice cakes that went out to friends and family. Does this practice ever end? I remember thinking as I caught sight of the arched eyebrow on her son's face as I made my way out the door. Two years she's been practicing. She's done everything from christening to wedding cakes. And she's still practicing. Maybe that's all life is ... one practice round after another. If there's no final exam, all that really matters is that you do the task before you as best as you can.

'I bet that right about now Mr Nunes is rifling through the kitchen looking for a slice of one of the four cakes he helped bake yesterday. He's going to be really disgruntled when he finds no more than a few odd crumbs left behind in empty baking tins. He still fails to understand Mrs N's logic of practicing her cake-making skills by baking cakes to give away. All those hours of effort seem like "such a waste if you don't even get to taste". Now this is a philosophy that's lost on Mrs N's daughter who hates fruit cakes in all their shapes and shades, but will still spend hours on end icing intricate patterns on the cakes her mum bakes simply because "it makes her happy". Hmm ... It's rather odd what makes some people happy.

'Now if you're wondering how Mrs N conned her entire family into helping her out, I'll tell you. It's no great secret. Mrs N, for all her enthusiasm, is a bit scattered. So she'll start a project, find something missing and then send her husband or son off on a treasure hunt. Or she'll have grossly underestimated the kind of time she has on her side. The only way to remedy that, aside from growing three pairs of hands, is to put the entire family to work. So while one whips the flour and the eggs together, another prepares the silver foil base and the third is sent out to purchase more eggs. There's no such thing as "too many cooks" in Mrs N's book.

'Now Mrs N's book has more chapters than I know of, considering she's spent over half a century here on Earth. I've begun this story somewhere in the middle, but I do think it's imperative that we go back to the beginning of Mrs N's cake chapter. Mrs N started attending a baking class because she fell in love with the delicate flowers she'd seen atop a wedding cake somewhere. Now it's pointless making flowers with nowhere for them to go, so she learnt to make the rich plum cake which, in case you've forgotten, is what I am. Then there's the marzipan and the fondant that go on top.

Now all this is just the base for what she's really interested in
... the flowers. This may seem like a whole lot of effort just
to have a place to put a few edible flowers, but try explaining
that to her. Besides, since she absolutely refuses to try her
hand at any cakes other than the rich plum variety, these
have now gotten so good than, even without the marzipan
and the other toppings, they're sumptuous. I've got to admit
that this blinkered focus, though I'd never advise it, does
seem to have a place for itself.

'What would possess a woman to come home exhausted
after a full-day's work and then stay up until three in the
morning baking? I still haven't figured it out. But my best
guess would be it's her way of breaking the circle. The circle
of going to work and coming back and then going back again
the next day just to keep the finances in order. The circle of
doing the things that need doing to keep her world-a-turning.
The circle of duties and responsibilities. Somehow stepping
outside the circle if only for a few hours appears to add
meaning to her life.

'"What meaning?" you might wonder if you stepped into
her house in the middle of a baking session. With aluminium
platters in all sizes, butter paper, essences, paint brushes,
bottles of colour and what-have-you spread across every
available surface, all you see is pure chaos. Make sure you
check the cushy armchair for cutters and crimpers before
making yourself comfortable. As you're finally starting to get
used to the disarray, your olfactory nerves wake up and you
think "Hola! What's that divine smell?" And before you
know it you're being served a slice of heaven.

'Is there a secret ingredient to Mrs N's confections?
Sometimes I'm tempted to believe someone up there is actually
listening to all those prayers she keeps murmuring while
stirring in the sugar, or hoping the oven doesn't quit on her,
or pleading that the clock slows down enough to let her
complete a cake in time. And after every "miraculous"

outcome she swears she's giving cake-making a rest. But two weeks later the household will be back in the throes of another cake-making episode.

'I'll bet Mrs N is starting a new cake chapter as I end this one. There's one last question I must pose before I'm food for thought. Did you know there's a right way to cut a plum cake so it won't crumble? You actually have to carve it like you would a piece of meat or bread, sawing gently back and forth till you cut all the way to the bottom. Very few know this and so you oft have occasion for sighs and phrases like, "That's the way the cookie (cake in my case) crumbles". But you know what . . . it doesn't have to be that way.

'Mrs N is a living proof of that. Ask her daughter.'

And that's where I come in to say my piece. My mother Ivy, who has been working with an airlines as a stenographer for the past twenty-six years, attributes all her blessings to 'the Man up above', which explains how she got this job while others with earthly godfathers and influence didn't. She grew up the 'hard way', though these are not, nor have ever been her words. She grew up in a chawl in Sewri, the third of four siblings. She's not different from a lot of the aunties of her generation who diligently went for sewing class and put it to good use for their kids, and are patiently waiting to sew stuff for grandkids. She taught herself how to crochet and knit and tat from books on the train enroute to college. She has been sort of running three households and playing mother to extended family long before she had kids. She's not one for travel and can spend endless hours at home doing stuff or watching squirrels prance about on the tree outside our home. She'll 'rest in the grave', she says. My mother, Mrs N, has always given wings to others and when she wants to fly, she bakes, swathes her creations with beauty and ends one more journey into rum-soaked happiness by putting those flowers on top.

*Averil Nunes*

# And She Rowed

It was the late 1960s. Our village, Vellattanjur in Thrissur district in Kerala, was struck by a famine. I was less than ten years old. Two crops of paddy were lost in a row. People had nothing to eat. They began eating anything they could think of—leaves of all kinds, roots and stems. Our house was one of the very few that had rice in what we call the pathayam, a storage cell.

My mother, Kunjathi, went through a period of deep moral anguish. She struggled to resolve the agony of being able to eat three times a day while most of the other villagers were starving.

Being forced to starve is something so remote to most of us. I saw people in our village doing things I had never seen before. Nothing seemed to matter to the people but food. Everyone was out foraging, gathering, and converting things to make them edible.

Parts of plants normally left to rot were picked up carefully by hand and taken home. Things that until then had been at the margins of our awareness—creepers, plants, shrubs, palm trees, everything that grew at the edges or between the crops—all came alive to our attention.

Thinking of it now, years later, I remember a story that is told as part of a folk performance in our village festival. It's called Malavazhi, the hill mother. The story goes like this:

Once it happened that Malavazhi came down to the plains and approached the goldsmiths, bamboo weavers, blacksmiths, weavers and potters to get something to wear. She did this so that all could recognise her and do her homage. But they refused to give her anything. After she left, the people of that area were struck by a famine. In panic, they went to a healer who told them that the famine was caused by Malavazhi, the mother of the hill, also known as Godavari, the sacred cow that suckles the earth. They repented and each made something for Malavazhi to wear. They went to find her and found her collecting the grains left in the field after the harvest. There they gave her the raiments they had brought. She put it on and danced, sickle in hand. At the end of the dance she gave them the paddy husk as prasadam to eat, in order to teach them that they shouldn't waste even a single grain produced by Mother Earth, even in periods of abundance.

Twenty years ago, I painted a picture to illustrate this story. Like all living stories, it doesn't stay in the past. If we remember it, it lives with us, even when we think we don't need it anymore. Even when we believe we've rowed past those waters.

So one night, when we were living our story, our mother explained to us how much the people in the village were suffering and asked if we'd be willing to make do with two meals a day instead of three. We could then give the families around us the rice of the third meal. I'm sure she must have given more than just that amount. But what stays so strongly in my mind is how she suggested to us children that we skip a meal to participate in what the others in our village were going through. Later, she began feeding us a third meal again, but a much smaller one, made from the same ingredients that the other people in the village were using.

My mother is such a mystery to me, especially as to how

she managed to row us through such troubled waters. It was around the same time my grandfather had become bed-ridden. Because he had such an overwhelming presence in the village, and because so many changes were taking place in Kerala, pitting labourers against land-owners who had hardly a few acres of land, his illness and then his death would throw us into another time of great turbulence. My father, who was speech- and hearing-impaired, (though a dreamer with founts of a deep, universal love in his heart) wouldn't have been able to guide us or weave together the loose threads my grandfather had left behind. There was only my mother.

We talk of courage as a force that carries us through hardship. But I don't think this word has much relevance to my mother's way of thinking. She was fragile and soft-spoken, and her face always had a smile, even if it was sometimes soaked in pain. She was forced to confront this new reality in front of her.

And she started to row. A rowing of compassion and suffering, love and endurance. Through one dark day. Then another. Then one more. With the oars of prayer. She was rooted in the real things, my mother, and yet, she was beyond them. My mother did not just row the boat. She *was* the boat, and the waters themselves. And everything she ferried across got connected to the truth that when it is dark, we must believe in light and must row on even if the shore seems unreachable.

*C.F. John*

# Changing Lanes

What do you do when your high-profile government job is so uninspiring that you have to drag yourself out of bed every morning? When you can't recognise yourself as you? When life doesn't seem at all what you thought it would be? And on voicing your doubts, you're told you're weak, irresponsible and a complete fool? Do you crucify yourself and carry on the same way, in that velvet-lined cage, for the sake of that sprawling house, white Ambassador car, safe job, pension, 'contacts'? And convince yourself that life will be rewarding next time around, in the next birth? Adjust? Resign to things as they are? Or do you search your soul to ask, 'What am I living for?'

Such a dilemma ended for me when I decided not be an unhappy government servant, full of self-importance, and instead gave up my job. I turned into a nobody, a nameless leaf on a tree, free to be myself.

The liberation didn't come about all of a sudden. It took me eight years to realise that my big dream had not really been what I wanted from life. Ah, how smitten I had been by the Civil Services Syndrome.

With stars in my eyes, I had slogged for the Civil Services exam, got through and was allotted CISF (Central Industrial Security Force). With a vague idea about what it entailed, I joined the training academy at Secunderabad.

Though demanding, the training period was exciting. At the academy, the day would begin at half past four in the morning with a clang on the door for tea. We would don our drill uniforms and at 5.30 a.m., jog out to the parade ground and stand in formation. After sweating it out for forty minutes, we would run to change into our uniform for the next training class. At around 8.25 a.m., we would sprint to the Mess to gobble breakfast, bathe, change, wear khakis and report for indoor classes by 9.30 a.m.

Keeping the eyes open during these classes was a battle. Lunch would be back at the Mess, where we'd walk down in the sun, always in step, with the course senior in charge of the batch. And then, a dreamless nap. Tea clang on the door at 3 p.m. Another change into drill uniform, walk in step to the parade ground for drill practice, followed by games. Over and out at 5.40 p.m. And then we were free to go to the room to nurse the day's aches and pains and crash out after dinner.

Yet, there was camaraderie, humour and bonhomie in everything that transpired there. I was even inspired to write poetry, the essence of which was:

How we scrubbed the rifles clean
While fate stood watching over us to preen
Oil on our T-shirts, oil on our knees
As we struggled to make our barrels and our futures gleam!

The future did gleam but not in the way I had expected when, after fifteen months, we were posted to our respective units. It was a regimented life with fixed duties and a fixed role for an officer. The years rolled by. I met people, many of whom I admired for their efficiency. But many, I found, went through their careers with little or no inclination for initiative. I had wanted to contribute to change, but I realised I had become part of the very system I had wanted to change. My enthusiasm gradually dwindled, till the day arrived when I found I didn't want to go to office at all.

I came to loathe every file and register that came my way. The window dressing, futile meetings and cynicism at work were depressing. I did not want to be caught in the vicious cycle of self-obsession, salary slips, promotions, plum postings and privileges that came with my office. There would be either too much work or none at all and there was hardly any scope for growth at a personal level. I felt my brain had stopped functioning, my appetite had shrunk and my spirit was stifled.

My parents were aware of my mental state but reminded me of all the toil that had gone into achieving the status and office I held. I was a 'gazetted officer' and there was nothing I lacked to lead a comfortable life. But they left the decision to me.

At work, clear lines were drawn, circumscribing personality and allowing limited space for an individual's blossoming. All the lofty idealism and ideas of fulfillment lay wasting now in a desert of sand and stone. According to my husband, if I wasn't happy, it wasn't worth it. Besides, I had little time for my children, who were being raised by the domestic staff.

A senior, a most extraordinary individual who had somehow remained immune to the calcifying effect of inertia all around, told me that it was my destiny to serve here. Things can only get better. Take each day as it comes, was his advice.

But the moment I tendered my resignation, I felt like a free bird!

After being shut away in an ivory tower for years, it seemed natural that I would opt for the most creative job in the world. Teaching children!

I didn't know what to expect or how I would react when dealing with eight-year-olds. Gone were the khaki-clad men with their mechanical salutes. Gone was the staff car, the 'to-do' lists and superficial, carefully cultivated exteriors. I stood before my posse of bewildered students, equally bewildered, but things felt right. I felt I belonged here. I was right. Within no time, I was part of the school routine. Life was busy, but the kids' energy rubbed off on one. Before we knew it, a year had passed. And I hadn't missed a single day of school! Anubha Goyal, my first headmistress who baptised me into this profession, asked me after a month of teaching whether I liked it.

My answer was buried somewhere in my aching, overworked throat and in my happily grinning heart.

Now, every morning, I spring out of bed and look forward to another day with my children, at home and in school.

*Harneet Brar*

# Armene Says Amen

Would a book motivate you to leave your job, the country where you have been living for the last eleven years and return to your hometown to make the lives of women and girls whom you have never met better? That's exactly what happened to Armene Modi when she read the book, *May You Be The Mother of a 100 Sons*, in 1996. The grim fact that screamed out at her as an educator was that an incredible sixty-one per cent of women in India according to the 1991 census were illiterate.

'A decade later, the 2001 census showed that women's literacy had increased by fifteen per cent but there are still millions of women who do not have access to education and are living lives of poverty and deprivation,' says sixty-year-old Armene who was then a Professor of English in Tokyo at the J.F. Oberlin University.

She decided to set up a project to increase women's literacy near her hometown in Pune and returned to India. Thus Ashta No Kai (ANK)—For a Better Tomorrow was born on October 1998. She says, 'Those of us who are privileged need to reach out to those who are not so fortunate. Had it not been for the throw of the dice, I could have been born in a village and my life would have been very different.' This is probably what motivated her to give rural girls a chance to control the dice of their own destinies.

Long distances to reach their schools and parental indifference were the two reasons why girls in Shirur Taluka, Maharashtra, were giving up their education even before Class 8. Armene recalls in horror, 'I saw young girls barely thirteen or fourteen years old with mangalsutras around their necks and babies on their hips.'

The distances village girls had to walk to high school were sometimes seven kilometres. The boys didn't face this problem as they were given bicycles. Armene thus started the bicycle scheme for girls by placing an appeal in the local newspaper asking people to donate cycles. Also her friends in Japan donated more than two hundred bicycles.

Initially, the scheme was such that the girl had to pay a deposit of Rs 300 for as long as she kept the bicycle. However, it was found that the bicycles were being misused by the men in the household, and since the girl didn't own the bicycle, she didn't take proper care about its maintenance. This resulted in most of the bicycles being returned in such a state that they could not be reused and could only be disposed off as scrap. Also, monitoring became difficult and so a better and more practical solution was hit upon. Now the scheme is simple in itself; the girl pays a fraction of the cost of the bicycle to her mother's self-help group. And since she owns the bicycle, she takes care of it and her contribution in turn helps the self-help group that comprises women who have organised themselves into cooperative saving and loan groups.

Till date, more than five hundred and seventy girls have benefitted from this scheme funded at a grass-root level. Modi's future plans include giving fifty to fifty-five scholarships each year to village girls who are interested in pursuing higher education. Initially the girls would only complete junior college. Now there is a tremendous increase in the aspirational levels and there are girls who are pursuing automobile engineering, graduate courses in law, pharmacy and agriculture, while some have got diplomas in computer education.

Like Armene, many of us are nudged by life to make a difference and to make the world a better place, but few respond to their calling like she did. Armene said Amen to change that started with her. Now it is our turn.

*Khursheed Dinshaw*

# My Students, My Teachers

'These small kids need you.' With these words, a well-wisher handed me an advertisement for the post of a part-time, spoken-English teacher for the primary classes. That sentence had the desired effect on me and off I went for the walk-in interview, armed with my eagerness and enthusiasm to make a positive difference to the lives of kids even though I had no prior experience in teaching.

'Our new semester will start three months from now. We will call you then,' the selection committee told me. A week later, the principal of the school called me with another challenging offer. 'Our Class 12 English teacher had to go on leave suddenly. There was an unforeseen accident and she has been advised to take rest. Are you up to teaching her students for just two months?' asked the principal. My initial reaction was pin-drop silence. Teaching five-year-olds had seemed like a fun idea, but seventeen-year-old, hot-blooded teenagers were another matter all together. I recalled all the terrible things I had done at that age and shuddered. Was it my payback time?

But I decided to step up to the challenge and bravely conveyed my acceptance. I had a quick preview of my future students in the corridor itself. 'Good morning Ma'am,' said one and before I could return the courtesy, her companion promptly told her, 'You idiot. She is not "our" teacher.' Nervous, I entered and was greeted by a near-empty class as most of the students were practicing for the annual-day function.

'There are just six of us and we don't have text books because they are not available in the market,' announced one six-footer, towering over me.

While this minor hurdle of few students and no textbooks was dealt with by getting photocopies of the required pages, the class bully, or 'bhai' as he had christened himself proudly, told me that he 'handled' all matters, not just of the class but also of the school as well so I should be warned.

Fortunately, I saw through his charade. He was just an insecure teenager who got attention by disturbing the class and bossing around the rest of his classmates. I had an honest talk with him and henceforth included him in all the reading and interactive sessions. Two weeks later, he came and apologised to me saying he wouldn't be a troublemaker any longer. Coming from him, those words really felt good. I was jubilant, more so since the rest of the teachers had warned me about the indiscipline and scant interest of these students especially when it came to English.

'They get decent marks in other subjects because they opt for answering in Hindi since they are so fluent in it. Unfortunately English happens to be their Waterloo. They are too weak in the subject and have no inclination to improve. Coming from a Hindi-speaking background doesn't help their case either. Most of them are children of defence troops whose fathers are posted to far-flung border areas. Their mothers are not highly educated themselves and are so busy single-handedly managing the household that they can't provide much of a support system for their older kids,' explained a teacher.

The students, however, had started opening up to me. I

was let in on what they had nicknamed the principal and my shocked expression had them burst out into peals of laughter. They were bright, with minds of their own, and didn't shy away from expressing their opinions. Our daily interactive classes bore results as the students started asking me questions instead of the customary nod I got when I asked them if they understood the subject matter. In turn, I learnt to be more patient and understanding. My family and friends were pleasantly surprised that I could teach supposedly rowdy students.

The students were my motivation for getting up and going to class everyday. In all this 'educational masti', as they called it, time simply flew and the day for me to leave dawned. When I had entered, I was a first-time teacher, and when I left, I was a student who would now never stop learning from life and from every young person who crossed my path.

*Madhavi Mone*

# Beyond the Smoke Screen

As Anna's fingers reached for the forty-fifth cigarette of the day, she was aware that she had plunged inevitably into the dangerous, smokey waves of addiction, and taken along with her all the normalcy associated with her life. Anna first burnt her fingers with a cigarette when she felt the need to measure up to her male colleagues at work. They all smoked—it was the done thing—and Anna didn't want to be left out. Her first smoke made her feel uneasy and giddy, but she puffed on. No one at home knew at the time that she had started smoking. It had started with five cigarettes a day, but it increased with time.

'I used any excuse I could get to smoke—I was tired, happy, tense or needed to alleviate my grumpy mood. Soon just about any everyday activity, be it having my breakfast, reading the paper or finishing my meal triggered my desire for a cigarette,' says Anna honestly.

She would get up in the middle of the night because her body would require an additional fix to carry on through the night. Not even in her sleep was she safe or free. This took a toll on her health, work and life. 'Since I was waking up at such odd hours to smoke, I was late, irritable, tired and started falling ill. In order to feel better, more alert and energetic, I would smoke, but, of course, it became a vicious cycle. I smoked to get better; but in reality all it did was make me more ill, so I smoked more,' adds Anna.

Anna's wake-up call came when she saw a close friend die of lung cancer. She did not want to be next in line. She made a promise to herself that she would quit and it is with great pride and a huge sense of achievement that she has kept her promise. 'It has not been easy. I have been to hell and back. The withdrawal symptoms included depression, difficulty in sleeping, irritability, frustration, anger, anxiety, lack of concentration, restlessness and an increased appetite. Nicotine speeds up the metabolism and affects sleep patterns, habits I had to break. Without nicotine, my body's sleep rhythms were slowly starting to return to normal automatically. But when I quit smoking, at first I felt overwhelmingly tired, my body was drained and exhausted,' recounts Anna.

Tobacco had only provided the illusion of energy and her body had long needed the rest denied to it. She started going to bed earlier than usual, because she needed that extra sleep. And it was also good because, when she was sleeping, she was not smoking. Anna would pat herself on the back when she woke up each day that she had made it and survived without cigarettes for one more day, and pep herself up by saying that today would be a little bit easier than yesterday. 'There are so many of us, women, out there. Our reasons for smoking vary from wanting to break stereotypes, wanting to fit in, being called hep and chic to just using smoking to escape from our daily pressures and stress. Being a woman who has been there, I understand. But for that very reason I say that it is not worth it. And we women are equipped to deal with what comes along when we quit smoking,' she advises.

Life is after all worth more than a puff of smoke and when you breathe in its blessings, you breathe out the reasons that make you reach out for something toxic.

*Sanaea Patel*

# The Big, Red, Nylon Ribbons

It was not so much the beauty of the sparkling earrings in the Antwerp shop window that arrested me. It was the shock of seeing the traditional, some would say old-fashioned, south Indian flower-shaped circles flashing in a Belgian Jewish jewellery store. Involuntarily, I walked in for a closer look. The owner said these were for Indian shoppers who came to Antwerp looking for diamonds. After thirty years abroad, the occasional twinge for traditional jewellery had left me and I rarely thought of wearing it, quite happy with the pretty rings and earrings I'd collected since the time I left India with my English husband. My daughter loves India and her Indian relatives, but she is British, with no passion for saris and jewellery. At least, not yet.

I've now reached a stage in my life when the children have grown up and the parents can spread their wings. My husband and I have decided to divide our time between Europe and India; finally, Indian events like childbirths and marriages, gruhapraveshams and upanayanams have become a priority. I am excited but nervous at the thought of going back. I have made my second home there but would I, could I, truly belong? Could I go back to being one of the middle-class Indians like my sister, my sister-in-law, my aunts and my childhood friends? I don't want shopkeepers to ask me where

I am from even though I speak fluent colloquial Kannada without an accent, knowing that, to my chagrin, they refuse to believe me when I say I am local. I understand now how my children must have felt when we brought them back to England after a childhood spent in Japan. I blithely told them it didn't matter, that they should just be themselves and make a few good friends, and in time they'd adjust. Why was this wisdom deserting me now?

Suddenly, the earrings seem to represent a feeling of belonging. They have a solid south-Indian-respectably-married-woman feel to them. These traditional jewels on my lobes would flash fire and announce that I too was an Iyengar or a Smartha—being a child of a mixed marriage. This last reality jolts me; this was the crux of the problem. I've never felt I really belonged to either community. Having been born in the north and with many of my growing years spent travelling the country with my army officer father exacerbated this feeling of not belonging, even to the south.

As a child visiting my father's relatives, I identified more with my Iyengar mother, to whom I was closer. I felt nervous around the Smartha women and felt vaguely guilty, without knowing why. My 'Punjabi dress' was commented upon, as was my and my sister's 'side parting' hairstyle. 'You must oil your hair, make a neat centre parting and tightly braid your hair into twin plaits. Use red nylon ribbons and tie big bows if you want some colour. And do put a red kunkuma on your forehead. You look like a Christian,' my aunt chided. I hated big, red, nylon ribbons. I just didn't belong.

My siblings and I grew up studying in military schools whenever my father was posted in the north where the medium of education was neither Kannada nor Tamil, but Hindi. My cousins, who never left their city of birth, were brought up steeped in the ways of our community. They were well-versed in all the customs and habits of their caste and community. They knew which side the salt went on the banana leaf. They knew how to crouch on the floor and 'sweep' the mess left on the floor after lunch with their bare, moistened hands. They seemed so capable. I tried to shake off my feeling of inadequacy by thinking I was more Iyengar than Smartha. Yet when I was with my mother's Tamil-speaking relatives, I felt different again, as my family spoke Kannada—my father's tongue was my mother tongue. When I tried to speak in Tamil, my mother's relatives laughed. 'Don't murder the language,' they said good-naturedly.

The feeling of rootlessness only intensified after marrying an Englishman, spending the first seventeen years of marriage in Japan and then settling in England. I was a gypsy who always found it difficult to answer a simple question—'where are you from?'

Could these earrings open the door to the middle-class, south Indian Brahmin society I was now going to be a part of? Would the costly blaze of ornament mark my status and make me respected and accepted? Was it worth dipping into our hard-earned savings to look like everyone else on those odd occasions when I went to family events where women eyed each other's jewellery? The pretty, traditional earrings suddenly became the big, red, nylon ribbons I'd refused to wear as a child.

Memories came flooding back. I thought with a mixture of guilt and amusement of the first thing I had done when I got married: used up our meagre savings to buy my mother a pair of traditional diamond earrings. My English husband, unaware of our custom of the daughter receiving jewellery from parents, had believed that we gave our mothers a 'thank you' gift. The truth was that for years I had seen my mother wear her simple stone earrings to all the occasions where the aunts and cousins flashed their diamonds importantly. I knew my mother wasn't regarded as quite their equal. I had sworn my mother would one day wear these earrings too, just as soon as I could afford them. Although she had never craved them, my mother had worn our gift proudly as a mark of a child who cared. When she died two years later, I carelessly sold the earrings, feeling no need for something that held little value when the wearer was lost to me. But now these expensive sparklers in Antwerp were casting their spell on me.

In the end, the underlying purpose of returning to my roots made my decision for me. It was to keep a promise made years ago to my mother to give something back to the land that had nurtured me. And to work for the cause as I'd planned, I would need to hang on to my savings. But it was not just about the money. It was about why I was going back and what I wanted to do with my life.

Yet, India was already getting to me even before I'd gone back, and not in the way I was hoping. I tell my Western friends there are different Indias, many I'm ignorant about. I know these different worlds will confuse me until I can find the India which I want to be a part of. I'd told myself that going back to my roots to find something spiritual was not just another cliché. After being a teacher for nearly thirty years, I was looking forward to volunteering my time and energy working in a school for underprivileged children. And yet here I was, gazing at the winking and beguiling diamonds, suddenly desperate to keep up with the Khannas.

I need those bright and beautiful children to sort me out. I hope they will help me find the purpose and homecoming, even the sense of belonging, I crave. I smiled wanly thinking, 'They have their work cut out!' as I handed back the diamond earrings.

*Rani Rao Innes*

# Over a Song and a Memory

What would you do if you knew you had just one day to live? We ponder over this question at various times in life. Some of us believe in bucket lists of things to do. Some of us believe in going about that day as we would any other day. The latter belief to me means your mother is in no doubt you love her and you smelt the roses this morning. I've ticked both boxes but there's one more thing to do.

God knows I wasn't good when I started my radio career. I remember those sleepless nights when I agonised about how more people were writing in to say that I was everything an RJ ought not to be—dull and boring with an annoying laugh and voice. No one seemed to appreciate my carefully selected pieces of trivia.

Feedback for radio hosts is instantaneous, often ruthless, and everyone has a right to dispense it. So you develop a mechanism to cope with it. Mine was the cold voice of reason, telling me that a good voice wasn't the only thing that mattered. And that not having such a great voice was not going to come in the way of a good show, and how I could compensate for the lack of finesse and voice quality with killer research. And then, just when I had lulled myself into this comfort zone, came this inland letter.

It was from a couple writing to tell me about how their

young daughter was mesmerised every time I came on air. There was the ubiquitous post script. She was autistic, they added, and didn't respond to much else. They thanked me. Nine years have passed, and I am ashamed to confess that I haven't thanked them back. Because in that one moment I'd made the lucky leap in perspective: from the defeatist 'It's okay to have a bad voice' to the more healthy 'Maybe there is more to this job than just having a good or bad voice'. For years I'd believed that there is always a personal motive, something 'selfish' to use a stronger word, in every act of kindness performed. I would always be seized by this thought when someone was nice to me, or vice versa. The letter, among other things, was also an example of how wrong I was. Kindness need not even be expressly intended for it to be felt. It was a letter of gratitude, not kindness, after all. No mega story this, and certainly no thrilling climax. But this isn't about one letter or one small change in perspective. To me it is bigger. It marked a moment in a time when I was truly beginning to grasp what I'd been told all along—life's big lessons sometimes arrive in small packages.

Getting a scholarship to this university, donating a percentage of your earnings to that cause, yes, these are milestones, worthy of celebration. But it doesn't always take a sledgehammer to drive a nail in. I'd be worried about sleeping through those subtle shifts in my life, about not attributing them to the people who helped cause them.

I have come to be grateful for the appreciation of strangers who were not strangers after all. There was something being sown each time a song I played touched someone. Something was being created each time a faceless name offered to bring me soup to the studios when I sounded like I had a runny nose. Over time something was born. I call it collective goodwill.

And to think we didn't have to lay down our lives for one

another. We just traded our love for a song and began to use first names and share Hindi film trivia. Never ceases to amaze me, how simple it all really is.

*Seetal Iyer*

# Many Paths, One Life

She was standing next to a stall when I first noticed her. Later I discovered that there were four such stalls, serving tea, free of charge, to the summit participants, nearly two thousand of them. The first two days of the summit, I was very happy to have my afternoon tea. But on the third day, it struck me that I must at least go and thank the person who appeared to be in-charge of this little convenience service, and so I walked up to her and we had the first exchange of introductions.

'No I am not from any tea company,' said Manik Damle, who had come all the way from Pune. I wondered what made her stand there, taking on hundreds of inquisitive queries, and she answered on her own as if she had read my mind. 'I am associated with an NGO that has tied up with this tea company and we work towards creating micro-enterprises,' she explained.

Later I discovered that their work included helping people with minimal resources to set up really small, but nevertheless self-sustainable enterprises like tea-stalls. I realised the work was not just limited to helping set up such establishments, but assisting and providing guidance to the concerned entrepreneur in managing and/or making it grow in the manner of a professionally-run enterprise.

I was quickly handed a form to fill up and submit if I wanted to be associated with the programme. I moved on with a promise to return with the filled form. Oh yes, in between all this, I had the brief opportunity to explain the kind of writing work I did and pleasantly found quick ideas and suggestions pouring in. I decided I would return soon, or may be later.

Luckily this time, the 'later' was not as late as it usually is in such cases. Shortly after this exchange, I spotted Manik and her colleague, Ajinkya Kulkarni, a person with a considerable amount of work experience in the developmental sector, sitting in the corner and enjoying a cup of tea. Surely, a well-deserved break for the two! Somehow, the conversation veered to my work. I spoke of the challenges I faced and Manik kept coming back with some solution for each one of them. In moments, she turned out to be the much-desired-but-never-met guide I had been seeking so desperately. Thanks to her, I now had leads to many people who could help me, either by contributing directly or who could potentially help me understand the wider context of my situation.

This was one heck of an NGO lady, I thought! Surprising, I thought, only to discover that she wasn't after all a 100-per cent–NGO-person. 'I am an engineer,' she said, smiling. I realised she worked for a large corporate organisation, while also managing a home with growing kids. She was lending time out of her official and home responsibilities to the kind of work she was involved with at that moment because she cared about issues larger than her own.

She exemplified something I have believed in for a long time—'What we do to earn a living is just a part of our life, and not the end of it'.

She was one of the few people I knew who lend their time to activities beyond the domains of their immediate bread-and-butter responsibilities. However, I am also witness to the mental conflict of such outstanding men and women. They increasingly find it difficult to strike the right balance between their passion and profession.

In some cases, I am aware, things go awfully wrong as the heart wants to take one road and the head draws you towards another. I had always wondered if we could ever find a formula to strike the perfect balance.

Manik Damle seemed to have nailed it, as she said, 'I lend my skills to the corporate world, which benefits from my contribution and in turn it shares with me the DNA that gets me access to doing bigger things and I benefit from that contribution. As long as this mutual benefit keeps happening, I will remain associated with the corporate world and still keep doing things outside.'

This simple understanding could have come only from someone who has mastered the juggling of multiple roles as part of her daily routine. She is seamlessly and effortlessly a home-maker, a mother, a story-teller, an engineer, an activist, a motivator, an innovator and a guide to people like me. How she does it is not important. That she does, makes it possible for so many of us to dream that it is possible to live many lives in one, and change the world for the better along the way.

*Puneet Srivastava*

# Memories of a Butterfly

My favourite quote is, 'Life truly is like a box of chocolates . . . one never knows what we're gonna' get'.

No doubt every one of us has been faced with a fair mixture of good, bad, bizarre, unpredictable, some predictable, experiences in life. We have all had our share. And in both known and unknown ways, these experiences have altered the course of our lives. Take my life. I had worked in advertising for a few years when a freak accident left me with a broken neck. I required surgery and more than a year of recuperation. Obviously it wasn't an easy time, and the immobility was especially frustrating. Although, having this free time, I would discover later, was in its own way a blessing in disguise.

To fill the void and boredom of being house-bound and largely immobile with a cumbersome neck brace, I slowly began to look for ways to occupy myself. Candle-making, something that I had learned and enjoyed as a child, was my first elixir. It was easy and meditative, and filled my days as I experimented with colours, contours and material. As I got stronger, I found myself at my make-shift, candle-making studio in the balcony of my room at every waking hour. I was not only distracted from my pain and thoroughly entertained, but I was happy and felt more energised than I had for years.

Over the first few post-surgery months, countless candles in a riot of colours began to fill my recovery room. I found that not only was I thrilled but guests dropping by to visit me had this wondrous look as they sat about in my colour-filled room.

That's when the journey of Memories of a Butterfly, my very own dream of a company, began. I realised, quite literally, that life was too short, and wasting it away doing the mundane was just not right. I knew that I felt happiest when being creative—a flair for design and aesthetics I had inherited from my family—and joyous colours and textures would have to be part of my professional endeavours. Over the next few months, as I ideated about products and concepts, numerous factors secretly surfaced, influencing me in untold ways, from which materialised my first bead curtain. Created while I was still mostly bed-ridden!

As Memories of a Butterfly emerged and flourished, so did my health. I made a near-full recovery and was able to put all my energy into my company.

Today, my products are a reflection of who I am but mostly who I aspire to be. The creations are free-spirited, boundless in creativity, buzzing with excitement, yielding yet strong at the core, constantly evolving, unique, unpretentious and grounded in purpose.

Not to say there were no setbacks and failures. In business, one tends to question one's sanity on a daily basis. But eventually the highpoints come, and the orders rush in, the appreciation is unconditional, and faith in life and creativity is restored. Every problem is eventually solved and delivers lessons vital for future success. With patience and self-respect, I have been able to nurture the company into an honest, creative, genuine and sustainable business. I have dreams that the company will soar higher, that I will expand its scope and that I will remain happy doing what I do.

I'm finally on the path where I want to be. And that's more than I could have said some years back. Today I work out of home in a wonderful little studio surrounded by beautiful beads, doing something that I truly enjoy, something that challenges me, satisfies me and gives me the freedom to experiment and evolve.

The most satisfying reward, however, is in having happy customers who wouldn't have imagined the joy a spectacular bead curtain can give them. To be honest, I have never been one for sweet-eats, but I am very happy with my box of chocolates and the constant surprises it throws up at me!

*Sreeti Mondol*

# Lessons Beyond the Syllabi

The blessings of the Internet! Had it not been for it, I would have lived the rest of my life with one of many unfulfilled desires. After all, it's not easy tracking someone you have not met for over nineteen years. Thankfully now, all one needs to do is to type a search string on a web portal and press 'enter' and you can virtually find anything or anyone!

I found that she had been awarded the President's citation for outstanding achievement some years back. It was surely the highest of all the honours, but it was not the only one. An array of awards and recognitions had been credited to her name. Interestingly, even when there were no awards nineteen years ago, when we went to the same school, we knew she was, quite simply, someone extraordinary!

No one had to tell us that she was an exceptional teacher. We simply knew it. It had become evident within a few months of her joining the teaching fraternity. She had never been my teacher; in the sense that she never taught our class. Yet, till date she remains one of the most profound influences in my life. She tops the long list of my favourite people.

Those wonder years when we were growing up and were not yet tall enough to put the basket ball through the hoop, she would step in the court, grab the ball and send it zooming towards the basket! She had been a university-level player and she showed us not just how to aim, but to reach our goals on the court and, on several other occasions later, in life.

I remember a pottery session where teachers and students were being taught intricacies of the craft by a potter and she, my favourite teacher, picked up the skill faster than any one of us and within no time was moulding and cutting beautiful designs. She moulded clay candle stands, toys and simple show-pieces. We learnt the true meaning of application and 'value-addition' that day!

From annual-day functions to monthly debates to youth parliaments to sports meets, and all those insignificant day-to-day activities of the school, she led us, always by example. With her around, we could find a way to channel our energies in the right direction even when we had no sense of direction. Thanks to her, we could find courage to run a marathon and finish it, and meet seemingly impossible challenges. Our personalities were being changed, refined and groomed subtly, quietly, even though we were perhaps too immature to even realise or notice the change.

Nineteen years later, when I set out to find her, I wondered if she would remember me. I would, of course, always remember. For me, there would always be only one Shinde Ma'am, but for her there would have been so many children. Soon, I had sourced her number and was dialling it anxiously.

'Of course, I do remember you, my dear!' It was the same reassuring voice at the other end—the one that I had listened to on so many occasions in the past, so many years ago. I can't really describe the feeling that coursed though me except that it was really fulfilling! We chatted for a while and I gave her an account of what I did. 'Wonderful!' she exclaimed. 'But find a place for this old lady somewhere near you and get me out of this place!' she said and went quiet.

I was instantly dumbfounded. I had not imagined her

saying something like that. All I was looking for was perhaps a sweet, innocuous conversation between a senior teacher and one of her old students. I had thought it would be just a simple conversation about common acquaintances, but somehow real life had crept in. She had given so much to us and to the system but what she had got in return, I had never wondered. My favourite teacher suddenly became an individual, a professional who had worked within limiting environments to bring out the best in children and herself. The work-place dilemmas, the games people in positions of authority play, the push and the pull; she would have gone through so much.

An efficient and popular woman with far greater accomplishments in an environment where mediocrity thrived would have been in a minority. I realised just how painful and frustrating it would have got for someone like her.

I recalled how a decorated police officer, incidentally another lady, had opted for premature retirement some years back because she was tired of writing reports on police reforms that no one was reading. Why do we do this to those who help us build our institutions? Why are we so disrespectful towards excellence?

Well, these might be questions much bigger than the scope of this story but I want to say to the woman who inspired it: Ma'am, thank you for all that you did for us despite the odds, and this time your student is not going to take another nineteen years to come calling. I will see you soon with a small solution that may not change the system that you worked with and against, but will nonetheless remind you that it was all worth it. Because, we remember. And because we will never forget. And that's a promise.

*Puneet Srivastava*

# When Dancing Equals Healing

Dance recitals never fail to move me.

Odissi performances always have me hypnotised, and when they end, I am left with a strange longing in my soul. An energetic Kathak and tap dance jugalbandi I recently had the good fortune to witness left me breathless and yet charged at the same time. Bhartnatyam, Mohiniattam and Kuchipudi, they all have me enthralled; folk dances have me tapping my feet to the beat; ballet has me swaying and sighing, and salsa has my heart pumping.

Yes, dance recitals never fail to move me.

But this was the first time that a performance had reduced me to a blubbering mass of tears. There I was, swathed in silk, surrounded by other bejewelled gentry decked up in their finest, and not caring that the kajal was leaving black streaks on my face.

The recital that had held me captive for eighty minutes and ultimately left me incoherent was a presentation of Rabindranath Tagore's dance-drama *Balmiki Pratibha*. The story-line is inspired by the popular legend of the dreaded dacoit Ratnakara, and how he undergoes a spiritual awakening to finally become the great poet-sage, Valmiki, author of the immortal epic the *Ramayana*.

It wasn't my first time watching a stellar performance of

one of Tagore's celebrated works on stage. But what was it about this particular performance that left me sobbing openly and unashamedly in the audience?

Part of it was because this remarkable performance had been put up by an unusual group of amateurs—the inmates of West Bengal's various correctional institutions. The 'lifers', to be exact.

This performance was the result of a novel experiment by the Inspector-General, Correctional Services, West Bengal, B.D. Sharma and celebrated Odissi danseuse, Alokananda Roy.

IG Sharma was keen to introduce 'cultural therapy' as a means to cure depression amongst the lifers whom he was in charge of. Alokananda, a firm believer in dance as therapy, was already working with juvenile delinquents to motivate them towards better and brighter futures. With similar beliefs and an unshakeable faith in the power of the human spirit, these two like-minded souls came together to introduce the inmates to a world of art, music, dance and culture.

It was during her sessions with her 'children', as Alokananda refers to them, that the idea of presenting Balmiki Pratibha to the people of Kolkata came to her, and IG Sharma readily jumped on board. While Alokananda took care of everything related to the performance, IG Sharma took upon himself all the administrative particulars that needed to be taken care of.

However, no one, least of all the audience, was prepared for what we saw. The performances would put professionals to shame! The inmates and staff of West Bengal's various correctional homes not only danced on stage, but also sang the parts, created the masks and props, spun the cloth and stitched the vibrant costumes that set the stage ablaze as hidden talents were unleashed.

And yet, that is not all. What finally left me, and every member in the audience undone, was when we learnt the history of Alokananda's Valmiki. When Alokananda first started her workshops, she would notice a rather arrogant and seemingly impenitent young man watching the goings-on from a distance. The young man was forever brooding, openly condescending and always aloof. He was also curious. Extremely curious, for he never missed a session.

It was on the day that Alokananda had narrated the story of *Balmiki Pratibha* to the inmates that Vicky was finally won over. His eyes overflowing with tears, Vicky humbly approached Alokananda and asked, 'Maa, may I be in the performance please?'

The man had gone through the same spiritual turmoil and ultimate awakening as the legendary sage himself. Day after day, he had struggled with his inner demons as he watched his fellow inmates give in to the therapeutic calm and beauty of dance and music, until finally, he realised that he wanted that for himself. Paying heed to the spiritual chaos whirling within, he finally succumbed to the lure of light and knowledge.

Alokananda had found her hero.

And what a hero he made! With Alokananda's gentle guidance and absolute dedication, Vicky did not just breathe life into Valmiki's role ... he was Valmiki reborn! When asked how he was able to interpret the soul of the lyrics so beautifully despite the entire ballad being in a language that is not his mother tongue, he shyly credits his entire performance to 'Maa.'

Alokananda's dedication to her 'children' is evident as she lovingly introduces each and every member of the cast and crew after the performance is over. Her tenderness towards these men and women whom we would not think twice about branding 'lawless, delinquent and criminal' may be surprising, even improper, to many, but it's genuine.

Maybe because she takes her role as their mother to heart,

and isn't it the very essence of a mother to love her child no matter what? But that, however, does not mean that she looks the other way when an errant child makes mistakes. And Alokananda doesn't. She is their mentor and guide, helping them to see right from wrong, trying to steer them on to the right path.

Has it worked?

Well, today Vicky, born Nigel Akkara, has been granted a full pardon and is now working with an NGO as well as pursuing his Master's degree. He and a few other ex-convicts, his fellow brothers in the correctional facilities and on stage, are living proof of how cultural therapy can turn one around.

Can this be likened to a modern-day miracle? My tears most certainly believe so. Then that would most definitely make Alokananda Roy the miracle-maker.

*Baisali Chatterjee Dutt*

# 4

# LOVE IN ALL COLOURS

*You never lose by loving. You always lose by holding back.*

—Barbara De Angelis

# Love Eternal

Geetha's life changed on 31 March 2007. Her husband met with an accident that evening while riding pillion on a motorbike. He suffered from a head injury and slipped into coma. After months in hospitals, he was finally discharged and taken home. There wasn't much else that the doctors could do.

Geetha—totally dependent on her husband till that time— was suddenly entrusted with the biggest challenge of her life. She was offered a job by her husband's employer and free schooling for her daughter. But she decided to move cities and live with her in-laws and to dedicate all her time to care for her husband.

In 2010, some of us friends decided to visit her city and check on her. We drove one early morning down the winding road that led to her house and a few hours later were welcomed by her elderly mother-in-law, daughter and a few curious neighbours.

Then Geetha appeared, looking like a picture of joy, hope and love. We were quickly shown to a room where her beloved lay, all skin and bones with tubes stuck into his body. She tapped on his shoulder and called his name out aloud, but in vain. We stood speechless beside him.

After a while, Geetha served us tea and snacks that she had

made for us. She did share her difficulties and her challenges with us, but without hopelessness and with a grit and determination to face adversities. She hoped and believed that her husband would one day stand up and share her life the way he used to. She was doing everything possible to find ways to keep that hope alive and to heal him. She spent her days talking to him continuously, keeping him clean and feeding him. As she shared the past three years of her life, not one negative word came out of her mouth. She didn't whine, groan or complain. No 'Why me?' Just a glint of determination in her eye as she said, 'I know he will be fine.'

It was time for us to leave and Geetha had packed a sack full of home-grown tapioca for us to take home. But I was returning home with much more, having met a woman of tenacity whose devotion was unconditional regardless of the circumstances that had divided her from her beloved. I had met an ordinary woman living an extraordinary love. A love beyond Valentine's Day gifts, dinner dates and reciprocal warmth. A love that was just happy to exist for its own sake.

*Lalitha Menon*

# Beyond the Womb

In life, we meet many people and a few leave in their wake strong imprints, for better or worse, and then there are some who seep into our hearts and create a pure connection and a bond beyond the politics of give and take, beyond expectations. A kinship develops between virtual strangers that is wordless and yet deeply profound.

I've been happily blessed with similar inexplicable connections. For me, the word 'Ma' stands for my mother and all that she means to me; one day, I felt what it was like to be a mother even though the person who evoked such strong emotions in me was a student. Right from the beginning, I noticed a certain innocence about him and felt drawn to it; I felt that the child, even though he was a teenager then, was trying to reach out to me. Small gestures of respect from him would move me immeasurably. Then one day, he wrote me a note saying that I was the mother he had never had, and in that one moment, I felt strangely fulfilled too. I felt at peace, as if a missing piece I had been looking for had been found and fitted back in my soul. But it was strange to discover a bond so deep in a rather formal environment, where he was one amongst many students. He often resented the fact that he could not be as close to me as he wanted, and would write short stories dedicated to his 'Ma', and I would read them and smile in wonder as to what I had done to deserve such heartfelt tributes.

Many times, many other students connected with me and said similar things. Another student I met a few years later often touched my feet with such great regard that I wanted to somehow be a better person to earn that kind of respect. He often shared his problems with me and I would try to help him in whatever way I could. The day he was to graduate from college, he had tears in his eyes and said that he was leaving behind not just his friends, but a mother as well.

A girl student, who I took care of in college recently when she fell sick, asked me for a hug and when I hugged her, she broke down and told me not just what was going on with her life, but that I always reminded her of the mother she had lost. When I walked back to the staff room after this encounter, I felt drained and wanted to ask God why I had never had a child of my own if I seemed to have been born to be a mother and with so much love to give. . . .

Were such students sent my way to remind me of the child I did not have or to compensate for the absence of one? There is never complete perfection in life, but I was to discover in the years to come that you don't have to give birth to children to love them and that children always respond to truth, to genuine affection and even if it comes from a teacher, not a parent, they reciprocate in abundant ways. Perhaps I was not given a baby of my own so that I could be sensitive to children who needed love and guidance. And in return, I have been made to feel many times over how a mother adored by her children feels. Though my arms have never known the joy of cradling a baby, my heart has never been empty.

*Navtej Sibia*

# Arranged Love

I believe in karma, whether it is good or bad. Be it my work, my interactions with family and friends, my conscience keeps me in check. No, I have not at all managed to create that fabled work–life balance. For instance, I am still clinging to straws, trying to hold ground with parents and in-laws, but something somewhere has worked to my advantage to bring me thus far in life. Was it my good karma at work when I not just met the right man by default but also found myself in the right profession?

I had enthusiastically chosen to study dentistry only to end up disillusioned thoroughly. I was convinced that I would not last even a couple of years in the profession, leave alone enjoy a thriving practise. I was fairly good at what I did back then in college, but it wouldn't have taken me anywhere close to where I am today. I started moonlighting as a radio jockey just as I was finishing college. For some aunts and uncles, I was just a 'radio presenter', but I loved my foray into a new world.

I was due to get my eyesight checked and to possibly get an exciting new pair of contact lenses, when something unforeseen occurred. My regular eye physician had changed his consulting address and my mother plainly refused to take me that far. Looking back, it seems like my mother and fate truly knew what they were doing. My mother somehow convinced me to see another physician, albeit in a charitable hospital, closer home. I had my reservations about meeting this doctor but nonetheless went along. It was lunch-time when we reached the hospital and we were assigned to an Iyer soul with so many letters under his name on the office door that I was fairly impressed even before I met him.

As we waited in the lobby, this man with slightly longer locks than I would have expected from a doctor sped down the stairs carrying his lunch bag. And he seemed to be the only one who had finished his lunch well in time for his afternoon consulting hours to begin on the dot. He called us in and my fidgety brain started thinking. Why would a doctor with so many qualifications be in an unexciting place like this? And why was he wearing pinstripes? The only thing I thought missing on him was a pair of suspenders! Did the guy have a serious colonial hangover since he had studied at the Royal College of Surgeons?

After the initial introductions, we realised we knew where his forefathers were from and he knew some of our distant relatives. After I was seated in the examination chair, he asked what I did, and I blurted that I was an RJ but had completed dentistry. He stopped and looked me straight in the eye and asked why. I said it was because I'd got the opportunity and because I enjoyed it and I think he made up his mind then and there as to what a thorough nut I really was.

Incidentally, both of us had finished from the same government college but many years apart. After the eye examination, my mother, overcome with curiosity, asked about his family and our man shyly said he wasn't married and that his folks were on the look-out for a suitable (read fair, homely, qualified) girl.

What do you know, my folks were doing the same thing,

looking for a decent boy for me. And at that moment it struck me just where my mother's questions were headed. I squirmed with embarrassment and hoped dear mum would not blurt out next that I was the suitable girl his family was looking for and that his prospective wife was sitting right in front of him! Fortunately, nothing to that effect transpired and I was asked to come again for a detailed examination two days later. We went again, and after the examination we exchanged numbers. He said my lenses would be ready in three days and he would get in touch. On the second day itself, I got a call from him saying my lenses were ready. The treatment was now over but phone conversations continued and then began coffee shop trips. His folks remained clueless and my mother was in a state of high alert!

After a few weeks, my mother decided the phone conversations had gone on for too long and took a friend along to the hospital and that lady right away went in for the kill. The good doctor did not know what to say or do and blurted that he had a few other proposals to consider! What gall! My mother came back fuming. Though our friendly chatting continued over the phone, our man was in a fix. His parents had sensed from his massive phone bills that something was going on, and it was time for the penny to fall.

With the little information they had, his family thought that their son was about to get himself a party-hopping, tequila-guzzling, nocturnal DJ (that's who they presumed I was!) for a wife! My mother, already impressed with her prospective son-in-law, had a bigger issue at hand—how to tell my father about the situation. It was decided that my uncle, who was distantly related to the doctor, would tell my father that he 'happened' to know a suitable boy's family. My father was greatly impressed with the doctor's profile and thanked my uncle for having got such a match for his daughter! Missives were sent, calls were made, families met and thus concluded an eye surgeon and his patient's tale of several coincidences and eventual matrimony.

The funny part is, we still haven't let the secret about our courtship out, and among the many who think our marriage was an arranged one, is also my father. The first few months after marriage were tough with expanding work commitments, illness in the family, my multiple commitments as a daughter, wife and daughter-in-law. And now we are expecting a baby. All this has led to some tough decisions that eventually have changed a lot in both our lives, but we continue to share great fondness and greater respect as a couple. I must have done something right.

All this has reinforced a belief that nothing in life comes to you without you either deserving it or working for it. Meeting my husband has been the best coincidence of my life. But I also have to thank my mother for arranging it!

*Shruthi Prakash*

# A Lifelong Gift

It's been six years since Reeva passed away. I still remember how my world turned 360 degrees right before my eyes when I heard that she was gone and how helpless I felt that I could not control or change what had happened to her. Reeva, ironically, always called me a control freak! Not that it helped when it mattered the most. But, even today, as I think of her, my heart begins to race and I feel a shiver go down my spine. Reeva, my best friend since school, my confidante, my partner in crime, battled with stomach cancer for two years before she passed away one morning.

Reeva and I had done it all, from sleepovers to studying together, from shopping to chasing boys, partying and gossiping. Reeva was an independent, loving, forgiving, God-fearing, and above all, a very straight-forward, bright girl.

The two years she battled with cancer were the most painful years of my life, but she never complained. She would read, cook for me when she could, talk on the phone even when she was tired, or try to drop in whenever she had the stamina, but mostly she would write. I would keep asking her what she was writing, but she never told me.

Reeva succumbed to her illness at a very young age, but did not leave without giving the world a piece of her soul. I say that because before she parted from me forever, she handed me her last gift to me. It was titled: 'To you, with love!'

The gift included a letter, a photograph of her in school and a diary in which she had written all her memories. The diary had a lot of information about her ordeals, but the letter is what I wish to share with you today. And this is how it went:

*Hi, my baby,*

*I am sorry I have to leave you like this. I know for the past two years, you have been complaining and fighting with God, but please stop now! I had to go. Besides, the pain was getting to me! But, now that I have gone, you my darling have a lot of work to do. So wipe all those tears, so that you can read what I have to say and get geared to execute all my wishes in your freaky, controlling manner.*

*First and foremost, let me begin with my Ma. I know she will be shattered at this moment, but stay by her side and pull her out of this grief. Always keep in touch with her. She has always seen you and me as her two daughters so don't ever lose touch with her. Tell her, she has loads to do. Before I went in for treatment, she told me she wanted to go to Maldives. I have booked her an open ticket. She can go any time next year and enjoy. Also tell her to join school and start teaching again, and quickly. The faster she joins school, the faster will she see more of me in every little girl and realise that her baby has not gone anywhere but is right beside her.*

*As for Kiah, my baby sister, tell her to stop cribbing. She can now use all my clothes, bags and shoes! Also give her all my cosmetic jewellery! That little elf! She kept eyeing it all the while. Be there for her, keep her away from all the useless boys and ask her to marry a sensible, educated boy who will take care of her and Ma. But more than anything else, ask her to study hard and become a fashion designer. I always made fun of her but she has the aesthetic sense to do it so tell her to pursue it. And from my cosmetic jewellery box, you take the black beaded set. I know you love it and you have been eyeing it from the day I bought it.*

*Okay, do me one more favour. Karan [Reeva's long-time boyfriend] has been extremely supportive, you know it! He told me if I go, he will never get married. He had given me a ring. Please give it back to him and tell him that when he proposes to the girl of his dreams, he must give her the same ring. Also give him a snap of mine on one condition—that he won't frame it and keep looking at it. I had taken them all from him, because he would keep looking at them and crying. Tell him, from here I will keep looking out for him and bring to him a girl who is just the opposite of me. A girl who won't complain, be possessive, message him a thousand times a day, feed him or argue with him! Also tell him I thank him from the bottom of my heart and that I truly loved him a lot.*

*As for you my lovely, there are no words that can do justice to how much I love you. I want you to fulfil all your dreams, go ahead and become a writer and write about our story, okay? Marry a level-headed man, who loves you and sees your heart which is made of gold. And the day you dress up as a bride, look in the mirror and you will see me there dancing, smiling and blowing kisses to you.*

*Tell Ma, Kiah and Karan that I love them very much and will miss them a lot. As for you, I know I am in your heart, your thoughts and all your decisions so don't worry because you won't miss me as I am always going to be a part of you.*

*Bye! Till we meet again!*

*Loads of hugs and kisses to all and thank you all for enriching my life!*

*Reeva*

Reeva's letter changed all our lives. Reeva's mother did go to Maldives and enjoyed herself as well. She also started teaching and today runs a nursery from her house only for girls and loves spending time with all the little Reevas in her life. As for Karan, he married Kiah (who *is* the complete opposite of Reeva!) and both of them have been blessed with a baby girl whom they have named Reeva. Karan stays with aunty and has become one of the leading cancer specialists in town. Kiah has a flourishing accessory business. As for me, I did become a writer and I did write our story—and I did marry a lovely man! The only thing that did not go according to her plan is the fact that I do miss her even though she is in my heart, in my thoughts and in all my decisions. And on my wedding day, I wept and wept and kept searching for her in the crowd. But I knew even then that there was only one Reeva and even though she was not with me on my wedding day, I was lucky to have had her in my life. Even if it was for a short time.

*Roma Kapadia*

# Stepladder to Motherhood

Oh, the joy of mothering a daughter! Yes, she is my daughter alright, though I am not her biological mother.

Before I crossed this bridge, I had heard and read enough to understand that the very connotation surrounding the word 'stepmom' indicated something negative. Little did I know that in the years to come, I would become one and live to tell the tale!

Much before tasting this uniquely flavoured motherhood, I was convinced that my maternal instincts were almost non-existent. In my teen years, and later as well, I had no skills to handle children, did not know how to soothe or cajole wailing babies or baby-talk adamant toddlers. I am afraid to confess that I considered almost every child as a little ogre! It wasn't surprising then, that all those who knew me were aghast when I announced my decision to marry a man with a six-year-old daughter from a previous marriage!

It did not help my shaky resolve to be a good mother that I was going to step into the shoes of a predecessor far more well-versed with motherhood—a loving mother who had succumbed to a malignant disease after a painful fight.

When I met the little girl who would eventually become my stepdaughter, the first response I received was anything but friendly. I immediately went into panic mode and was overwhelmed by huge waves of conflicting emotions. What was I thinking? Was I prepared for unfavourable stereotypes and tags? Society's cynical glances, pressures and unrealistic expectations? Yet, despite these misgivings, I went ahead with my resolve and with complete awareness that life would from now on be flavoured with the above ingredients. And there I stood, at the threshold of an emotional minefield.

Months before we would be wed, my fiancé and I geared up to work together as a team on matters connected with child-raising, with me in the role of a friend and a guardian rather than a premature mother.

I had prepared myself that I would not be addressed as 'mum', and to be honest, I didn't have the slightest expectations of being called the same. My mind began working overtime as I imagined the various names I could be called: 'Hey There', 'Auntie', 'Steppy', 'Other Mother', 'Spare-Mum'! I knew I would have to go out of my way, more often than not, to prove my worth. But nothing, absolutely nothing in my wildest dreams or in my months of planning had prepared me for this—I was called Mamma on the very first day after we were wed!

For every biological parent, there is a teething period of nine months to get ready for the big moment. For me—new to the role of a mother, harbouring only aspirations of being good friends for life—motherhood hit me like a truck!

With all my inhibitions and hang-ups, trust me, I was totally and completely unprepared to take in this child's innocence and her yearning for some mother-figure behaviour. It was emotionally draining, at first, to be called Mamma, but then the word sank in, slowly but surely.

And I've always wondered what it must have been for her in the early days. As awkward as it is to be known and tagged a step-parent, being a step-child must have been just as hard.

It's been three years now and counting! Each day is a revelation and a discovery for us both, mother and child. Way back then, when she was just six years old, I was awed by her amazing sense of perception and maturity! And she continues to amaze me even today.

The day the realisation dawned on me that she was now an intrinsic part of my life as my daughter, it was a life-changing event for us both. Because it was then that I transformed into 'Mamma' without any prior warning at all.

About a year ago, I had to travel abroad for a few days and alone. The nights preceding my departure were filled with discussions on how she would manage in my absence. To the best of my ability I tried to placate her that I would be home soon even before she knew it. On the night before I was to leave, she cried bitterly and, needless to say, I felt terribly guilty throughout my journey. The next two nights, as we communicated via the phone, she would plead that I return and never leave her alone again. I was left speechless. What was going on in that little mind? I had comforted myself with the fact that since she is extremely attached to her father, he would make up for my absence, but no, she was not that easily soothed. Ironically, post all the business trips her father has undertaken, I hadn't seen her shedding a single tear!

I do admit, we have had some not-so-easy-times, and the near future may hold situations that may get a bit difficult to handle during the adolescent years. Whenever I am compelled to reprimand bad behaviour, I am sure she wishes I vanished into thin air, or views me as the 'Wicked Stepmother'. And just for this I would love to settle scores with the Grimm Brothers and a certain Mr Anderson, especially at night when I squirm reading aloud 'wicked stepmother' stories to her.

What then would I have going for me in the future? With a few lessons in patience, some skills learnt the hard way, a great deal of that time-tested listening ability, I hope that my

daughter and I will find a way to cross another bridge the
way we crossed the first one when she first called me
'Mamma.'

*Carol Pereira*

# A Sip of Lasting Love

A bunch of us colleagues were reeling from Monday morning blues and decided to meet for a tea break before starting work in our office. We have these sessions once in a while to lighten our collective mood or to bring in the weekend, but mostly we have these sessions without any reasons whatsoever!

We are a group of five. Rahul was the first guy I spoke to when I joined the office six years back. He is the jovial sort and its fun being with him. Sneha is a headstrong girl and I see a lot of me in her. Ashley is the serious kind. Nidhi is an ebullient girl and I am Anjuli. To define myself is difficult, though people often call me volatile. I guess that's what I am—funny at times and serious occasionally.

So with sips of tea, the talk session started.

'So guys, what's up?' Nidhi initiated the discussion as usual.

'Hey, Ashley is going to be a dad soon!' Rahul shouted.

'Congrats!' I said cheerfully.

'Thanks!' Ashley replied, visibly excited.

'Isn't it a great feeling?' I chirped.

I was thirty and single; thoughts of becoming a parent, or even a spouse for that matter, were alien to me. In fact, the whole idea of living with someone and taking care of them baffled me, given the fact that I had been living alone in

Mumbai for the last six years and considered myself to be absolutely independent.

'You know,' Ashley said, 'it took me five years to convince my parents and Shreya's parents to agree to our marriage. But all's well that ends well, and now I'm going be a dad!'

I remembered the lanky guy in his mid-twenties who had joined the office three years back. He was sincere and hardworking and got many accolades while he was just a trainee. He got a promotion last year as he was the brightest amongst the people who had joined with him. But there was tension always visible on his forehead. Then one day, Ashley introduced Shreya to me. He had known her for more than three years and they had gone to the same college. Shreya's simplicity drew Ashley, though he knew for sure that they could never get married. He was a Christian and she, a Brahmin.

When love would not listen to reason, they tried to talk to their parents but failed to convince them. There were setbacks and tensions and they almost resigned to the wishes of their parents, but then the heart has its own compulsions. Their persistence and sincerity bore fruit and one day Ashley got a call from Shreya's mother.

She had recently lost her husband and both mother and daughter were grieving, so Ashley did not know what he was about to hear. But his happiness knew no bounds when the gentle voice on the other end said, 'Beta I want to meet your parents to talk about your marriage with Shreya.' Ashley could not believe his ears and called her back to confirm what he had heard and Shreya's mother laughingly repeated herself. It took some more time to convince Ashley's parents but finally Ashley and Shreya got married.

'It's always nice to have a love story in your life, I wish I had one too. A love story like a roller-coaster ride surely rocks,' Nidhi said wistfully.

'Love is not a Bollywood movie, Nidhi. It just appears

rocking on screen. Relationships come with a lot of responsibilities and you cannot just enjoy the fruits without working hard for them,' Ashley said in a serious tone.

Ashley's story was not just about love, it was about the belief of a woman in her man and vice versa. The story was about standing up for each other against all odds and not many couples today can do that.

'I think, to keep a woman happy is very simple. Just let her know that you care, that you are going to be with her come what may and she will be yours forever,' said our wise Ashley.

As I was moving towards my work station, I thought of Amit, someone I had met through a colleague. He was someone who had been by my side from when I'd first moved to Mumbai. When I was roughing it out all alone, he was the shoulder I cried on when things went wrong in office. He was happier than I was when I got appreciation. He was someone who understood my pain, my sorrows, my demands, my happiness and my aspirations. He was the one who tolerated my angry SMSs and my irritable PMS phases. He never complained and I just took it for granted that he was someone who was always going to be by my side.

He understood that I wanted to be this strong, independent woman who wanted to conquer the whole world. I knew he loved me; yet I wanted to be by myself. Independence was fascinating to me and I did not want to let go of it. But what I had not understood—till that second—was that being together with someone does not mean losing your independence, it does not mean dependence, it means interdependence.

I reached my workstation, picked up my phone and called Amit.

'Will you spend the rest of your life with me?' I asked.

'I thought you would never ask!' I could hear him grin at the other end.

*Anjuli Dhiman*

# Love Alive

On a rainy day, when all the greenery glistened, Tia was born. Her parents, Anita and Madhav, were ecstatic when they first took her in their arms. She was a bright, chubby girl with a twinkle in her eye and such soft, pure skin that she actually looked like an angel. Anita and Madhav were proud parents of this girl who was born to them after nearly twelve years of their marriage.

Years went by and Tia was soon ten years old. She was a bright student and performed very well in sports and cultural activities as well, but life had taken a turn for the worse. Madhav had lost his job and had started drinking heavily. Anita kept working and tried her best to meet household expenses and fund Tia's education. But all that she did was just not enough, and eventually, the outward lacks began to impact the inner mechanics of the family. Anita and Madhav began to have minor and major squabbles and Tia was caught between their warring egos.

Tia grew more and more reticent and melancholic, and her performance in school started deteriorating. She started staying aloof from all her friends. Anita saw the change in Tia, but did not know how to deal with the situation. Things just did not seem to work in any positive direction for the family. Madhav wanted to provide for the family, be a loving father and husband but he was getting increasingly crushed by a debilitating sense of failure.

One Sunday afternoon, Anita decided to take Tia out to a fair to cheer her a bit. Both of them were silent all the way to the fair. They sat in a couple of rides, ate candy, bought a doll, but nothing seemed to change their mood. Later, Anita and Tia sat on a bench in the park. Both sat silently as they heard the birds chirping around, the children's laughter around them. It was a perfect, bright afternoon, but both of them were merely onlookers, not participants. There seemed to be only one connection between them—and that was silence. The silence was such that it spoke a thousand words.

Anita began to reminisce about how happy she and Madhav were in the earlier days and when Tia was born. Everything was so beautiful and then things changed. Today, everything seemed bleak and hopeless and beyond change or redemption.

Suddenly Anita and Tia saw a little boy hurtling down a slide and his mother catching him at the bottom. In a flash, Anita realised what was missing in her family: it was the very feeling of support and togetherness that everyone wanted in life. It had been a long time since this feeling had made itself visible in the form of a joyful smile on her daughter's face or her own. Or Madhav's for that matter.

But before Anita could process this feeling, Tia got up, sat herself on her knee, held her hand and said with a smile on her face, 'Mommy, I know things have really been bad lately, daddy too is not at his best. Everything will be fine. All I want to tell you is that I love you very much. And you are doing a great job. I want my mommy back. I miss her a lot. Can you please get her for me?' Hearing this, something green like a new sapling broke from Anita's frozen heart and the world looked as clean and fresh as the day when Tia was born.

She burst out crying with a smile on her face, as though she had yearned to hear those words. Both mother and daughter hugged, laughed, played together and went home after a great time of bonding that they had missed out on for a long time. Anita had a feeling, deep and strong, that nothing would ever get the better of her love for her family. And she was right. The family survived the passing storm to become closer and happier than ever.

Anita often looks back at that perfect afternoon in the park when it had taken just one gesture of love to heal her spirit and put her family back together. And wonders why love is withheld when it is the only miracle we all need to reconnect with ourselves and each other. She knows today that love is a living force and it's the only thing that can make life worth living.

*Aditi Shah*

# The Perennial Bloom

In a surreal, predawn hour, as I sit holding my mother tight, I suddenly remember the story of the perennial bloom. Rain or draught, snow or bush fire, the eternal flower always held its own in a garden peopled by seasonal beauties. I don't know at what precise point this tale jumped out of Thakuma's repertoire of bedtime stories and settled into a deep groove of my subconscious. With the sagacity of a six-year-old, often misconstrued as precociousness, I had discarded the story as a make-believe yarn.

But now, as a grown-up woman, in the melting darkness of dawn, as I look at my mother's hand clutching a sepia-tinted photo of Baba cutting the ribbon at the inauguration of the Bengali colony in the capital, the fragrance of the eternal bloom suddenly becomes palpable. And it is no figment of my imagination. Only, the flower in question is a death-defying love that bloomed like a thousand-petalled Brahmakamal—a rare mountain bloom that lives a lifetime in a day. The love between my mother and Baba was rare like this Brahmakamal and it lasted through life and beyond it.

As a child, I found it most natural that two people married to each other should be so obviously in love. Only later, as a battle-scarred woman, did I realise that the unstinting love and commitment my parents shared was a miracle that a majority of us wouldn't experience. Ma was seventeen and Baba all of twenty-two when they got married. And Ma fainted on her saat phera. Our grandfather attributed this to her day-long fasting, but once the newlyweds were alone, the true story behind the fainting spell and weeping came out.

Ma, having grown up on Sarat Chandra and the Bronte sisters, made the dramatic statement that this marriage was against her wishes and her heart belonged to someone else. The groom, already besotted by his dusky bride, took the punch on his chin. Being a man of principle, he did not find her statement blasphemous. A truth should never be swept under the carpet, he believed. His only reaction was, 'Then why the hell did you not get married to that bloke?' Ma, playing the perfect tragic heroine, said her Prince Charming was in prison for his alleged involvement with the anti-British, clandestine nationalistic movement.

Instead of feeling scandalised, humiliated or hurt, Baba took his bride's hand and solemnly promised that he would give her so much love that in a year's time she would have forgotten 'her imprisoned hero'. He used the same diligence to win his bride's love that had fetched him five gold medals and record-breaking marks that could not be bettered for thirty years in his law school.

Our parents loved me and my siblings to distraction, but somewhere they had created a space just for themselves that no one could encroach on. Even after a lifetime of being together, it was not uncommon for Baba to hide a surprise gift for Ma under a pillow with the active connivance of his children. Despite his high-profile government job, he never forgot to call her up from office at least three times a day just for a chat. And Ma, whose intuitive powers were always very piquant, uncannily read Baba's mind or some impending ailment that was yet to plague him. Reading out poems to each other or writing evocative dedications on their favourite books were things I thought all married couples do!

Baba passed away a broken man after the sudden passing away of his favourite son. His loss was a part amputation of our collective consciousness. But at that moment, our pressing need was how to protect Ma from her twin bereavement. As usual it was our narrow, blinkered mindset that made us feel that Ma needed protection. Because she always said, 'Don't worry. He has just gone to the other side of the veil. He is with me now, even more than ever before.'

It was no truism but a rock solid truth. Two days after Baba's passing away, the secretary of the Bengali colony, of which Baba had been the driving force, called up to ask if we had Baba's photo for the memorial ceremony they were organising in his honour. Not just any photo, but the one clicked at the inaugural ceremony. They had misplaced their copy and could we please send them ours? There were so many pictures of Baba but that particular one was missing. We went into a tizzy and turned the house upside down to find it but without any luck. All through this, Ma sat impervious. Her only comment was, 'When the time comes it will surface.' On the third day, in the wee hours of the morning, Ma shook me up from sleep.

Her exact words were, 'He came and told me where to look for the picture.' She smiled at my obvious disbelief and said, 'But he is always there.'

Then we went to my brother's military chest that had been referred to in her dream. Ma unhesitatingly reached for the top drawer that had been returned to us after our brother's death by his regiment. The photo lay there, waiting to be claimed.

*Sanghmitra Paal*

# The Mother

It was a fine morning and a hazy mist hung around the village. I was on my morning walk along the narrow country road. The trees formed a green arch and whispered of serenity and peace. Situated four hundred and fifty kilometres south of Paris, off Limoges on the Plateau de Limousine, the village Villa ra José is occupied by hardly a dozen families. An Italian, a Russian, American and even a Chinese are among the villagers. My friend and art collector Richard Regis has a fine farmhouse here, and he has converted a large, well-lit, wooden space upstairs into a studio for me. I have been painting here for a couple of months now, creating the most colourful and exuberant series of works in my entire career as an artist—The Kites. The very air and light in this part of the world transports one to a surrealistic realm. It inspires me to think afresh, to see anew. The night sky is lit with countless shining stars and sometimes I'm tempted to lie down and gaze at them the whole night with Vincent van Gogh's 'Starry Night' playing in my mind like a song.

On this morning, I continued to walk along the tree-lined path, occasionally greeting a fellow early riser. The fine village folk love having an artist amidst them. It is the beginning of the Nineties and I am here, in this remote corner of France, to start a new phase in my artistic journey. Memories began to unfold in my mind; memories of my struggle, my formative years.

I had lost my mother at the age of seven, just six months after the demise of my father. My own life was like a novel, for I had run away from my home at the age of sixteen from chauffeur-driven comfort to end up on mean streets and railway platforms of a large city I knew nothing about. The beautiful city of my imagination, where an artist would be embraced, did not exist. A total stranger in a metro, I had no money, no friends, no woollens even to protect me from the cold. I did odd jobs in roadside garages, dirty workshops, ramshackle teashops, construction sites for a little food and shelter. But there were days when there was no food and no shelter and I slept on railway platforms and even cemeteries. But I had decided not to go back to my family till I found a way to become an artist. In retrospect, I feel that those one-and-a-half years on the streets made me a man and became the best university of my life. I began to realise the significance of those experiences because they enriched my palette.

Soon after my art education in the early Seventies, I began to experiment with different mediums and materials. It was like groping in the darkness without any particular direction. Abstract and Tantric art was the fad of those days. Tantric art was out of question for me and so I veered towards abstraction. After many false starts, towards the end of the Seventies, a series of paintings began to take shape. The works were inspired by my time as a technician in an aircraft factory and emerged from my day-to-day engagement with countless wheels. The series was called, yes, 'The Wheels', and became very popular subsequently and won the highest academy award, began selling a lot and every industry house wanted to posses one. After riding high on 'The Wheels' for a while, I began to realise that I would end up as a wheel painter if I did not change track.

I almost stopped painting for a while and began to read a lot. Albert Camus, Franz Kafka, Jean Paul Sartre, Ernest Hemingway, Vaikom Muhammad Basheer and even Harold Robins! These readings helped me to understand their life lessons and how they shaped their works and even destiny. But emotionally I needed an anchor, and at that juncture, I came across the works of the great German artist Käthe-Kollwitz. I came across an article where I was stunned to see a work in black and white that almost looked like a drawing but with much more intensity and substance. The painting was called 'The War Widows' and depicted a lot of despairing women hunched together, their wailing children clinging to them in fear and a lot more that would haunt me for months to come. It was a masterpiece. This one work cemented my direction and philosophy for my future works. And possibly life.

I began painting a series, this time, depicting figures in a very realistic form. But after the success of 'The Wheels', the critics were very touchy about these works. They advised me to drop the digressive approach. But I was very sure where I was heading. Instead, I dropped the critics.

Käthe-Kollwitz became not only an inspiration but a maternal figure to me and somehow, strangely, a surrogate mother figure guiding me through life and art. Though I was very careful not to imitate her in my work, I began to sense her immense influence on my thinking, philosophy and direction. She helped me discard a lot of confusion and misdirection. During the early Eighties, I had a chance to work at Garhi, the artists' community studios set up by the National Academy in Delhi. I worked there for over a year. I did a series of works titled 'The Pipes,' inspired by drainage pipes where people on the fringes of life sometimes live, have children and even die. The series came from pain, anger and helplessness. As an artist, I cannot help reacting through

my work to inhuman conditions and inequalities. Yet again,
I went back to Käthe-Kollwitz for inspiration before I began
work on this series and did a series of lithographs. Her
philosophy and compassion for the downtrodden helped me
in formulating the entire series which won a lot of critical
acclaim.

A decade after my first series inspired by Käthe-Kollwitz,
I am here, standing in this magnificent light in a remote
corner of France with a series of exuberant paintings waiting
to unfold. Is this exuberance emerging from those traumas in
my life? I do not know. But I am leaving for Berlin next week
to study and work at the Käthe-Kollwitz museum there. To
be nearer to someone who has been a mother in absentia and
a great inspiration to me. A woman, I realise, does not have
to be in your life literally to change its course forever. Käthe
was not an Indian, but she had the spirit of an earth mother
and mothers don't know nationalities. They only know love.

*Yusuf Arakkal*

# A Drop and an Ocean

My mother spent a good sixty years of her life being a mother and a wife with little thought to any other aspiration. She faced life's vicissitudes with courage and hope. She lost two children at an early age and raised the three of us with a passion that went beyond the call of duty. Like a brave soldier who gives his life to defend the country, so too my mother would gladly do if such a situation had ever arisen where she needed to defend her children.

Five years ago she had her first stroke. She was terrified and confused like she had never been before. She regained her speech and there seemed little damage to her cognitive abilities, till the second stroke came as the doctor predicted and truly took away all her confidence and will to survive. Several times she pulled out her feeding tube and would look at me imploring that I let her die in peace.

Every time I tried to care for her by feeding her or cleaning her, she would push me away. I realised why she was doing this. She wanted to take care of her children, she did not want us to take care of her. In a flash I realised how much of her love we had taken for granted over the years. We demanded love and attention from her and we always got it. I sat down beside her and explained to her that she had taken care of me for fifty years. Won't she give me the opportunity to return some of that love? Somewhere in her confused and damaged mind there was a moment of understanding. She allowed me to care for her. It was I who became the parent and she the child. I understood what she must have gone through caring for us, like so many mothers do without even for a moment considering the magnitude of their devotion.

She lived for another six months. People often tell me that I did a wonderful thing by being by my mother's side for six months. The fact is that she was by my side for fifty years. What I had done for her was a mere fragment, a pale imitation of love compared to her selfless dedication.

The Buddha mentions in one of his sutras that even if you offer your life, it cannot repay the debt of gratitude you owe to your mother.

*Mahesh Dattani*

# The Lonely Singer

That night, my wife, Megha, and our six-month-old baby were sleeping peacefully and I was working on my laptop, when suddenly I heard a bird in the backyard. I wondered what kind of a bird would 'sing' at midnight and went to the window to listen closely. The bird was making very sweet sounds and each chirp was different.

Just then, our baby woke up and Megha woke up too, to rock him back to sleep. As the baby dozed off, I told her about the nocturnal singer and she was amused; we listened to the lonely, midnight song together.

We debated as to if there was more than one bird in the concert but that seemed unlikely, because even though the sounds varied, the voice singularly belonged to just one bird. We forgot about the episode in the morning, but then our singer returned at night for an encore and soon we began looking forward to the music. In the deep silence and solitude of the late hour, the songs acquired a soothing, sweet melancholy and I even entertained the idea of recording the notes.

Megha, however, was beginning to worry about my obsession with the bird. She did not even want us to listen to the sounds now, leave alone going out at night to look for it. Bad souls sometimes draw attention to themselves and attract people in the middle of night, she explained seriously, and added for good effect that one should never follow unnatural sounds. I laughed, but Megha insisted that she had her reasons. When much younger, she lived amid the mysteriously beautiful hills of Himachal Pradesh for a while with her family, and every night she would hear footsteps of someone walking the length and the breadth of the home. But no one else would ever hear the same sounds—not her elder sister, not her parents, and no, not the house help either. The sound was only for her ears and no one else could catch it. With time, she learnt to ignore the unseen intruder, but then an overnight guest, a younger cousin, woke up in the thick of night to ask who was walking around the house so late! Megha had almost jumped out of her skin then, with the realisation that the voice was not in her head. The story was attributed to restless souls and put to rest with time. I had often tried to reason with her that, with age, we hear less and less of lower frequencies, and perhaps some sort of animal had been walking in the vicinity, making low frequency sounds that no one older than her could hear. Megha, of course, told me in no uncertain words that I was just being my usual foolish self.

So, as it happened one night, it was around two in the morning and the bird was still singing outside. I decided to look up the internet to see just who our daily visitor could be. But nothing came up and almost a week passed and, unfailingly, I would be up late working and the sounds would come, and I would enjoy them for a while. Then one night, I could stand the suspense no longer and decided to look up the web one more time and came across a perfect answer.

The bird singing outside had a name and a good reason to sing so wistfully. Our Indian garden in an American neighbourhood had, in fact, been playing host to a lonely mockingbird. Mockingbirds, which are very common where we live, don't really have their own song, like a mynah or a koel would; they just listen to and imitate other birds. So they make a variety of sounds. And if there is a lonely male mockingbird, he is known to sing loudly at nights to attract mates. It's actually not a very uncommon thing in these areas. The more Megha and I read about it, the more it made sense to us. We began to feel for the poor lost soul and it made us realise just how important it is for every living being to have someone to share a song and a life with. In a strange way, the lonely bird brought Megha and me closer, and we began to value each other afresh with the realisation that in a world filled with souls hungry for companionship, we had found each other.

Then a few days later, Megha noticed a mockingbird sitting on a wire during the day and, miraculously, there appeared another mockingbird who came to sit next to the one who must have been lonely for so long. The wait for a mate was finally over.

We did not hear any songs that night, and haven't heard them since.

*Rishi Chhibber*

# Love of My Life

Most of the women I know are closet romantics, too afraid to confess that they believe in the kind of love where two people meet and say to themselves even before anything has begun or ended, 'It is love already'.

What is love anyway? The eternal question with no one certain answer. Here is what I think. Love is awareness of the other in a way that erases otherness. It is knowing a person in a way that goes beyond what they wear, what food they eat, their favourite colour and so on. I don't think all the relationship quizzes that ask such questions have been able to crack it. Who cares about what anyone eats and what the song of their life is or which side of the bed they sleep on? If it is love, you are branded by a glance that transfigures a moment as commonplace as a chutney sandwich into a memory you would possibly take to your death bed with you. If it is love, that is.

Love is when absence is fullness. And when you remember everything—the bad posture, the unfiled nails, the scruffy shoes, the wrong word. And when you remember all this with a feeling that everything is perfect and right and just the way it should be. When you talk to this person as if you were clinging on to a life jacket. When you feel the need for them in the duvet of your skin, in the pang in the pit of your heart and when you feel that need is just too small to capture the miracle of what love really is.

And it *is* a miracle. Isn't it? What are the chances that, in a world where nothing ever goes according to plan, you would meet someone who can bring you to life with just one glance or a smile? Forget about having someone and being with them till eternity. For a moment, just imagine the magic and the wonder of finding someone you can love. Even if it is just for an instant.

So did I find the love of my life? Don't know the answer to that question. Not yet anyway, but the moment when I thought I had love in the palm of my heart and the moment when I lost it, my life expanded, changed, became richer. Years later, in my late thirties, life went into a gentle spiral and everything fell apart in noiseless pieces. My idea of love too crash-landed somewhere between dream and reality. But it was a strangely liberating time because all this made me fall back on nothing and no one but myself. I began to paint seriously after twenty years of half-hearted doodling and had my first art show. And I became an RJ at forty. I was finally goaded from within to write a book I had wanted to write from the time I was eighteen. And joined a dance class and even did a stage show because the soul-numbing loss of one dream demanded that I start another and do something more than just curl up under my quilt as if a truck had hit me. Though I admit I did a lot of that too because it was easier to do that than to face squarely a life of challenge, a serious health alarm and an uncertain future among a few other frightening things.

But here is the thing. The biggest realisation of all that struck me through it all: that the love of my life is really life itself. And as long as I'm alive, I'm going to live with hope rather than fear, though truth be told, there are days when I feel paralysed with panic, wear my pyjamas through the day, sleep too much, watch too much TV, wallow in self-pity, but I also know that there is always something to be grateful for in everyone's life. I am so blessed to be a mother. To have friends who over long-distance lines, listen and talk and share wisdom we have earned painfully together over the years.

I'm grateful for the work I love. The sunlight that filters through the sea froth sheers on my windows. The music I got to play on air along with the poetry that is unfurling again within. The pink lamp hanging in my new bedroom. And the blue ones gleaming softly in my freshly-painted living room. And yes, for that love for small pleasures and great realisations that has survived everything. When we love life with all our heart, we find that we are loved back. Maybe not in the way we imagined, but by a rose-tinted dawn that kisses us on the forehead and gives us another gift-wrapped day just when we thought that the dark night would not end.

*Reema Moudgil*

# Where Memories Dwell

My husband and I started our life together in a home borrowed from my father. Our building with self-contained flats was attached to a couple of chawls—and as is common knowledge, there's little privacy in tenements of this nature. Adding to this trespassing of psychological territory was the familial pressure to get on with your life: own a house, a car, further the family line. So, after having lived there for three years and not having got on with any of these three things, it was with a sense of relief that I packed the last of my household in a carton and loaded it in a truck. We were finally headed to our new home. For me, there would be no looking back; this place would be a closed chapter.

This is why the gush of emotions I felt when I crossed its threshold recently after five years—not out of choice, but out of necessity—was a little shocking and surprising. It was enough to make me sit on a rickety stool in a cobwebbed corner, and stare ... at the dusty floor, patterned in places with tracks of something going about its business. At the water-smudged kitchen platform, where some past rain had found its way in. At the peeling living room walls that had once been painted a pleasant blue.

Then the memories came knocking.

The glass insets of the window ventilators we'd painted

a friend in orange and blue. The wrought-iron curtain ds with leafy finials the fabricator had to do and redo because he couldn't get it right. The sooty smudge on the wall left by the diya, which illuminated a motley collection of gods. The arched windows whose deep sills accommodated my little garden and from where, early one morning, I'd watched, bleary-eyed and horrified, a tomcat stalking two mewling kittens. The unpainted portion of the wall where our wardrobe used to be. The kitchen where my cook whiled away time, telling me how nice her mutton biryani had turned out the previous day, and then lamenting she was simply too rushed to prepare the salad for me. The deliberately colour-coordinated meal of chicken in white sauce, palak raita and steamed rice that I'd cooked for my husband—only to have him comment how he missed a little bit of red (and spice) for dinner.

Echoes of days spent together. Everyday joys and sorrows. Togetherness and tiffs. Disappointment and fulfilment. And, most importantly, the hope of a bright tomorrow. They say home is where the heart is. And though I have my heart firmly lodged where I stay now, I guess I've left some of it behind, in that place I used to call home ...

*Rupali Sebastian*

# The Woman in the Mirror

I missed my mother and her smile. It had been almost a year since I completed my graduation, got married and came to Delhi from my hometown Kolkata. I had started building a new family life and a career as a teacher in a public school. I enjoyed it, but I missed my mother.

My childhood memories came alive whenever I was with the children to whom I taught creative things in class. I remember how my mother guided and helped me to prepare my projects in her unique way throughout my school days. Her concepts inspired me to grow as a creative person in all aspects. She always tried to emphasise the value of beauty in every form in life and her ideas guide me even today.

I was kept busy by life, and I rarely had time to speak to my parents. In 1980, we did not have mobile connectivity— and I did not have a landline either!

Whenever I had a free moment though, I remembered my mother in her colourful, heavy-bordered Bengali cotton saree, sindoor on her forehead, beautiful long hair casually left open after a bath, bangles on her hands and a gold chain with a delicately designed locket. She looked graceful and happy, and like a woman who had been greatly loved and cared for by her husband. He had never allowed any unhappy moment to touch my mother. So I did not worry about them. They had each other.

Almost three years passed and I was now busy taking care of my one-year-old baby. One Sunday, I was relaxing with my baby at home when there was a knock at the door. I opened the door and found my neighbour standing there. He anxiously asked me, 'Where is your husband?'

I said he was out of town, wondering about the reason for his unease. He said 'There is a phone call for him from Kolkata.' Then he added, 'It is not for you,' when he sensed I was about to move forward to attend to the call. After a fraction of a second, he answered my questioning look, 'Okay, just inform him it was his brother's call. His father-in-law is no more.'

It took me a moment to realise what he had said. I mumbled, 'His father-in-law ... my father ... my father is no more?' The man at the door said, 'I'm sorry, it happened at eleven in the morning today.'

This shocking news was totally unexpected and disorientated me. I looked at my baby, trying to come to terms with reality. My heart wanted to fly to reach my family home at Kolkata, but I had to wait for my husband to return and I had to get my leave sanctioned at the school, which would probably be approved after six days. I was helpless. My job was not yet confirmed and I had to follow the rules.

I spoke to my mom; she was calm and steady. She said, 'Don't worry, take your time.' It was incredible to me that her voice was normal—as if nothing had happened. I couldn't sleep or eat or think. I reached Kolkata after ten days, suddenly nervous about meeting my mother. The main door was open and there were people everywhere. Preparations were on for a puja on the thirteenth day. I found my mother making tea for a few of our relatives, who were sitting and gossiping as if some party was on.

I was shocked to see that my mother was wearing a widow's attire, only a white dhoti without any border. She was without any ornaments. No sindoor and hair tied in a topknot. I felt as if her beautiful life had been snatched away suddenly.

She gave me a lifeless smile when I asked, 'Is this necessary?'

She replied, 'The relatives convinced me that I must do this for your father.'

I knew she was being forced to do all this to satisfy social norms expected by the relatives. They were not allowing her to remember my father's words to her; he always insisted that she dress up and look beautiful, no matter what. He had always just wanted to see my mother happy and these careless visitors were enjoying a get-together, oblivious to my mother's feelings.

I went to the bedroom, took out a saree that my father liked, and asked my mother to dress up as she used to before. She changed without saying a word, as if she had only been waiting for someone to tell her this. Her tearful expression made me sad. She was my mother, beautiful and graceful, and no one was going to take away her life from her. We shared an emotional moment, hugging each other and feeling my father's absence, and yet feeling his presence around us.

My mother looked at herself in the mirror and whispered, 'You know, he told me with his last breath, "Please keep smiling, I will be with you always even when my body is no more".' She smiled, 'Don't you feel he is still around?'

'Yes ma,' I answered, between smiles and tears.

*Saswati Chaudhuri*

# The Language of Kindness

The bulging bags left at the front door surprised Rina. She took them inside feeling glad Tokyo was a safe enough place for visitors to leave presents unattended outside the door when the owner was away. But a bigger surprise, shock rather, awaited her. She gasped when she opened the beautifully and carefully wrapped presents and saw the contents. She stood for a long time staring at the letter, swallowing back tears.

It had all started with Keiko San sending her two lovely children for English lessons—twelve-year-old Yuki and ten-year-old Yutaka. Keiko was in her mid-thirties, petite, neatly attired, rather shy and very pretty. The children were bright, particularly the elder daughter, and keen to learn English. Their father was the manager of the local Juku, a tutorial school—one of the many that most children went to after school. Jukus were cram schools where students were prepared to pass exams. English was one such subject taught just to prepare students for taking exams rather than as a tool for communication. Keiko San was keen for her children to learn to converse and communicate in the real world, not just pass exams. She was overjoyed at finding a willing teacher near her house who actually taught in the prestigious Waseda University. She had a part-time job and paid the tuition fee herself. Rina thoroughly enjoyed teaching these well-mannered children and also looked forward to the few minutes when she and Keiko would chat when she came to pick up the two children after their lessons late in the evening. However exhausted after work, she never failed to arrive on time, with the third and youngest child smiling and gurgling in the basket of her bicycle.

Rina usually insisted Keiko come in for a cup of tea as these chats helped improve her own spoken Japanese. She also knew the mother barely got a break between office work and housework. She was always moved by Keiko's gentle smile and calm demeanour; Keiko never seemed to complain about the work or the long hours. Being a working mum herself, Rina recognised the effort needed to multi-task as Keiko did, and admired her patience tremendously. She knew the husband left early in the morning and didn't return till late at night after his drinking session with colleagues. And on Sundays, it was 'business golf' of course. Keiko was left to manage the home and upbringing of her three young children almost single-handedly. The mother had one ambition—to give her children the best possible chances in life.

One evening Keiko was unusually late. Surprised and rather worried, Rina tried to appear nonchalant and got the children to share in the family meal. Again, she was touched by the hesitation and good manners of these beautifully brought-up children. Finally, Keiko arrived, third child in tow. She asked to speak to Rina in private; she explained that her husband's Juku had to shut down because of falling numbers and, consequently, he'd lost his job. Rina knew how painful, humiliating even, this conversation was for the mother. But worse was to follow. She said she'd taken on extra hours at work to bring in more money and the daughter was required to stay home after school to look after the baby. She could not send the second child alone either. They also had to move out of their house and into an apartment. The children were heartbroken.

Rina was desperate to continue helping the family but she knew their sense of honour too well to even suggest teaching them for free. They would lose face terribly and perhaps she'd lose their friendship too. She saw a way out. She pleaded with Keiko not to stop their lessons when their English was improving rapidly but to send them on Sunday mornings instead, when the parents were home. Rina said that unfortunately she could not teach on a Sunday, but her daughter, Mia, older than Keiko's eldest by two years, could help with reading and writing, and certainly with conversation practice. It would also help Mia by giving her invaluable practice, as she also wanted to teach English when she grew up.

Keiko wanted to pay Mia something for her time, but Rina found it easy to refuse. She explained that because Mia was not a professional, she could not accept any fee but would see it as free teaching practice. All of them would benefit. Since the children were longing for this and Mia clearly wanted to help, the mother gave in gratefully. Rina felt she'd scored very cleverly. So the two students began coming in for an hour on Sundays. There would always be times when the daughter was busy and Rina, of course, had to step in. And many were the occasions when Rina would find she'd baked too many cookies or cakes, and asked her young students to help finish them. They could not forget the youngest, so some were packed to take home too. This continued for a few months.

One evening, Keiko arrived unexpectedly. She had disturbing news. The family had to give up the apartment they were renting and so had decided to move the following week to their hometown, a village about a hundred miles from Tokyo. It was a sad week for everyone as all the children had grown very close to one another. After the last class was over and the children had gone back after a little 'farewell party', Rina realised she had made a stupid mistake. She had forgotten to ask for their new address and contact numbers and did not know the location of the apartment they had moved to in Tokyo. She and Mia rushed to the old house and asked around, but none of the neighbours knew where the family had moved. It dawned on her that there was no way for her to keep in touch with the family. It seemed unbelievable she would never see dear Keiko again or see the progress of her beloved students.

It was a few months later when she came back from a day out that she found the bag outside her front door. Inside, beautifully wrapped in delicate washi, Japanese rice paper, she found a solid gold 24-carat pendant for herself, traditional Japanese clothes for her husband, a delicate golden bracelet with charms for Mia and a rather special watch for her son. Most precious of all was the letter. It expressed affection and gratitude for all the kindness and generosity of the teacher and her daughter. The last two sentences read: 'When all around me was dark, you gave me hope. You showed me what it is to be genuine and how to live and relate to other human beings.'

With tears in her eyes, Rina thought: 'No, my dear, it is you who has taught us the true meaning of generosity and honour. It is easy to be generous when you have enough to share. I could not force you to accept my charity. You have too much self-respect and did not want to owe anyone any obligation.' There was no address on the letter. And yet, two women from two different countries had found each other.

*Rani Rao Innes*

# Care In a Package

Lata came to work for my family when my brother and I were toddlers. She was hard-working, honest and affectionate. Despite her less-than-privileged background, Lata never let her poverty define her. My mother encouraged and treated her like an equal, and so, Lata became family. I was nine when the incident that changed our lives occurred. Sprawled on my bed, I was reading a Famous Five book when I heard the sound of sobbing nearby. It seemed to be coming from the kitchen. Incensed voices hinted at an argument in the making. Aware that my mother would be furious if I was caught eavesdropping, I crept towards the kitchen surreptitiously. Reading that book had taught me a thing or two about stealthy investigations.

As I got closer, I heard familiar voices, one of which belonged to my mother.

'Are you certain, Sanjay Singh?' I heard her ask the driver sharply.

'I'm telling you, bhabhi,' he replied. 'She is the culprit.'

'All lies,' shrieked Lata. 'You know I would never steal anything from you, bhabhi,' she cried.

Something held me there, as I hid behind the kitchen door hoping for a sign perhaps. Some intimation of her innocence. I recalled Lata narrating stories from her childhood about being hungry, homeless and deprived. She always emphasised that her parents had taught her to handle those situations bravely, but with integrity.

'Calm down, Lata,' soothed my mother, 'I believe you, but I need to hear what Sanjay Singh has to say.'

Sanjay Singh's words rang fallacious even before they were said. I sensed trouble ahead.

'I was on my way to my quarters, bhabhi,' he declared. 'When I crossed Lata's room, I happened to look inside and saw a large packet of sugar lying open on her cot.'

He paused. 'That's when I realised I have solved the case of the disappearing sugar, bhabhi, and I came straight to you after telling all the other family members,' he concluded smugly.

The silence seemed to linger. Then, with tolerant perception, my mother said, 'Sanjay Singh—Lata has worked with us for over six years. Never have I had a problem like this before.'

'But bhabhi . . .' he interrupted.

She cleared her throat, indicating that he should stop talking. 'It is only in the last few months that I find this problem with the sugar, Sanjay Singh,' she said. 'Which happens to be around the time that you started working here.'

I felt hopeful again.

'I don't doubt for a second that when I go up to Lata's room, I will find the sugar there,' she declared.

Lata gasped, but my mother continued, 'However, I suspect the sugar has been planted there by someone who is threatened by Lata's position in this family.'

Silence.

'I believe that person is you, Sanjay Singh.'

Lata began to cry. I could sense there was relief in her sobs.

'I no longer require your services, Sanjay Singh,' my mother said coldly. 'Please go pack your belongings and then come see me to settle your salary.'

Sanjay Singh was at a loss for words. He stormed out miserably.

Lata broke down, whimpering as my mother consoled her.

I quietly retreated. With each step, the sound of her cries subsided, overcome by the noise of the afternoon traffic outside.

Lata didn't come down from her room for the rest of the day. My mother said it was because she was sad.

The next morning, as we were leaving for school, Lata met us at the gate. My brother and I shrieked when we saw her. She smiled in delight as we ran into her arms.

'Bye Lata,' we yelled as we dashed into the car and looked back at her from the window.

'Bye,' she replied tenderly as she waved farewell.

When we returned from school later that day, Lata was gone. When we asked why, my mother told us that some of our family members still suspected Lata of pilfering sugar out of the kitchen supply. Since she didn't want Lata to lose her self-respect, my mother told her to leave. Lata begged to be allowed to stay, but my mother insisted, and I could tell she was very upset. 'I hope Lata understands why I made her quit,' my mother said softly. 'She wouldn't have been content if this family constantly mistrusted her. I made this decision for everyone's happiness, but most of all, for Lata.'

Seven years passed. One morning, Lata showed up at our door unexpectedly. She couldn't stop gushing about how wonderful it was to meet us. There was no hint of a grudge, much less any furtiveness, after all that had transpired.

Lata told my mother she was currently working as a housekeeper with a family in Washington D.C. She was merely back in India to conclude visa formalities. When she inquired about my brother, my mother informed Lata that he was studying in the US. My mother stated how miserable he was eating dorm food in his university, and how much he missed eating Indian food.

Lata took my brother's address from us and promised to look him up if she could upon her return to the US.

At the door, Lata said, 'It took me some time to understand why you made me leave then, bhabhi.'

My mother became uneasy. Lata smiled and continued, 'You were concerned about me, bhabhi. You worried about how everyone would treat me following that incident.'

She kissed my mother's hand. 'You made me go because I would have been unhappy around the others and their distrust in me. Thank you, bhabhi, your actions made me realise how much you cared about my dignity. And I will never forget that.'

And once again, Lata left.

Weeks went by, as did life. One night, my brother called home and told my mother that something remarkable had happened. He had received an enormous package from Lata, containing many Indian snacks and goodies, with a note saying it was the least she could do to show her appreciation for my mother's love and kindness.

As it turned out, Lata continued to send my brother care packages once every few months for the next two years. There was never a return address on the parcels, only a PO Box number, but she always enclosed a note sending her love and good wishes.

The last time my brother heard from her, her note stated that she was accompanying her new family to the country of their next posting. As a result, she wouldn't be able to send any more food packages.

We haven't heard from Lata since. But her love, thoughtfulness and compassion will never be forgotten. For Lata, sending the packages was never about the food. It was a token of affection and care for our family, her family.

*Jaya Kaushish Dhawan*

# One True Love

I was fifteen and it was a Tuesday afternoon. For months, we had exchanged glances and shared jokes in front of two seventeen-inch monitors in computer class. It was on one of them that I saw his girlfriend's photo, he was practicing his Photoshop skills on it. That's when I understood that just because someone constantly flirts with you, it doesn't mean he loves you. Yes, that's what I had thought, 'He loves me.'

It took me a decade, one filled with numerous minor flirtations, major heartbreaks and a variety of relationships—from the nearly perfect to the utterly dysfunctional—to understand that love is bigger, better and more wonderful than I could have ever imagined at fifteen. And I wanted to experience it for real. I had looked for it at places and through channels that conspire in books and movies to make you bump into your true love—libraries, parties, coffee shops, airport terminals, common friends—and conceded defeat. Serendipity had failed me.

I was twenty-five, just the right age in our magnificent country to let your parents find you a groom and live happily ever after. Suddenly, an arranged marriage seemed romantic. 'If the basics are right,' my mother said, 'the rest will fall in place.' In no time, she was ready with endless copies of my kundli and to tap into a social circle that spanned the whole globe. My horoscope was enjoying many cross-continental journeys that I had always dreamed of. I loved my mother, but once again, I had begun to look up to her, as though I was five and not twenty-five. She could find me love, she could do anything. What a great feeling it was!

But as great feelings go, this one didn't last too long either.

Armed with a fancy tray, holding cups brimming with the beverage of the groom's choice and snacks handpicked by my mother, I hoped to meet the love of my life. And in a matter of few weeks, I met three—in my eyes—totally unsuitable men. One of them hated animals, the second one didn't want me to wear jeans and the third one, I couldn't quite put my finger on the reason.

In a year, I had met many men. Some rejected me. Some were rejected by me. Some connections fizzled out. Some had expectations I could never fulfil. It was the dating game all over again. Except this time, all first dates included two pairs of parents and numerous relatives. 'When the families are involved, things will be taken seriously,' my mother opined.

She soldiered on and often consoled me (and herself) with contradictory statements. 'You can't expect these things to work out overnight,' she would say on one day. And on another occasion, 'You see, something will work out overnight, we'll have to be ready,' she'd say to my bemused father, who was relegated to the role of a complacent assistant in the 'get-the-daughter-married' project. While it had its lighter moments, the whole process of presenting my-best-possible-self to one guy after the other was getting tedious. It was getting harder to explain to my joyfully enthusiastic mother, why I didn't think much of the 'highly-educated guy' who asked me, 'What is Tolkien?' or why I just couldn't be with someone who said 'communicate' when he actually meant 'commute'.

I was tired of playing the good girl. I began to date

somebody who was the antithesis of 'a suitable boy'. He was from another religion, had barely passed his graduation exams and had no steady job. It was a reckless affair, but something I needed.

As expected, it didn't last.

Without giving myself time to heal from a year's worth of rejections and rejecting, and another six months of a dysfunctional relationship, I was back in the market. I had managed to exhaust my mother's social connections and there was talk of placing an ad in the matrimonial classifieds. I shuddered at the thought. My ad would have read: dark, not convent-educated, not homely either, as works in media. In the classifieds game, I wouldn't stand a chance.

I needed another medium where I could express myself better. With an allotment of two hundred and fifty words per profile, matrimonial sites seemed like a better option. I tried it and met a variety of delightful and interesting people. Almost all of them were from out of town, so chat, phone and e-mail were usually how I got to know them. With no gawking relatives and salivating parents watching me say (type), 'Ya, I tried pot this one time . . .' I opened up a lot more and got to know prospective grooms much better too. Things didn't always work out, but many of them remained friends and I was even invited to the wedding of one of them.

As I had hoped, I also met a very special person through the site. He was smart, successful and had a fabulous sense of humour. We exchanged over a hundred emails, chat conversations and international telephone calls for over four months. Then he came down to India and never visited me. My impression was that he was making the trip to get engaged to me. Swift, simple and smooth. The way these things happen in arranged marriages—to other people.

I was too heartbroken to go on. I half-heartedly tried talking to a few more people—with my mother reminding me constantly, 'Don't waste four months, decide within one month.' I tried to analyse what happened to Mr No-Show and had many fascinating theories. But it was the lesson learned when I was fifteen that comforted me the most. Just because he flirts with you incessantly, doesn't mean he has fallen in love with you (or in this case wants to marry you).

The promise of a situation or one made by a person isn't always sacrosanct. These things happen and it's best to move on.

After looking for love, for about a decade on my own and about three years through my family, I have decided to give it a break. To take some time off and fall in love with myself. All those decisions I had put on hold are now out of cold storage. I quit my day job and pursued my dream of working from home, something I always thought would be best to do with the security of 'marriage'. I travel alone and enjoy my own company or those of the others I meet on my journeys. I am learning a new language and I pick up words to describe feelings I have not truly felt since that Tuesday afternoon when I was fifteen—feelings like peace, calm and joy.

*Aarthi Gunnupuri*

# Rebels In Arms

I must've been eleven and my sister, about nine. It was an age when impulse ruled. Calculated afterthoughts came later.

'Bhaiyya' is what my sister called me. And, was I a bully! I still don't know who taught me to be that way, but I never missed an opportunity to show her who was the boss. But then, life has a way of teaching us just how strong those are that we usually take for weaklings.

It so happened that, one day, we discovered a new restaurant near our house, one of those places that brandish their 'pure vegetarian' credentials. Our parents decided to take us there and we bragged a bit about it among friends in our apartment, enjoying their jealousy and anticipating mouth-watering delights.

So we went and, like us, most of the people in the restaurant seemed curious to check what the new place had to offer. After scanning the menu, as any judicious middle-class family would do, from right to left (first the prices, then the dish), we all decided what we wanted. I settled for a Veg Club Sandwich. Needless to say, my biggest fan, my sister, also settled for the same. I really don't remember what my parents settled for, but it was definitely not a Veg Club Sandwich.

Their order came slightly earlier than mine and my sister's. So obviously it vanished soon. I restrained myself from trying whatever they were having. 'We won't dig into what you are having and we won't share what is ours'—the lines were drawn on the table. After a while came our sandwiches. Soft stacks of white bread slices holding together slices of tomato and potato smeared in green chutney, with a generous topping of cheese and ketchup. My sister and I started devouring them without a sound.

But halfway through the plate, I realised the treat was bigger than my stomach could take. I surreptitiously looked at my sister. Yes, she was also going through the same agony. We both had this it's-too-large-for-me-to-finish look written on our faces. But then, our egos wouldn't allow us to accept defeat and let my parents share the spoils.

We were eating slowly, so slowly that my insightful father asked, 'Can I help you finish it?' 'No, no. I (burp) will finish it,' I managed to say with my mouth full.

Many minutes later, my sister and I still had to work our way through a quarter-full plate of food. So we began to gulp water after every morsel. But still, the plates looked unvanquished.

My father, unable to bear our struggle, volunteered to pick up a piece from my plate. 'No!' I said. It was humiliation! But he was in a mood to bully me with his friendly smile. Notwithstanding my protest, the bread started approaching his wide-open mouth. 'I'll walk away if you eat it!' My threats seemed, well, childish to him. And in went the piece of sandwich.

'That's it!' I declared. I stood up at once and walked out of the restaurant. I paused, expecting a voice to call me back. Nothing! More insult! I started stomping away towards our house. 'I swear I'll never go with them to any restaurant. Or ... maybe that's too much ... I'll go with them, but I'll never order a Veg Club Sandwich,' I said to myself.

Then a faint, familiar voice fell on my ears. 'Bhaiyya!' I

turned around. My sister was walking towards me with equal vehemence. 'What are you doing here?' I enquired. 'No Bhaiyya, even I won't eat with them. Let's go home.' A deep sense of camaraderie swept over me. I felt like a general on the brink of losing a battle yet finding solace in the unconditional support of his closely rallying troops. Once again, I looked in the direction of the restaurant, perhaps trying to imitate some angry Bollywood hero swearing revenge and then walking into an angry sunset.

That episode made me look at my little sister as someone who was strong enough to not just take my insults but also to stand by me when I had painted myself into a corner. My sister hasn't changed still. She is still the same loyal, innocent, hero-worshipping little girl as far as I am concerned, and I, on my part, try a little harder to deserve her unconditional love.

By the way, one-and-a-half hour later, my trusted lieutenant and I were back at the same restaurant with our parents, occupying a different table and devouring a far more manageable chocolate ice-cream, while our parents tried their best to contain their laughter, fearing another domestic rebellion.

*Sagar Haveli*

*Reprinted by permission of Lavanya Karthik*

# 5

# BEYOND ADVERSITY

*If you want the rainbow, you've got to put up with the rain.*

—Dolly Parton

# Role Reversal

'Moti', 'Shahi-nahi-hai'—these were just two of the nicknames that my schoolmates had bestowed on me. I would come back from school crying every day, hating my name and my plumpness, and I would hide my head in the most comfortable place in the world ... my mother's lap. It would immediately give me a sense of security. Then she would smile and put her hand on my head. Such simple gestures, but I would be a transformed soul.

She was constantly giving me pep talks. 'Don't bother with what people say. Work hard instead and be the best that you can be, and then they will notice you for what you are. Being fat doesn't mean being ugly, my beautiful daughter, you are the most beautiful person on this earth.' These words were like my mother's mantra for me; she would chant them to me every day.

It was her faith in me which served as encouragement and it gave me that burning desire to excel at what I did. And so I studied really hard so that I could get into the college of my dreams ... and I did! Both my parents dropped me off at my hostel and my mother left me with her gentle words of faith, encouragement and trust ringing in my ears.

I broke that trust not once but three times, when we were caught by the hostel warden for going out without permission.

Both my parents were called. I was scared but she was very calm as she told me, 'Remember that in life, whatever you do will make or mar you, so be careful what you choose. Have fun, definitely, and enjoy yourself, but always know your limits.' Still that unshakeable trust in me! It made me cry in shame for days afterwards; it was worse than being scolded or shouted at. She unknowingly gave me a life-lesson that helped me while bringing up my own kids.

When I first started working, she came all the way to bless me and her unbridled joy knew no limits as the years passed and I started getting noticed for my work. Whenever I won awards or my pictures would appear in the newspaper, she would be ecstatic, her pride in me evident for all to see.

However, I truly believe that all the awards and accolades were her doing! The credit should go to her. My success is a result of her faith in me. Yes, whatever I am today is all thanks to my mother. It was she who gave me all the courage and support I needed to face the world and not be plagued by negativity; to believe in myself and to never lose faith in God.

And today, she is frail, old and partially deaf. The mother, who had put all her trust in us, is today suspicious of our every move. The mother, who had the magic touch when it came to comforting us, now refuses to be comforted by us whenever she starts crying like a child.

After my father's death, our mother's personality changed completely.

The same woman who would sit till late at night to knit me the most beautiful sweater that I wanted to wear the next day to a school party; the same woman who would give me milk at three in the morning; who would spend sleepless nights during my board exams just to make sure that she was able to wake us up at odd hours to study, now glared at her two daughters as if they were strangers with ulterior motives.

It killed us, the way she looked at us now. Would she ever be the same?

Our need for our mother is still enormous. I worry about so many things ... Who could I call when people let me down? Where should I go when all I need is someone to just listen to me and comfort me? I can think of no one other than my mother—the person who tenderly and patiently cared for me; taught me to walk and talk; read to me and made me laugh. No one delighted in my successes more; no one could comfort me better in my failures. She disciplined me when I went wrong and gave me the courage to face the storm. She taught me how to always smile even in the worst of times. Who would do all that now?

I decided to visit my friend, a doctor, and seek his advice. He said that the trauma my mother was experiencing was typical of a spouse who loses the partner s/he was so dependent on. She would heal, but it would take time.

The doctor's words kept coming back to me that night, 'Losing a life-long partner is one of life's greatest pains. One thinks of all of the thwarted desires that die along with the person we love. We want that person to be with us still; we desire their presence, companionship, or blessing; we long for the connection we once had, or possibly desire to say one last thing. She is a single person once again and you must understand that she is trying to come to terms with that.'

The look in her eyes kept coming back to haunt me and that's when it hit me! That look that we believed to be of distrust and suspicion was actually the look of an old woman asking for understanding and support!

Once again, after so many, many years, I was ashamed of myself. How could I sit and cry and worry about my needs when the woman I loved most in my life was in such anguish! Wasn't this the same lady who stood by me at all times? Didn't she need me now more than I needed her?

It was time for me to comfort her. To show her the depths of my love for her. To be there for her the way she has always been there for me.

I just hope she can forgive me for taking so long to understand.

*Shalini Nambiar*

# Love Lost, Life Gained

Reetu was caught in a dilemma. She paced about her room, fidgeting nervously with her wedding ring. Early that morning, she had seen a message flash across the mobile as it played out the tune, *What I Miss About You*. This missive on her husband's mobile had caused her mind to flip-flop between bleary confusion and plain disbelief. Never before had she experienced this dreary feeling in her twenty years of marriage with Nilesh. Never before had she doubted the love between them. This happenstance was to serve as a litmus test for Reetu to find out whether faith too was enmeshed in their relationship.

She'd found it queer when she read it the first time. But as she mulled over it, she couldn't help wondering if her relationship was on the verge of a break-up.

She decided to call the person who had sent the message. Reetu dialled the number from her mobile and waited. She felt the portents of doom fall on her when she heard a click followed by a dial tone. It played the song again. The words of this ditty buzzed in her ears for long—'The sharing of secrets we thought no one else knew, That's what I miss about you . . .' Nilesh had once mentioned that this song was special to him because someone dear to him had liked it too.

'Hello,' said a woman's voice, interrupting the song. Reetu

could not think of anything to say. She wanted to find out who this person was, and at the same time she did not want to embarrass her husband in any way.

'Is this Sophie I am talking to?'

'I am afraid you have dialled the wrong number,' said the voice before cutting the line.

Reetu went over the message again in her mind. It had read: 'Nilesh, I am happy that we could finally meet yesterday. I know we drifted apart some time back, but I want to make up for the lost time ... can we bring the spark back in our lives and light up the love between us again?'

She waited for Nilesh to come home that day. She met him with a warm smile and hugged him tightly as he entered the room. Tears glistened in her eyes as she began to think that she may be torn away from him forever.

'What's wrong Reetu? Why are you crying?' asked Nilesh.

Reetu knew that she couldn't hide her emotions from her husband for long. She explained to him at length how she had chanced upon the message on his mobile, and how this had shaken her belief in their love.

And then it was Reetu's turn to hear the shattering truth. Her husband had been in a relationship with another woman for the last fifteen years but had stopped meeting her since the last year. He also told her that he had considered a divorce a long time back. What stopped him was the thought of their two children who were now studying abroad.

If she was hurt and angry, Reetu didn't show it. She chose to hear Nilesh out quietly for the next one hour. However, the next day, Reetu left the house without saying a word. Not that she didn't want to cling to the faintest glimmer of hope or save her dreams from shattering. She left because her trust had been broken ... the trust that she had unconditionally placed in her partner. She made up her mind to walk out of his life forever because she no longer wanted to share her life with someone who had not valued her or their shared love enough.

I wonder now, if it is tough to walk away from a world that you have created bit by bit over the years. Are the memories of old times enough to bring a semblance of happiness in your life? Should women accept loss of trust as part of their lot? Should they put up with a marriage that turns out to be a sham after decades of caring and sharing?

And then I see Reetu, my aunt, who is all of fifty today. She catches my eye and smiles. The creases on her pretty face hide a multitude of quick-silver emotions. But not one emotion out of all of them has a trace of regret. When the foundation of her love crumpled, she did not want to put it back together. She still doesn't want to have it all back. She cherishes the moments she spent with her husband, but doesn't wish to relive the old times. She has moved on and in doing that has taught all the women who know her, including me, that love is not just an arrangement, it is a commitment. And when this commitment is dishonoured, the least we can do is to honour ourselves.

*Pooja Nair*

# My Daddy Strongest

On a hot, June day, the world as I knew it changed forever, when a phone call from my mother broke the terrifying news that my father had been diagnosed with pancreatic cancer.

It was on 18 June 2002 when the doctors decided to operate on him. It happened to be my birthday and I wondered if I would be given the most important gift of all—the gift of his life. Before he was taken into the operation theatre, my father looked at all of us, as we tried to fight back our tears, and said, 'Don't worry. I've talked to the doctors and they have told me that I will be fine. Wait for me ... I will be back soon.' Yes, he came out after the surgery, seemingly fine, though we knew and so did he that all his pain and misery was not over.

Yet he promised me that he would be fine when I, his daughter who was also a mother of two, would make time to see him next and visit him from another end of the country.

Doctors had granted him maximum one or two years more to live, but that information was not enough to make a fighter like my father give up hope or to stop living his life, which had never been too kind to him. When he was just ten, he along with his parents and two younger sisters had to abandon their affluent home in Lahore during Partition. He being the eldest of the siblings had to help his father earn a living and had even sold balloons as a child when most children of his age were busy coaxing their parents for treats.

At times, he had also studied under the lamp-post at night and it was a huge achievement for a person who had battled such odds to retire as a professor. He was the one who always taught me that the battles of life are won in your mind. Never be a pessimist, he would say, look at the positive side of each situation.

When I made another trip sometime after his operation to check on him, he was thrilled and laughed, and said, 'See, I kept my promise. I am alive!'

Yes, I knew by then that my father always kept his promises. He had kept a promise many years back when I was in Class 3 to teach me to play Raag Yaman on the sitar for the school annual day function. He was the happiest when the local newspapers carried a picture of his 'talented and all-rounder daughter!' I remember the next day when I came back from school, there was a gift lying on my bed with a tag which said, 'For a great sitarist of the future' and there was that newspaper picture of me playing the sitar. I could never be a sitar player, but this small gesture instilled great confidence in me and also the will to excel in every task I have taken up since then.

Soon the doctors declared, 'Don't take him anywhere. He can't handle travelling'. By now, the end was near. We all knew it. My father was weak, in pain, physically not an iota of his original self, but still smiling. 'Till the time I don't feel like leaving this world, no one can take me away, and when I'm gone my daughters will do the last rites. They are no less than sons,' he declared and told the doctor cheekily, 'And I will come back again and trouble you again.' The doctor too smiled back. But we all knew that he would not come back to the hospital again.

Back home, it was a shattering experience to see him in so

much pain, and yet his will power was amazing. Then one night, he gave up and told us to collect wood for his pyre. He told us to take him down from the bed and place him on the floor as it was his time to leave. And true to his word, he left us that very evening.

When I had to light his pyre, how I wished I could snatch him away from the cruel clutches of death and carry him away on my shoulders just as he had done once when a rampaging bull was heading towards me when I was a little girl. But whenever I feel lost, I remember his words, 'Always look for some positive point in adversity and you will never fail in life.'

*Kanan Gautam*

# Full Stop

She didn't know when the sense of finality hit her. This was not the first time her husband had come home in an inebriated condition, after his return from the rehab centre. And she knew it would not be the last time he would come home drunk. Drunk. Somehow, she hated even saying the word to herself. The word had a foul smell to it. She remembered how it had all started and how she had ignored all the signs that something was amiss.

The number of times he had gone out with friends just for 'a couple of drinks', or had downed innumerable pegs because he was 'stressed' were plenty. Her mind travelled back to the time when she had fallen in love with this man, who now stood before her looking like the mess that he had turned into. He had been handsome, smart and well educated. She was an extrovert, a happy-go-lucky girl who loved life. Together, they made the perfect couple. Their parents had not approved though. After fiercely fighting their disapproval, they had eloped and got married in a temple, in bona fide filmy style. Little did she know that her world was to undergo a dramatic change.

This had been going on for seven years now; but for her it seemed like forever. Such was the devastating effect his drinking had on her, that she could not remember ever feeling happy and carefree. Every time he abused her in a drunken stupor, she had told herself that she would no longer tolerate it. That she would walk out ... only to change her heart the next day when he 'behaved'. She had almost walked out on him twice earlier, once during their fourth wedding anniversary party, when he had insulted her in a sozzled state in front of a hundred guests; and next when she had her pregnancy confirmed and had come home eager to tell him the good news only to find him passed out drunk. But like all other previous occasions, she had convinced herself that she could and would change him. Like a naïve teenager, she had thought that with time and love he would change and give up his habit. But habits are like weeds that are sometimes impossible to eradicate if left unattended for years. His drinking progressively worsened and he took her with him, arms flailing helplessly, into a dark void without a bottom.

She felt a tug at her sleeve drenched in tears. It was her tiny, three–year-old son, Siddharth. He was shaking her, crying, yet trying to soothe her; when instead it should have been the other way round. She should have been the one calming him, shielding him from the emotional chaos that seemed to devour them every time the man of the house returned reeking of liquor.

Suddenly she felt something shift inside her. It was the sense of finality finally that told her that the time had come to put a full stop to this sordid tale. Like a bolt from the blue, courage she had never known before enveloped her in its light. She wiped her tears, pulled Siddharth close to her and went to her room and locked it. Time to sort her life, she thought. She had postponed this moment enough, thinking that she must sacrifice her happiness for her son's sake. But enough was enough. She could no longer ruin her life and that of her son's for a man who did not value his family enough to clean up his act.

The next day dawned and her husband woke up as if nothing had happened and started calling out her name. But there was no reply. First, he thought she might be in the bath. But then, an hour passed. She was still nowhere to be seen. And where was their son? He was not there either. Where on earth had she gone with him? Then fear began to rise in him like bile. When he was not drunk, he was a different man. The man she had loved so very much. After searching for her, he spotted the little note peeking from under her pillow. It was for him.

'Amit,' it said, 'I am sick and tired of your drinking and your careless ways. All these years I hoped you would change, but now I have no ounce of hope left in me. And I am not going to allow you to ruin my son's life. So I am taking him away, far away from you. I want him to grow into a fine young man, full of promise, love and goodness. I want to give him a life you could not, cannot ever give him. And I don't want him to see you again.'

The story does not end here. The little boy turned out to be everything she had wanted him to be. And his mother? She is a decisive woman today, at peace with her decision to end a story that had no promise, to begin another that, like her son, keeps growing new joys everyday.

*Sonali Brahma*

# Raindrops

Raindrops kiss my car window and a few drops trickle down, as if trying to win a race, one faster than the other. I hold one of them on the tip of my finger. But it soon flows out, finding its destination.

I see her stretch her arms, trying to embrace whatever she can of this love from the heavens. Her face is held high, facing the skies. It glistens with the raindrops and a smile that refuses to die.

Meet Meera. She has been selling flowers at traffic signals for a few years now. Every evening she has to tour the nearby graveyard and collect flowers from the tombstones—and steal the memories, some happy, some wilted of loved ones and sell them to others. The sun has scorched her skin and the harsh light penetrates her unseeing eyes. She envisions colours flashing before her eyes at times—green and blue when she is in the graveyard, pink when she smells flowers, and grey when she is selling them.

But the only colour she really sees is black.

Once, as she sat by the pavement clutching the earnings from the day, she met an angel. His paternal touch fell like drops of healing water on her scarred, mud-covered skin. He was a florist who had been observing her talent for identifying flowers by their mere fragrance. He took her under her wing and let her be around fresh flowers in his shop during the day and, in the evening, he sent her to an evening school for the blind.

Now, every evening as she leaves the shop for school, she stops by the graveyard from where she used to steal flowers from tombstones, this time in gratitude that she does not need to steal those precious blooms of love anymore.

Now, meet Radha. There she is, banging at my car window, selling a newspaper at a signal, just like many others. But she isn't merely selling the newspaper. She doesn't just tell me, 'newspaper lelo,' or 'aaj ki taaza khabar'. She actually reads out the headlines, talks about some hot Bollywood gossip, and even sports! Her face is bright with wisdom.

I am stumped by the entrepreneurial skills she demonstrates just to sell a two-rupee newspaper at a signal. Not only this, she has small plastic bags that contain change for various denominations of money. Her resourcefulness is exemplary.

Meera and Radha are like the raindrops that trickled down my window but each has a destination of their own. There are many more such real stories of courage that animate grime-stained young faces and fragile frames but stay undiscovered and wait in vain to be heard and shared. Those few seconds before the signal turns green, there's a lot that we miss in the chaos and commotion outside our windows. All we need is to capture these little raindrops and give them a direction. Listen to them as they whisper, 'I wait here for you to give me more than just a coin. With an open palm, I wait for yours ...'

*Vaishali Shroff*

# On a Sun-Baked Terrace

Right from my childhood, I had ambitions to pursue medicine or engineering. My family is educated and very open-minded but my father was keen that I finish my studies and marry. As I set out to become an engineer or a doctor, my father discouraged me from following either of the professions. But then he was always defining rules and this time I decided to do what I wanted to do.

When I was twelve, my family moved to Maharashtra and I could not because I did not know Marathi and would have had to appear for a compulsory Marathi paper in Class 10. I chose to stay in Chennai along with my uncle, his wife, two children, and grandparents. Slowly, I began to feel unwelcome and things came to a head when the arguments became ugly.

One night, after a particularly violent argument, I cried endlessly. Then, the time came for my board exams. It was hard to find a place where I could sit quietly and study. So, I crept away to sit on the sun-baked terrace to study and none of the hardships deterred me from doing well and studying. My Class 10 board results were good and I got into the much-longed-for science stream. First milestone achieved! Then came the time for the Class 12 board exam and I would study in the garage or on the terrace under the water tank. Today, my tenacity boggles my head especially when I remember how I once suddenly ran a high fever and passed out and there was no one except my grandfather by my side. But such odds made my resolve to make something of my life stronger.

My mother could not spend as much time with me because her duties as a wife controlled her life. And my father had his own issues, though I know in his own way, he loves me a lot. Those four years saw me focused on my goals. There were no extracurricular activities, no outings, except for when my parents came. There were times I'd simply sit alone and cry, cry, and cry, praying for courage and patience. I found ways to grow. I learned a whole lot about managing and living in the real world on my own. Learning to ride a bicycle was empowering and I felt as if I was taking charge of my life.

I got a hundred per cent in maths in my exams and my average in the other subjects was also ninety per cent and above. But the joy was short-lived because it was tough to get admission in colleges in states one had not studied in. In one case, I was even told that my university was not a recognised one and my board marks were not relevant! During this period, I went through a lot of sadness and loss of confidence.

Then one day I decided to write to Rajiv Gandhi who was then the prime minister of India. I wrote that I was a brilliant student, that India was one country and yet I was not able to get admission on the basis of divisions that I could not understand. After posting that letter, I forgot about it and got admission in a college in Nagpur. Then one day, my mother called me and told me that Punjab University has directed a college to give me a seat that I could take up now or the next year. There was no end to my joy. The joy of getting admission in a good college and above that was the joy of getting the better of a divisive system. Today, I am a senior area manager in a multinational company and have overcome many challenges with the knowledge that if I had not taken the decision to follow my dreams, my success would not have followed me home.

*Sonia Sant*

# Fire-Engine Courage

Though frail and emaciated, Vimla seems to have an inexplicable inner strength, which comes from real battles and relentless strife. She attributes it, however, to her work with a local NGO. That indeed was a happy twist in an otherwise convoluted tale of pain and misery.

Vimla was married off at fourteen and had her first child at sixteen. She must be about thirty now, but the years have not been kind to her.

Her husband works as a house painter but his work brings in occasional money and long periods of uncertainty. She stays with her family in a small room which serves as a home. The family bathes in the kitchen and has no access to a toilet. From her meagre wages, she pays Rs 700 as rent and shells out Rs 300 for the electricity.

After her fourth child, Vimla realised the importance of family planning and getting in touch with an NGO for women like her was the beginning of her inner awakening. After giving birth to three children at home, she went to the hospital to make sure she would never get pregnant again. She knows what she missed out on and how education could have changed her life and her determination to keep her children in school against all odds has only strengthened with time. Her children study at the municipal school where they get a noon snack, and aso help out at the NGO. Vimla does some quilting work at the NGO from 11 a.m. to 6 p.m., and occasionally carries her work home.

Dehumanising urbanisation has leached rural areas of its populace and Vimla knows she can never go back to her village. 'There is nothing in the village,' she says. 'No land, no cattle and more than that they do not let the girls study there.'

More than poverty, she wants to fight ignorance that disempowered her. 'I want my girls to study and be smart and not foolish and ignorant like I was. They should be able to make the choices, I wasn't,' says she. Her deepest regret is that the freedom to make her own choices could never be hers. 'I did not study so I did not understand many things. My daughters will study and be intelligent and aware. I know they are studying in municipal schools but I tell them to work hard because then their life will change. I love all my children but I love my daughters more. I want to make them strong.'

For someone who could have been scarred for life by her travails, Vimla displays delightful positivity as she says, 'Everything is destiny but I am going to work as hard as possible to change it.' Nothing about her is submissive. Not the red polyester saree, the red, printed polyester blouse and yes, the bright, red lipstick that announces to the world that she is a woman with a fire-engine's courage. It does not matter that her red saree and blouse are the only pair she owns. She washes it in the night and wears it to work in the morning. Like a badge of hope and courage. Her dangling trinkets make merry music like her laughter and I realise as she walks away that sometimes the word 'heroism' has the wrong gender. And that sometimes a hero can walk in your life in a cheap, red sari and an untold story of homespun grit.

*Anu Chopra*

# Prayer Puff Girl

In 2005, my mother—after battling a long illness—had slipped into a coma. She lay on the threshold of death, hanging by a thread on life support. Every day threw up a new medical complication—one more bed sore, thrombosed veins from long-stay canulas, fluctuating blood sugar and blood pressure, low saturation. A constant series of stomach-knotting emergencies over three months. To the hospital staff and some doctors, we were people who had long over-stayed our welcome. One doctor remarked during his rounds of the ward, 'Oh! Mrs Bijur is still here? Maybe we should build a separate section just for her.'

My mother thankfully was deep in a coma, insulated from such hurtful taunts. To me, it felt like someone had pushed a knife into my already bruised heart, and was twisting it spitefully. After three years of hospitalisation, painful gangrene, dialysis, an amputation, a failed vascular surgery and now a coma that sucked every bit of dignity from my mother's life, I felt hopelessly inadequate to handle this new insult. How much longer was it all to last, I wondered, and not for the first time. Prayers would not form on my lips. If out of habit a prayerful entreaty escaped my lips, the words sounded hollow.

I did what seemed like the only option: I went back to

school, to the Sisters of Cluny, who had taught me to pray. I had suffered a crisis of faith. Their faith was rock solid and enduring. I knew they could intercede and pray for my mother.

To say that I got an admission into my school on the basis of a 'little white lie' would not be far from the truth. My mother was watching us two girls, my sister and me, fast outgrowing play school. No one at home, least of all her husband, my father, seemed to want to send us to a regular school in a hurry.

I think my father fancied a rather unconventional education for us, but my mother would have none of this new-age ideas. Plus, she was the only one among her three siblings who was not schooled at a convent. So, she couldn't think of any other school for us but a convent.

Prompted by other mothers who were far ahead of her in the admissions race, my mother landed up at the school on a day when an entrance test was being held for the boys. Admission tests were long over for the girls. We were waiting near the parlour, she told me many years later, when a Sister came out, saw my mother and me, and said, 'Oh, didn't you come yesterday? Please come this way, but I hope your daughter won't mind sitting with the boys for a test.'

My mother answered for me, and I was blissfully unaware of my complicity in her plan. So we went along with Sister, I cleared the test and how that incident came to pass is still a mystery that only my mother, the Sister and their God know. That was in 1974.

Sister Marie Therese, the principal of my school, came to see my mother at the hospital one evening. I think in that little prayer session, my mother and the Sisters of Cluny and their God made their peace, and the little white lie was deleted from that great balance sheet of sins and good acts.

My faith in prayer was reposed although I still was a long way off from forming even a remotely prayerful plea. My mother passed away a fortnight later. But since that day, prayer has come back slowly but surely in my life.

The good, bad and ugly as prescribed by all those many years of moral science lessons, assembly speeches, prayer meetings are cast in stone for me. I must confess here that when I pray, it is not always for the most important issues like world peace and eradication of hunger. I pray for that too. But I also pray that I do not get stuck in a traffic jam or get delayed for an assignment. I pray that my cook does not take unscheduled leave when I have an important early morning meeting to attend, and that my presentation goes well.

I was once asked by a distant relative, if I shouldn't reserve God's intervention for more befitting things. Little does she know that at school we challenged long-established weather systems and diverted the course of the monsoons, only so that we could have a rain-free sports day, which we have, with a certain impudence to the weatherman, held slap bang in the middle of the monsoon, for all these years. We've prayed for electricity supply to be restored in the middle of a teacher's day concert, we've prayed for the health of our students, their parents and our extended families, to reverse disease, misfortune and all manner of obstacles that the fates dare strew in our paths.

So there's a prayer in my heart and a song on my lips always. Those hymns we learnt in school are a memory mainstay and I have caught myself humming them unselfconsciously, as if a musical entreaty will finally move the Great God on High, if not my rather out-of-practice soprano voice. There is a steely tenacity and an endurance in me now that survives the small wrongs and the big tragedies with the belief that this too shall pass. And if all should fail, I always have a prayer as the final bail out.

*Anupama Bijur*

# Mamo's Faith

'Please be careful and come back in one piece. You are the only one I have.' These are the words that Mamo says before I leave home everyday.

Mamo has taught me a lot by just being herself. She has taught me to be independent, to always believe in myself and, above all, to have faith. She has a very different aura, my mother. Mamo, as I call her, has always been my pillar of support, the one who nurtured my thoughts, believed that I could do the impossible, and smiled for me through excruciating pain and sorrow.

She exemplifies the phrase, 'A woman's heart is like an ocean and can hold a million emotions'. I tell her very often that, 'God made you when he had a lot of patience and spare time!'

Mamo's life has always been full of struggles since childhood. As a child, she wore a single set of school uniform for almost three years and then began to work from the age of thirteen to help reduce the burden on her family. She worked three jobs not just to earn her college fees but to fend for her family. The most brilliant in the family, her dreams of becoming a doctor could not be fulfilled because she could not afford the fees. Her bad luck did not cease here. Her family's non-cooperation caused her to lose an IAS seat, in spite of clearing the first two exams with flying colours. This did not deter her, for she continued studying and, today, is the most qualified in the family. Mamo's ambitious flight was grounded, however, before take-off with an early marriage at the age of twenty-two, though she still pursued her education.

Destiny had a lot of turmoil in store for her and an unhappy marriage followed. Owing to physical abuse, she lost her first child and three more after that. She had no one to talk to, no one to tell what she was going through.

Mamo was almost driven to the point of suicide when she decided to own her life and make her own decisions. That's when she moved out of her husband's house. A brief reconciliation with her husband followed and the only good that emerged from the brief idyll, says Mamo, was me, her only surviving child. Mamo says I gave her the hope to live on.

She showered me with unconditional love and fulfilled every wish of mine. Mamo made sure that I got everything that she did not as a child. We were happy as a family; just the two of us. There came a point after which Mamo never went back to my father and never looked back because she wanted me to be different. She wanted me to live freely and without any fear or sorrow. With time, I became everything she had hoped I would be. I became all the children Mamo had lost. As I grew, so did Mamo's happiness.

Today, twenty-eight years down the line, I have established myself as one of the very few female bike stunt specialists in the country. And Mamo feels proud when someone tells her, 'Hey, your daughter did that stunt really well!' She enjoys watching me give competition to guys on the road and off it. She always encourages me to challenge myself and not limit myself. Though Mamo regrets not living her own life fully, ironically, she also considers herself blessed and thanks God for giving her ample opportunities to grow stronger.

Most of all, she is grateful for me. Today it is because of her that I know how priceless a gift life is and that we all need to value it irrespective of what lies behind or ahead of us. For many of us, life is like a bed of thorns but somewhere we fail to remember that it is the thorns that guard a beautiful rose. Each one of us women is a unique, beautiful rose, and once we know that, we will flower and fill the world with a joyous fragrance.

*Dominique Toretto*

# Enough

Once again my friend Sanjana sat before me with blood-shot eyes. She didn't need to tell me what had happened. Another fight, as had been the norm in the last few months. Her relationship with her fiancé had become strained since her future mother-in-law decided to impede the impending marriage of her only son.

The reasons were crystal clear. She was unable to let go of him, unable to accept not being the only woman in his life, unable to see him go to someone other than her for advice, support and love. The man in question wanted to change the woman he had fallen in love with and wanted her to play his version of her, no questions asked.

After months of silent agony, Sanjana handed me an email she had drafted. 'It's my final communication to him. I can't take it anymore. My health, family and self-respect are getting affected by this. It's not fair to punish them for my inability to end a stagnant and suffocating relationship,' she said.

The letter read, 'You know, you were never present when your mom and I were alone. You don't know what was spoken or done. You heard both of us but you defended your mother at all times. I guess you believe that it is your duty as a son to always see her point-of-view.

'I like meeting people as I am a people's person. It is

natural for a woman to connect with others and make that small yet important difference in someone's life even if it is for a short while. You grudge me that, you want me to be at your beck and call 24/7, have no life of my own just because I am a woman you are going to marry. I won't do it anymore. I owe it to myself to be the woman I am, to do what I want to do, wear and say what I want to and meet whom I want. I know my limits, my upbringing has been the same as yours, yet I give you your space as an individual. Where's mine?

'I met a twenty-one-year-old today who told me matter-of-factly about his twenty-nine-year-old girlfriend. There was no awkwardness. This guy didn't need to tell me. But he did. What hit me was that I have never been acknowledged in your life. I never hid you. Why should I? I made a choice that I was proud of. And I believe that I was not doing something wrong. But I never got that strength and courage of conviction from you. You felt you were betraying your parents if you gave me that standing even though I never forced you to be with me, and it was your choice all along.

'I don't regret anything—the time spent with you, the person I became for you and the hope I had for us. But I don't want to live each day harbouring helplessness or lamenting the growing distance between us, because in doing that I am only harming myself. You were my entire world. But it is time to move on to a newer one. There will be times I will remember you, but then time will heal that too. I know for sure I can't live like this for the rest of my life. I wish you well and thank you for being a part of my life. The chapter you lorded over is over. A new one will soon unfold and I am ready for it. It is a woman's nature to be soft yet strong, dependable yet vulnerable, to give yet to know when it is time to take.'

Sanjana had finally decided to take her share from life and I looked at her with a surge of respect. It was as if she had grown into a woman and decided to steer her own life on a new path, one which this time would not be marked by tears or scarred by one-sided sacrifices. One where Sanjana would not be reduced to a shadow, but become a real woman reaching out for the sun.

*Hemant Patil*

# Willpower Inc.

The first time I saw Shernaz Poonekar, she was at a social gathering, had fallen off her wheelchair and was trying to get back on without any help. At our next meeting, she was counseling a spouse on understanding the needs of her recently disabled husband. That was three years ago and even today I can never tell what this gutsy lady will do next. A lifetime's disability or let us just say, special ability, has only spurred her on to live her life to the fullest and to make a positive difference in the lives of others.

Spirited and indomitable are adjectives coined for Shernaz. She has won the 1978 Indian Arjuna Award for sports (in the disabled category), is a world-class athlete who has won twelve gold, three silver and six bronze medals at international sports events. This is not all. She has dedicated herself to the betterment of the disabled, drives a three-wheeler, nurtures a healthy daughter and enjoys a full life.

None of this was easy for her, especially at a time when the differently-abled were openly discriminated against. But her mother, Gover Irani, was the driving force behind her daughter's success right from the start. While most schools pointedly refused to admit Shernaz, Gover saw to it that she went to a regular school.

By the time Shernaz was ten, she had accepted that she

would never walk again. But not wanting to miss out on anything, she would drag herself on the floor to play catch and cook with other able-bodied kids.

Her meeting Dr Jeroo Manchershaw, a physiotherapist, became instrumental in her rehabilitation. She advised Shernaz that, since she was never going to walk again, it was more sensible to strengthen her arms. So Shernaz did the only thing she had learnt to do. Everything. She lifted weights, swam with her hands rather than her legs, and did hand exercises. She involved herself in special sports where she competed against boys in swimming, short put, discus throw, 100-metre-wheelchair races and javelin.

Shernaz went on to win many international championships. 'At my first international games at Tel Aviv, I lost miserably. After my many wins at Mumbai, I had thought that I would win international medals easily, but the reality hit me hard. An Italian coach told me not to give up after my defeat since I had strong arms and it was just a matter of time before I won. Those words encouraged me to forge ahead,' recounts Shernaz. Thereafter there was no looking back for her. The American Wheel Chair Games in 1977–78 saw her win four gold, four silver and four bronze medals.

Her father modified a three-wheeler for her but locked and put it away because he felt it was too risky for Shernaz to ride. But his rebellious daughter had other plans. She broke the lock in more ways than one and moved to another city to live on her own, away from her sheltered life. 'I should be able to take care of myself before I get married and have a family. I didn't want to be a burden on anyone, be it my family or husband,' was Shernaz's thought at the time.

Later she married a surgeon in the army, five years younger to her. When it came to starting a family, she was told that age and her disability would make carrying a baby to term or even conceiving difficult. But for Shernaz, this was just another challenge to overcome. She went right ahead and had a healthy, normal, baby girl.

A diabetic who has had a mild heart attack, Shernaz till date has no time for self-pity or hopelessness. Instead she uses her life and achievements to inspire others. The last twenty-eight years have seen her counsel parents, spouses and specially-abled people regarding general and specific situations, acceptance issues, rehabilitation and more. She also provides wheelchairs, crutches and calipers, and medication to those who cannot afford it.

When she looks back, she realises that, 'A family must accept disablity as an opportunity and not as an impediment. Specially-abled children need to be taught everything that able-bodied kids learn. They must be taught to be independent in the smallest of things, right from bathing and dressing themselves.'

Today people seek her guidance because she has shown that real ability has nothing to do with body and a lot more with how you use your life. 'Have a zest for life and a strong will and nothing will stop you,' she says. And as always, Shernaz Poonekar knows what she is talking about.

*Khursheed Dinshaw*

# The Here and Now of Memory

Today, it takes all her concentration to just shell peas. If she stops even for a few seconds her mind blanks out and she looks in surprise at the peas on her lap, wondering what they are and how they got there in the first place. Shelling peas is one of the few activities that my mother can still perform. It's a strange disease, Alzheimer's, for it takes away the one thing that defines you—your memory. Everything you learnt from the time you were a child, you now begin to unlearn. In under a year, she's forgotten how to cook, how to wear a saree, how to dress herself, how to bathe and how to brush her teeth.

Watching television was one of her favourite activities. Today she's forgotten how to handle the remote control, how to switch on the lights, how to fold clothes, how to eat from a plate, how to read in any language, even how to speak! Bizarre! There is no other word for it. And, we've been informed that soon she will unlearn how to go to the toilet, how to rinse her mouth, how to swallow and how to even walk. A kind doctor explained to us that it was like the opposite of growing up. Just like a child learns something new every day, an adult with Alzheimer's unlearns all that she has learnt in a lifetime, one step at a time. My mother is only sixty-four years old. Sometimes, the unfairness of it all makes me very angry.

I sink into a strange depression, but most of the time, I try to follow my younger brother who says that we should learn to accept our lot in life and try to make the best of it. My mother looks at us sometimes like she has no clue who we are but most of the time there is a flicker of recognition, and there is still comfort in our company. And, then there is the blank expression, which could mean anything or nothing.

The woman who single-handedly raised two kids, put them through school and college, looks into the mirror in confusion. She can't recognise the real from the image.

My mother, probably like most mothers, is a super hero. Our father died when I was fourteen and my brother was eleven, and she raised us with a single-minded dedication. She could speak, read and write in five languages and was learning a sixth in her forties and taking exams. She was an excellent singer and sang in four languages. Won prizes for singing at every competition. Her greatest regret was that she could not pursue classical music. She tried really hard to get us to learn music and dance. Since we had the aptitude for neither, we dropped out soon enough and she didn't insist. She didn't insist too much on marks and grades. She wanted us to have fun. She had a great thirst for information and knowledge. She read everything she could lay her hands on. We subscribed to three film magazines and two news magazines. She bought weekly magazines in Malayalam, Tamil and Kannada and got lifestyle magazines and glossies in English from her office library. And she read the daily newspaper cover to cover. She was a current affairs expert and got most of the answers to the TV show Quiz Time right. 'Remember that Daniel Ortega is being opposed by Violetta Chamora. It's an important development,' she had told me when I was preparing for my annual school quiz in Class 10. Needless to say, Nicaraguan politics didn't figure anywhere in the quiz, but I couldn't help boasting to everyone that my mother knew everything there was to know in the world, including developments in countries we didn't even know existed. Today she can't speak a single language. Words are an alien concept to her. And yet, when we sing an old and familiar song to her, she looks like she remembers it.

How is it possible to erase a lifetime of memories? Millions of fragments and shards stored somewhere in the brain? I have no clue. I only know that at the end of the day, it doesn't matter. It doesn't matter that she doesn't remember. It doesn't matter that she can't tell us stories like she used to. It doesn't matter that she can't go out with us like most other mothers or advise us when we are confused and troubled. We, her children, have left our childhood behind and have been transformed into her guardians. We look after her like we would a child that needs to be cared for. We sing old songs to comfort her, crack corny jokes hoping she'll laugh. Today we have reconciled ourselves to the fact that her disease is not reversible. She's lived a full life. She is loved and is cared for. Her abilities or what she remembers are not important. The fact that she is our mother and that we love her and want her to be comfortable and happy is the only thing that counts. By forgetting her memories, my mother has rekindled ours and made her presence in our past and our present more vivid than ever. Now each day arrives as a gift because she exists even if her memory does not.

*Nirmala Ravindran*

# Mother Courage

During my years in Mumbai, Drs Joe and Mary D'Souza
were very well-known in the suburbs fronting the wide
expanse of the Arabian Sea. Their beach-front chamber was
often referred to as Dr Albert Schweitzer's den by adoring
patients. Like the famous missionary physician of Africa, the
doctor couple's compassion and diagnostic skills drew patients
from all over Mumbai and from all walks of life. From
industrialists, film stars down to the poor fisherfolk of
Koliwada and middle-class clients like us, all got the same
warm, compassionate treatment from them. Their most
endearing quality was that, even after forty years in the
profession, they had not developed the hard crust of
impersonal detachment which often makes doctors immune
to the psychological and emotional needs of patients.

It so happened that my mother-in-law lay in a coma after
a brain stroke and Dr Joe D'Souza volunteered to come home
twice a week to check on her. We were overwhelmed by his
kindness, knowing very well what a busy schedule he kept.
But this story is not about the good doctor: it is about an
incident he narrated to me.

That particular morning when the doctor came home, his
usual bonhomie was missing and he looked a little
preoccupied. I followed him to the door, silently praying that

everything was alright with him. He must have felt my concern, and without any preamble he answered my unasked query. He was very worried about one of his patients, a three-year-old boy stricken with a rare stream of leukemia. The child's father, a well-known industrialist, had spared no efforts and cost to save his only child. But doctors all over the world gave the same verdict. There were no happy tidings in store for this family. As a healer with immense experience, Dr D'Souza knew that the chances of the child's survival were nil and it was a just a matter of days before the game was up. 'But it's the mother I'm worried about. She just refuses to accept the reality. She is convinced her child will live because God has told her so.' For the first time the doctor appeared helpless. Along with her family members, he was now more worried about the mother and was looking for means to shield her from the impending tragedy and trauma.

A few days later, the doctor came on his weekly visit to check my mother-in-law. After he finished with her, he turned towards me and said, 'I want to tell you about a most amazing experience I have had.' Since my last encounter with him, his little patient and his mother had given me sleepless nights, so even before the doctor could finish I blurted out, 'Is the child alright?' The doctor smiled and said, 'The answer to that is something you will have to draw from what I am going to tell you.'

After he had spoken to me last, the doctor got a call from his young patient's house in the wee hours of the morning. A calm voice said, 'Doctor, it's all over. Could you please come over?' It was the voice of the child's mother.

The doctor did not have the nerve to face the mother alone, so he requested his wife to accompany him. When they entered the room, the little child lay on his mother's lap as if a lullaby had put him to sleep. The mother sat quietly stroking the child's hair. 'Doctor, I told you my child will not die, How can my faith be wrong? See how His words have come true!'

The doctor did not want to break her heart and thought that if this was how she wanted to keep her equilibrium, so be it. As he got up to leave after some time, the mother's next words took his breath away. She said, 'Doctor, you must be thinking I am being delusional. No, I'm not. For the first time I've accepted the reality. My child is no longer living in this body but I knew that he would remain with me somehow. And he has. Today, a dear friend has delivered a baby boy.'

The good doctor took his leave but I was shaken to the core. My grandmother's belief that faith can move mountains and that a complete surrender to a higher power opens the third eye of human consciousness made a tentative entry into my being, though, to be honest, I did not fully comprehend the stoic faith of the bereaved mother till decades later when I met a young woman at a meditation centre in Bangalore.

As a freelance writer, I was visiting the centre to write a story about how young and restless Indians were turning to their spiritual roots to gain control of their lives and emotions. After the meditation session, I interviewed a group of young people, all doing exceedingly well in their chosen professions. While I was speaking to them, a young woman in her late twenties attracted my attention. I had never seen her before in the ashram. There was an unmistakable aura of peace and serenity about her that perfectly blended with the ambience of the ashram. I approached her to ask her a few questions and opened the conversation with a, 'Are you a software professional?' Before she could answer, her mother standing next to her spoke up, 'No, she is just a mother.'

I asked next if they were first-time visitors to the centre. It was the daughter who spoke this time. They were long-time devotees of meditation and believed in having a spiritual discipline in life. She was from Hyderabad and had come to

Bangalore for the medical treatment of her two-year-old child. Politely, I asked how the child was doing now.

Her answer took me years back in time when she said, 'My child passed away yesterday. In my meditation, I saw him in an angel's lap, playing and laughing. No sign of pain. He appeared very happy.'

And the mother smiled. She seemed happy too. This time, I had no choice but to believe that faith is bigger than loss and that when a mother chooses hope over sorrow, she does so not because she is weak but because she is stronger than anything that life can throw at her.

*Sanghmitra Paal*

# Never Fear

Framed in silver is a photograph of a four-year-old girl with a cat on her lap. The lap of the girl is too small for the cat, a Turkish Angora, who sits regally as only a cat can, even in the smallest of spaces. The photograph is in black and white, and the little girl's dark, curly ringlets complement the dark poetry of the cat.

What the viewer of the photograph does not know is that the girl has had the cat on her lap all afternoon and has refused lunch, refused to go back home from her grandmother's, braved the urge to go to the bathroom, all so that she does not disturb the cat. Her parents have given up and gone home hoping that when they come back in the evening, the cat would have jumped off so that they can at last take their daughter home.

One day this little girl was sitting by the fireplace in her home in Sweden and was looking at the pictures in an encyclopaedia. She looked at one picture and pointed it out to her mother, who looked at it and then at her and said, 'Yes, I know you will go there one day and never come back.' The picture was of the river Ganga with an accompanying write-up on India. My mother's journey to a strange unknown country must have begun then. It was a journey that ended many years later with her ashes immersed in that river.

But this is not my mother's story. It is not about her life in India. It is about the immense inner strength and compassion of an individual who, with a smiling face, braved two traumatic marriages, a deep, spiritual crisis and almost terminal cancer. An inner strength and will-power that no spiritual guru can take credit for. Her greatest gifts to me were courage, and a determination to smile and live life no matter how bleak or how short.

When she was diagnosed with grade four, stage three endometrial cancer, my mother made me sit down and listen. I had been avoiding this 'talk' with her, because I knew she was going to tell me that she was going to die, and I, nearly twenty then, did not want to listen to her. If she did not talk about it, I thought, perhaps, she would not die.

I blocked out every thought of her death. It was in the garden one afternoon when she finally insisted on the talk.

'Look, Amma, you are not going to die,' I said, before she could say anything. I was shivering under a blazing sun. I was biting my tongue so that the pain would stop me from crying. I did not want her to see me cry.

The fear I felt was crippling. Panic surged through my head. How would I, the cats and the dog manage without her? The cats who loved her so much and would cuddle with her all the time? Memories of childhood flashed by. A kitten she had saved when I was a little girl. A pup I had brought home and she had welcomed. An injured raven that she nursed and taught to fly again. Our numerous animal rescues over the years. We had several cats and a dog at the time of her diagnosis. Would I be able to look after them as well as she had?

She smiled and told me that the cancer was very serious and that her death was a very real possibility, she would naturally fight it with the best treatment even though it was diagnosed in an advanced state. She also told me that she was very peaceful about it. There was no denial, no rationalisations and no intellectualising. Just a calm acceptance. She told me that death was nothing to fear, it was merely a transition, a change of clothes. Death would never change what we had. Death would not stop the love she had for me. I know that this is what anyone remotely spiritual says. However it is the way she said it. It was really not a big deal for her. It calmed me. It made me begin to accept the possibility of her going away.

She worried for me, yes. She hoped that I would complete my Master's degree, get a good job and be independent. 'Never depend on a man,' she told me. 'Never be in a situation where you have to justify asking for a few hundred rupees from your husband. Don't marry if you do not want to. Have friends, but do not tie yourself to someone just because everyone says that you must get married. Pursue your interests, build a career and be independent, man or no man,' she added.

The months that followed saw her in and out of painful radiotherapy and chemotherapy sessions. After four months, the cancer lost. Her tumor, when operated, was only a centimetre of dead tissue. The doctors were surprised but happy. They had not expected her to live. She remained cancer free for five years after that in excellent health. Then one day she fell inexplicably ill. No diagnosis could be made and she was gone in three days.

In her last hours on the ventilator, I repeated to myself the conversation we had had. I smiled at her and told her that it was okay and she could go if she wanted to. I would be okay and I promised to look after all the cats, the dog and myself.

When I returned from the hospital, I saw Meera, one of our cats, with her paws around my mother's photo, her face nuzzling it. She had never done that before. The next day Chitti, our black cat, began to hysterically tear the skin off her paws. I picked her up, hugged her and told her that I was her mother now and we all would be fine.

Looking back, I know that on the afternoon of our 'talk', she gave me the greatest gifts a mother can give her daughter—the gift of courage that is always within.

She remained fearless till the end and gave me part of that fearlessness, not just to face her death but to face anything that came my way. I did fall into a black abyss after her death but I never forgot her words. There will never be a day when I do not miss her. If I speak about her to anyone, the tears will flow, even now, six years later. That is not my weakness. It is the sorrow of not being able to show her that I kept my promise to her. Maybe she knows, anyway. But it is this that I would like to share with you. If everything that can go wrong in your life does, be fearless. If you are fearless, nothing—not even death—can conquer you. You will walk proud and a smile will never leave your face.

*Yasmine Claire*

# A Long Walk Home

If something is to go wrong, it will. Or so, Murphy's Law says. I had hoped though that the 'something' in question wouldn't turn out to be my life itself.

So we, three business partners, once classmates and good friends, were now seated in a chartered accountant's office to dissolve the interior design business we had nurtured for five years. Samir turned to me and asked me if I really wanted to do it. After all, this venture was my brainchild. I'd been compelled to sacrifice my engineering degree in its final semester to start this business. I was the sole bread-winner for my modest family of four and this was my only source of income. And starting afresh at such a juncture appeared to be a proposition out of question for a girl like me, who had walked on an artificial leg since childhood.

Yet I was firm. I had been let down by another person I had once trusted to supervise my sites but who, in fact, had subjected me to untold harassment. Without another thought, I grabbed the dissolution contract and signed it.

On the way back home, my mind began contemplating repercussions of this inevitable decision. All the brand equity, all the goodwill that our business had built up over years must have possibly gone down the drain the second I signed those papers. How was I going to survive in the future? How was I going to start my new enterprise? For inspiration, I turned to look at how I started my life, twenty-seven years back.

Born to a family that had prepared itself to welcome a baby boy, I was left to grow up on my own—unattended and unwelcome. Naturally, at the very first opportunity available to them, my parents flew abroad with my infant brother, carelessly leaving me behind alone in the hands of destiny. An unmarried aunt paid for all my bills and expenses. Possibly there was something of her own isolation that she could see in my fate. Caring neighbours peeped into the house often to check if I was still alive. Of course, I was. A six-year period of preparing my own food, washing dishes and doing laundry, cleaning the home, studying, preparing myself for school and coming back home safely to the horrors of a lonely night passed. I loved the awe and praise that the onlookers showered on me, too young to realise that all this was not normal.

But there was more to come. One fine day, on my way back from school, I met with an accident while crossing the railway tracks. I lost my right leg thus, at the age of nine.

Amongst hordes of known and unknown visitors, social activists, relatives and friends, my parents too visited me at the hospital. They had a flight to catch back at the very hour my second immediate surgery was scheduled. Something deep within instructed that there was a long battle waiting ahead. My aunt carried me to Rajasthan to get the famed 'Jaipur Foot' installed. I began walking and running normally within a month of using my prosthesis. Guess we shouldn't boast about braveries we commit simply because life does not leave us with an alternative anyway.

Those were my adolescent years—my body height increased every few months and though cracks in the prosthesis cut through my flesh every day, it wasn't practically possible to visit Jaipur and have the leg replaced that often . . . especially when someone who wasn't responsible for my life and birth would have to bear the expenses for it. Thereby I used to limp through, till the difference between my real and artificial leg measured a good few inches in height.

In spite of brilliance at academics and fine arts, an over-cautious school management denied me entry into even basic sports that I applied to participate in. At an hour when socialisation and external encouragement mattered the most, I withdrew to explore an inner spiritual world . . . and lived there totally secluded from the outer environment till long after.

I had another surgery on the leg during the crucial higher secondary year of education. Subsequent bed-rest for several months ensured that I couldn't earn enough credits to enter architecture, despite burning the midnight oil in the final term. But 'Never say die' is what life had taught me. And I admitted myself to the degree course for construction engineering. By now a guilty father,.who had returned from his overseas pursuits, agreed to pay the curriculum fees.

Little did I suspect that he had spent away all his remaining fortunes on living a larger lifestyle than he could afford, and had now returned to India, expecting that his investment in my higher studies would oblige me to feed him and the family forever thereafter. Back then, this very urgency of supporting the family I had never had sparked off the idea to enter business. But today, that business stood dissolved. I dared not ask myself if my family would stand by me in this low phase.

Expectedly, it did not and so I left home one day with the confidence that if a six-year-old girl could survive alone, why couldn't I? My new enterprise took off successfully. The workforce of our old firm followed me loyally, contributing extra work hours at their own will. Goodwill, reputation and market credit followed suit. Somewhere along the way, everyone saw their own triumph in my perseverance. Four years since then, I've bought a house that doubles up as my office in suburban Mumbai. The office of an unfortunate engineering dropout that ambitious architects seek employment in. I live in this apartment now with my aunt who had supported me, and yes, the family still visits often.

Whatever Murphy's Law might say, in the midst of every struggle, I somehow suspected that something would still go right. It always remained my first thought. And so in life, beware of what you think. Because what you think about most intensely, is the only truth.

*Aamrapali Bhogle*

# The Medicine of Faith

My story is not about the triumph of good over evil. It's a story about the power of faith.

It is about the moment when every door in life closes and we feel completely drained of all feelings, and the moment when we turn to God, reconnect with Him and suddenly everything seems to fall into place.

I have not been a religious person but I do believe in living right. When my husband got a great job in Dubai, we moved there with all the excitement and eagerness that comes with moving base to a new country, but little did we know how we would be tested in the near future. My husband was in the Merchant Navy then, and we had sailed together with both the kids for a long while. After my elder son went to the third grade, we had decided I would not sail as his studies were getting affected. So I had lived alone often with my sons and had handled many of life's situations on my own, but I was not prepared for what I went through in Dubai.

My husband had gone to Chennai for work and my older son, who was twelve years old then, woke up complaining of a stomach ache. It was 22 May. I gave him some jeera water and asked him to miss school for a day and rest at home. The next day he went to school, but soon I received a call that he had developed stomach pain and wanted to go home. I picked him up and he went to sleep at home and all seemed well. He seemed fine on 24th morning, which happened to be his birthday, but when he came back from school that evening, he could barely walk.

He came home in tears, and was running a high temperature. After he removed his uniform, I gasped in shock. His knees and ankles were swollen and red and he had a million red spots all over his legs. I was in cold panic, and for a moment did not know what to do. He just could not walk and collapsed. Picking him up in my arms and asking my younger son, who was just seven then, to not open the door to strangers, I rushed him to a hospital near my house. The pediatrician was almost as jittery as me on seeing my son. A series of tests were conducted. Soon the reports came and the doctor informed me that my son had rheumatoid fever and needed to be hospitalised. I had heard of this disease but did not know what it meant exactly. She went on to tell me that I had to administer penicillin injections to my son for the rest of his life if he did not improve. The final straw came when she told me that he had a heart problem. I was in a state of shock. I called my husband and he said he would fly home immediately.

After another battery of tests, a heart specialist saw the reports and declared that my son had no heart problem. Same hospital but two versions! Still in shock, I immediately took him to a renowned pediatrician in another hospital, who again conducted tests and completely ruled out rheumatoid fever. She said my son had Henoch Schonlein Purpura (HSP) and so he was given medication accordingly. This is a relatively rare condition and, if not treated quickly, could affect the kidneys. All through this my son had severe stomach pain and abdominal cramps and was on an I.V. drip. The next day, my husband arrived and decided to fly us to Mumbai as we were scared and confused because of all these conflicting diagnoses of my son's illness. Even with so much pain, my son never once complained or cried. On seeing his strength, I gained the courage to not break down either.

We drove to Lilavati Hospital, in Mumbai, directly from the airport. The senior doctor there confirmed that my son had HSP and the treatment continued. She said that there was a slight chance of it manifesting again within a year. My son still had the red dots all over his legs as his blood capillaries were affected.

I was under much stress and decided to take him to my parents' home in Coimbatore. My mother is an alternative healer and she encouraged me and my son to meditate. The medication continued, as did the meditation, and soon we began to see some positive results. My son recovered and has not had a relapse ever again. He is completely cured. I still remember being all knotted up for one year and panicking every time he complained of stomach pain or had a fever. But, every time he recovered, I began to believe in miracles that we were too preoccupied to notice before. We all meditate and pray as a family even today. This episode also made me relish and appreciate all the relationships and blessings I have in my life.

I am not an atheist but I never had the time or inclination to think of God or thank His grace for all I have. I needed a jolt in my life to realise that, at the end of the day, we need to listen to our spirit when our mind is screaming in fear. I have realised that peace of mind is just a prayer away.

*Kala Raju*

# Angels with Fur

Here are a few things one must know about cats. They are not dogs. Every cat is a unique individual, but all share some traits. They are grooming fiends, obsessive, compulsive cleanliness freaks and hate dirty litter trays. They love on their terms, never on yours, and are otherwise pretty straightforward beings.

If they love you, they will show it. If they don't, by God, you will know it. And they are fiercely protective about the children in their human families. I should know, because every time I raise my voice at my son, Bella, my cat, leaves which ever cushion she is snoozing on to bite my hand in no uncertain terms. And this ain't no love bite. It has teeth and purpose.

All these lessons are relatively new because for a long time I did not know much about the cat universe that exists in the haze beyond my gaze. Cats never intruded in my version of existence till one day my eleven-year-old fell in love with a stray. I passed the two of them by occasionally, trying not to get sucked into the sticky, sweet, compulsive bond that sometimes develops between animals and humans where one babytalks and the other fidgets in embarrassment. Having lost a stray pet as a child, I wanted no part of this hopeless, heart-breaking love.

I remained fastidiously aloof. Even when my son pleaded, 'Ma, see how she is sitting in my lap? See how she likes being tickled under her chin? How soft her tummy is?' I inched close tentatively once or twice but could not bring myself to touch her.

Then Snowy came home and I decided to lock eyes with her. I kneeled to reach her eye level and she looked at me intently. When I nodded, she came over and changed my life and made me over, starting with my heart. Snowy wore her heart on her sleeve. Literally. She was a beautiful but emaciated Calico cat with bold patches of brown, white and black and there was an unmistakable heart printed on one of her shoulders. To say that she was a cat would be an understatement. Beneath all the fur and the jelly she carried around, there was also a spirit that recognised mine, one that always said to me, 'What's the big deal? Just let go!' She was receptive to everything around her—to humans, their feelings, their voices and to her own needs. If I was getting irritable, she looked at me with a glance that could not be mistaken for anything other than, 'Tone it down ... will ya?'

You had to behave around this lady who always slept on the pillow designated to her and nowhere else. She never entered the kitchen. Never tampered with things. She would come to the ground floor every morning mewing loudly, and when I opened the door and called out to her, she would climb three steps at a time to reach my second floor apartment. She would immediately go for her bowl, polish off her first meal of the day and then curl up to sleep for an hour or two. She would leave near noon and then reappear again the next morning, exactly at 6.30 a.m.

Then we discovered that she was pregnant. It was the thick of summer and she was restless and moody. She began to come more often and to stay in longer. She began insisting that I put her to sleep. If I was busy at my computer, she would mew loudly and insistently till I came over to her. Then she would fall on her back in delicious abandon, ready to be tickled and stroked. If I didn't oblige, she would jump on the keyboard. She would close her eyes and display more bliss in the few moments she was being stroked under her chin than most human show in their perfectly abundant lives. Sometime later, her three babies, her rather glazy-eyed mate and she made their home in the dump yard of an automobile repair shop opposite our balcony. Maybe she chose the space so that we could keep an eye on her family. We saw her feeding her children till she was spent. She would stroke them, lick their cup-cake faces and only occasionally push them away if she was tired.

The idyll was interrupted when a wild tom cat attacked the kittens. Snowy fought him till he sneaked off limping but then one of her kittens went missing and so did she. My son and I cried occasionally watching her videos, her pictures and tried to rescue the remaining two kittens but could not reach them through the junk.

The heartbreak I had dreaded was here. I talked to her in my head and then one day she was back, tired and wounded, and she slept without food or water for over twelve hours. She left at midnight and we never saw her again. We watched over her two kittens till one of them grew old enough to wander off.

Her mate and the last of the three kittens are almost the same size now and start mewing every morning for a two-egg omelette.

She is gone, I know decisively, but she made space in our home and our hearts for Bella, a pesky little thing who has arrived with her own set of lessons. She is teaching me boundaries though she does not observe any. She is teaching me how incomplete a lady is without fastidious grooming, and that humans make the biggest mistake when they want their version of love to be everyone's.

She is her own mistress and she does not like to be petted much but she follows me every morning throughout the twenty minutes I take in getting ready for office. Then she bites me on my ankle to say goodbye. And this is a love bite though sometimes it hurts just a bit. And when my son does his homework, she likes to be close, just in case he wants something.

I have learnt in the last two years that cats have more emotional poise than humans. That they scratch your wrists but heal your spirit. That they are meditative yogis who need the freedom to just be. And that they are inviolably unique and would prefer it if you did not tamper with that fact. Most of all I have learnt that love must be welcomed, even if, like a cat, it comes unannounced and leaves suddenly.

*Reema Moudgil*

# Green Hope

Tough times do not last, but tough people do. This is not just a quote or a random phrase. It means exactly what it implies. Problems and tough situations are blessings in disguise. They arrive to wake us up to our inner strengths, hitherto untapped potential or undiscovered mental acumen. The tougher a situation, the more resilient the person facing it becomes as she harnesses inner strengths and becomes more centred, aware and focused.

My thoughts race back to a terrifying night ten years ago when I was woken up by an incessantly ringing telephone. Maybe the phone call in retrospect was divine intervention to wake us up and save us from a horrendous end. When I woke up, I found bright flames licking at the front porch of our house. We had sublet the front portion of our house to a garment dealer who had set up shop during Onam. The electric wires passing overhead had short-circuited and the whole shop had gone up in flames and the fire was slowly finding its way towards the rest of the house. I ran out with my daughter and husband, watched the scene, terrified and unable to act.

I called out to my brother, who lived right behind our house, to summon the fire brigade. By the time they arrived, the garment shop was in cinders and the front portion of our beautiful home was charred beyond recognition. Telephone and electric wires needed to be reinstated and the flames had also singed another business complex that belonged to my sister. But luckily the damage was restricted to just the side portion and not the interiors. Our neighbour's plush French windows were shattered as well.

I was too numb to even cry! I was banking heavily on the rent from the small garment shop to tide over a financial crunch, and now not only had that source of income been destroyed, but I would also have to repair the damage done to my home.

The neighbours were magnanimous enough not to ask for compensation but there was the media to face, the electricity board to chase, the officials from the fire department to answer to, and the police to explain the accident to. I needed money desperately to put things right and asked a close relative for help, promising to repay a small amount each month from the meagre teacher's salary I earned, but to no avail.

But God helps those who help themselves. After I had done everything possible to raise some money, help came from a totally unexpected source. My father-in-law lent me or rather sent across some much-needed funds. My pride had not allowed me to ask him but the money came when I needed it most.

I began to set my house in order by employing people who would repaint and refurbish the house and clean out the charred remnants of the accident from the grounds. An inch-by-inch walk to your goal is usually a cinch and slowly but surely I managed to divert my salary and other savings towards renovation. My brother-in-law, a hardware businessman, pitched in and slashed prices on cans of paint.

I braved the relentless reconstruction all alone but I am proud to say that I learnt to trust myself and I realised that

I am strong and not the shrinking violet I had assumed myself to be.

I discovered deep reserves of confidence, inner strength, peace and calm that I had not known earlier. And soon my house looked more beautiful than ever and the charred tree in the yard started growing green leaves all over again. A new lease of life! Yes, a new lease of life for me too and an awakening of sorts. If it had not been for that unfortunate incident, I would never have realised that I have a strong heart and a spirit that refuses to give up.

Today, years later, I still think of that horrendous night but not with regret. It was a hard nudge from the Divine, asking me to wake up and be aware that when life throws me a ball, I had better be ready to catch it. I have leased the house since and have gone to another city in search of new and varied experiences. I now face every situation with the awareness that God does not give us any situation that we cannot handle. The tough times did not last after all. I did.

*Valsala Menon*

# When Silence Is Not Golden

It was raining so hard you could barely hear the sound of those pair of feet as they hurried down the road. Finally, they reached their destination as they entered a well-kept house, right at the end of the road.

'There you are Ruchi,' smiled the mistress of the house as she opened the door. But the smile was short-lived, as Ruchi lifted the hem of her sari to reveal the bruised skin on her feet. She had been beaten again by her husband.

What would you do, if Ruchi worked for you? The lady of the house decided that it was time to go beyond mere sympathy and do something for her house help. Within days, she enrolled Ruchi into an institute to learn a beautician's course so that she could rebuild her life. Ruchi poured her heart into her new challenge even as she continued to help around the house.

'Now, I did pay half the fees for Ruchi's course,' the lady in question told me, the day I heard this story from her. 'But the other half I made her pay from her own pocket. You see, I did not want her to be totally dependent on me. Besides, the money she was paying herself would make her work harder!'

And their hard work paid off. Today, Ruchi is a successful beautician in town. And her pocket, may I mention, contains a lot more than that small amount of money she once had.

She is today an empowered, fulfilled woman and she sure has made the woman who changed her life very proud of her!

Instead of putting up with an intolerable situation, both women did something about it, but they are not the only ones doing it. I recently heard another story where a domestic worker and her daughters used to be beaten up by the man of the house who was not only an alcoholic but also blew up the money the wife earned. Once the daughters were old enough to protest, they, along with their mother, beat up the man when he tried to raise his voice and his hand! The last I heard, he had cleaned up his act and sobered up. There are many women who go through worse situations, mistaking their silence for resilience, not realising that it takes just one act of courage to break the cycle of abuse and pain.

To be a woman takes more than just the ability to endure. And, you are not a woman till you have learnt to stand up for yourself and say *no*.

*Aparna Srivastava*

# Mother India

Remadevi is not extraordinary. And yet, she is nothing but extraordinary for her mere decision to continue to live. It is brave to die for a cause, but sometimes it is braver to live for it.

Remadevi first hit headlines in November 1995 when she gave birth to five children in a single pregnancy—four girls and a boy. The media celebrated this event with gusto. All the babies were healthy enough to have a good life expectancy and so the media followed their progress for a few days. The happy father was shown choosing dresses and toys in fives and, in general, they were all deliriously happy. The babies were given very similar-sounding names, and they provided enough feature material for magazines from time to time.

When the quintuplets joined school, almost every newspaper in the state showed their photograph on the front page, dressed in identical uniforms, carrying a water bottle and bag each of the same colour, posing in front of the auto-rickshaw that was to take them to school. They were a curiosity everywhere they went, and their father Premkumar became a minor celebrity. He would take all five of them on his arms and shoulders together and ride around on his cycle. He would scold his wife if she ever reprimanded the children about anything. He couldn't bear to watch the pain when the children were being vaccinated against the routine illnesses at the hospital. He was a caring and protective father.

The family initially had had two businesses, a bakery and a stationery shop, both with good turnovers too. But soon, the business went into a dull phase and their income started to dwindle. Then Premkumar contracted a spinal illness which needed expensive treatment. When the medical and living expenses started to rise, the family finances stumbled and finally crashed. They had large debts which they repaid by taking a loan. To salvage the situation, they sold a share of their property and some gold. It was downhill on skids thereafter.

Then they went into the classical debt-trap by borrowing more money on high interest. When the interest was not paid in time, Premkumar was harassed by the lenders and he began to tell his wife that he wanted to die or run away from life.

In February 2005, the family hit the headlines once more. This time, not for a good reason. Premkumar had committed suicide. He solved his problems by just deciding not to hold on any longer. Remadevi was left behind to take up the reins of a family of five children and a bad balance sheet.

Time for some grace under fire, and true grit. She just decided to be there for the kids, no matter what. The woman who depended on a pacemaker attached to her body to keep pace with life decided to not let her husband's suicide disturb their children's lives. She did not lament and curse fate, nor did she blame anybody. She just focused on strengthening the lives of their children, even though she could'nt understand why her husband had killed himself.

She had been a typical housewife, dependent emotionally and financially on her husband, till he gave up on life. After his death, she also discovered that she had a severe heart problem and underwent heart surgery. Her health is now so bad that she cannot carry even light things. But she keeps her strength in front of her children and shows them by example that life is meant to be taken on and not left halfway.

Like Paulo Coelho's Veronica who 'decided to live', this woman too outlived her disappointments and lives on fruitfully. Premkumar chose the easy way out, while Remadevi holds the fort even with fading strength. Life is sometimes unsparing, but the woman who does not give in is the hero of her story and, one day, she will write her own happy ending.

*Suneetha B.*

# Ma

Ma was dying and she knew it. She'd been diagnosed with breast cancer and had her first mastectomy at the age of fifty-five. The biopsy report said 'stage 2-B', which, I learned later, was a euphemism for 'stage 3'. Post-secondaries, her second mastectomy happened three years later, and it was then that she sensed that the end was near. It is more than two years now since she has passed away, but she lives in our memory (and the memory of all who knew and loved her) as the embodiment of love, grace, dignity and beauty.

I remember clearly her determined courage when she was diagnosed with the dreaded disease. My sisters and I just went numb—it was too much to take in all of a sudden; but Ma and Dad, working as a team as always, took prompt action, and without getting into the controversies of second opinions and conflicting advice from different sources, opted for immediate surgery, and by the next evening the diseased organ had been severed away. By that time we had managed to get a grip on ourselves and were concentrating on the task of mentally preparing Ma—and ourselves—for her chemotherapy.

The doctors told us that hers was one of the fastest growing strains of malignancy known to medical science and her chemo medicines were commensurately strong with their equally strong side-effects, apart from the usual debilitation, weight loss, hair fall, etc. They gave her four weeks to recover from surgery before subjecting her to the rigours of chemo. She was up within two, deaf to all protests and admonitions, determined not to be a burden on her two married daughters (or for that matter, on her unmarried one), her sister or her sisters-in law, all of whom had planned to take it in turns to stay with her during her treatment. She spent the next two weeks planning out the running of her home and the hired help, so that there would be the minimum possible disruption in our lives.

This was when we really appreciated the bond between Ma and Dad—the way they synergised their strengths to create a support structure, an almost tangible edifice of love, much stronger than their individual strengths. When her hair fell out overnight, the sight of her beautiful, thick, wavy strands lying in bunches all around her was traumatic, and not just for her. And Dad joked and said, 'You are my true companion, even sharing my increasing baldness,' making her laugh. He then went on to plan the different kinds of wigs and stylish hats he'd buy her, 'So that I can have a beautiful wife with a new look every week', was how he put it.

I feel blessed in the surety that no matter what, we are always there for each other as a family. Even if we are physically absent, we are with each other in spirit, and not just in the clichéd sense. I can find no better illustration of this than the fact that even though I had to accompany my husband to a job posting in the US, halfway through Ma's chemotherapy, I would dream of her frequently. And even though everyone back home made it a point not to let me know when her blood reports were not good, or when she developed extensive skin infection during radiotherapy, or when her finger- and toe-tips and nails degenerated as a side-effect of the chemo, I always knew something was wrong because of my dreams.

I returned from the US fifteen months later, to find her horribly weakened in body, but indomitable as ever in spirit— making all our favourite pickles, drying herbs for our kitchens by the kilogram (I still have the dried mint and the pickles she made for me), cooking delicacies for us when we went over for our weekly visits. Perhaps her biggest joy at that point of time was spending time with my daughter and my sister's son, pampering both her grandchildren with their favourite foods, toys, books (though she was as strict with them as she had been with us about standards of behaviour), and most of all, playing with them like a child. Her biggest worry at the time was my youngest sister's marriage.

At the back of her mind was always this desperate desire to see her happily married and settled in life. In that extremely weakened state too she would draw lists and make us shop for the necessaries of a wedding (in case something materialised, she knew she would'nt be able to handle everything at once in this state). We would protest at the incessant demands she made on herself; she'd always say, 'I want to leave behind pleasant memories. I want you to remember your mother as a positive figure, not as a sick, querulous, weak, old woman. Besides, all this activity keeps my mind off my body's ills.'

And then came the second big shock. After two false alarms (minor tumours that turned out benign, but which nevertheless had to be surgically removed), she was diagnosed with secondary malignancy in her other breast a little more than three years after the first mastectomy. I had gone with her to collect the report, fully expecting a third false alarm, and read the word 'malignant' in the report in a daze, looking at it again and again, willing the whole thing to be just a nightmare. Ma took one look at my face and plucked the report out of my hand.

'It's nothing,' I said, hastily pulling myself together. 'Yes, I can see that on your face,' she said. After she had been examined by the oncologist and the date for pre-operative tests fixed, she said thoughtfully, 'I know I won't live to see your sister's marriage.'

Cutting short my protest, she continued, 'I don't think I have much more to give you all. I just hope the end comes before I become a total burden. But promise me something: there should be no lack at your sister's wedding. And just look after your father as best as you can. Fortunately, he is a very peaceful soul, but he's going to be very lonely. Leaving him alone is going to be the hardest part of dying for me.' Then, she finally broke down.

Nine months later, she was gone. She battled her cancer bravely to the end. The last month in hospital, with the malignancy rapidly spreading to her bones, and then her liver, ravaged her body, but could not daunt her spirit. She would receive all her visitors with a smile and joke with them, enduring the intolerable pain which ultimately necessitated morphia patches. Ten days before her demise, she insisted on celebrating Dad's birthday in hospital, distributing sweets among the doctors, nurses and the paramedical staff.

During her final week, when smiling and banter became physically impossible, she gracefully declined to have visitors in her room. She was most peaceful when Dad was at her side. And that is how she finally died, looking at Dad. Even now, when faced with any problem, it is of her that I think, and as in life, so in death, she never fails me.

*Parul Gupta*

# A Team of Two

Single parenthood is not for the faint-hearted. That about sums it up.

Those who have been on this particular road surely know what I am talking about and will need no explanation past the first two sentences. But to those who find the very idea unthinkable or strange or even unacceptable, may I say that few other paths will lead to such stark self-realisation, nor indeed will the world and the people who you thought of as your own will be so clearly revealed to you.

One may end up raising children alone by several accidents of fate. But those who choose to do so voluntarily are no less than heroes no matter the compulsion that may have driven their decision.

My daughter was a product of pure love, but her father did not feel up to the responsibility and took off. Since I was pathetically in love, I behaved like a pitiful cur around him, even excusing his cavalier behaviour towards us. It pained me greatly when I finally faced up to the fact of the sort of man I had chosen. Yet out of such a marsh was born a pure and beautiful soul and she has been entrusted into my care— a fact that makes me ask, 'What on earth was God thinking!'

I knew raising a child alone needed time-management and sacrifices, but there was to be more.

There was the morbid curiosity of people who suddenly came up and wanted to know how 'she, the little doll', was and whether her father came to visit. They backed off quickly when I told them he doesn't and stressed that our well-being does not depend on it, in fact, we thrive on his indifference! What knocked them off completely was that I didn't seem sad about it at all!

In middle-class areas like the one where I live, it seems the common perception is that the children of 'women like me' grow up by magic or a maid. Therefore my hands-on raising of my daughter puzzled everyone. There were many smirks and asides as they watched me go through the normal routine of school-bus drops and doctor visits. The glamorous actress brought down to middle-class motherhood!

I am thick-skinned to moralistic barbs or preaching, but it's only now, after almost four years of persistent 'normal' parental behaviour, that I am no longer subjected to such nonsense any more. It is also, I believe, a result of the fact that a direct question about my single parenthood will elicit a direct and honest reply and most people don't know how to handle that.

These three years have been a wild roller-coaster ride of the kind not yet invented for common public use. The slightest achievement on the personal or professional front takes me to great zooming roaring heights—because finding and completing an assignment is very tough—and the slightest disappointment plunges me into dark, tunneling opaque depths. And through it all is the constant shadow of loneliness and the echo of empty rooms when I need advice or another voice to help me solve a problem.

Let me explain this a bit. An actor is expected to work for a minimum of fourteen hours a day and crèches don't operate for more than eight. At best they accommodate a child for twelve hours, for extra money. Also, unlike a technician, an actor can't send a replacement even during severe illness.

So when I have an assignment, my typical working day begins at 5 a.m. I cook and pack my daughter's breakfast, lunch, school-tiffin, milk and a snack-box in their respective dabbas. Then I prepare her school bag and my kit for the shoot, after which I wake her up, put her and myself through our respective morning routines and drop her to the crèche between 8 and 8.30 a.m. Then I go to work.

I make it a point to leave the shoot at 7 p.m. to collect her, failing which I am in all sorts of trouble since the crèche shuts down at 8 p.m. We head home, shopping for the next day's requirements on the way. I give her a wash, dinner or milk, whichever she wants, and put her to sleep. Then I wash all the dabbas for use again the next day, iron her uniform, prepare whatever I may need for my shoot, load the washing machine for a quick start the next morning and collapse into bed, always finding that I have forgotten to do something or the other but too tired to get up and do anything about it.

Now that it's been a while since I faced the camera, I do all the housework at a much slower pace and eat too much out of depression and wonder if I will ever set a 5 a.m. alarm again.

What keeps me up and running even through high fevers and bad stomachs and back-aches is my daughter's firm belief that Mama knows everything; and if it is broken Mama will fix it and if it hurts Mama will heal it and if she behaves badly Mama will not hesitate to tell her so. Sometimes I catch her making mistakes just to see if I am paying attention to her. I also catch myself venting my frustrations on her by being tougher on her than required.

I feel really bad when I realise that she and I will never have the benefit of a father-figure who will bring equilibrium to our relationship, who will give her another perspective to her own life and thereby, to mine. That I must be like a kaleidoscope to her, through which she can see all the colours that life has to offer her, a gift that children being raised by both parents take for granted.

I wonder how I am going to see her through math and skating, weekends and annual days, adventure and homework without limiting her vision because there is no one else but me to open up another window. Will she suffer greatly because there is no male point of view to refer to easily or regularly?

These are fears that lie under the bed all night, every night, along with the mundane fears for our financial future, the roof over our heads and the food on our table. Will I be able to provide for us adequately? It is a burden that cannot be contemplated for too long or too often. I am not that strong after all.

I have not been out with friends for years now and over time I have stopped missing the lack of a social life. Sometimes though, when the sounds of a party waft in through the window, I feel sad and am simultaneously repelled by just how pathetic that makes me sound! I have a magnetic sticker on my fridge door that sums up my life's ambition at the moment—it says, 'I don't need a man to keep me happy but a maid is essential'. Maybe then I will be able to catch a late-night movie.

However, I like this time we have together now, regardless of the hardships. I am the centre of my child's universe and she needs no one else around. In time that will change, however, and she will find her own feet and her own friends. But we have had a singular journey together, so far, and I trust it will at least be interesting the rest of the way. And I know that my daughter and I will always make a great team.

*Mona Ambegaonkar*

# On My Own

When the day is done and night falls, and you give up on catching up with chores that never end, do you realise that most of the time was spent in just organising the things that needed to be done, but that the actual doing of them is yet to happen? The good thing is that you are putting into place the things that will make the completion of the task possible. Would you call that an achievement—I stay awake pondering over this and other questions like it.

It took me two years of paying monthly instalments to buy a two-bedroom apartment in Mumbai. I paid for it entirely on my own and furnished it from scratch with loving care.

When my daughter was born, I sold that flat—on very bad advice from her father—and was homeless for six months, living out of suitcases with a newborn baby, going from my sister's place to my mother's, at the mercy of their whims.

One day, my daughter's father called to say that all my things, which had gone into a storage facility owned by his friend, had gone up in smoke. That was my entire life. My computer, with all my files, my notes, my scripts and stories and other ideas for further development; my furniture— beautiful old wooden pieces made of walnut and teak and rosewood, a four-poster bed with brass trimmings that cannot be found for love or money today; my clothes, my entire kitchen, my treadmill—everything was just a pile of ashes. The only things I had managed to save were my books which I had refused to put into storage.

I should have known then that he was planning a ditch since he did not think that news of this magnitude deserved to be delivered in person and had actually begun the conversation on the phone by saying, 'I will tell you something, but only if you promise not to be upset.' And I did not get upset on the phone. I did that later, walking round and round the building in the dark of late evening. Ten years of my life, my own home, wiped out and I was told about it only on condition that I would not be upset—he did not want the burden of my grief.

Ironically, I had been working in my sister's kitchen that same day, watching this huge pall of smoke rising from somewhere in the Jogeshwari area of north Mumbai all morning and had pointed it out to her when she got home. We had both wondered what was causing it and the amount of destruction it so obviously indicated. I had been watching my life burn, in more ways than one, without knowing I was doing so.

Then I began to look in earnest for a home to take my baby to. The dependence on people who could barely contain their impatience with us and their eagerness to see us gone kept me going even though I was recovering very slowly from a C-section and had no one to talk to or hold on to when the going got tough. No kind words from anywhere and the desolation of those months in the confinement of the rooms in my mother and sister's homes, where I was left to tend to my baby in an isolation of disapproval, still fills me with suffocation. I can still feel my head hurt and my eyes swim in tears that sneak up like traitors.

Then I found this flat that I have now been in for over three years.

I still remember the day I took a lift from its previous owner to the bank in Nagpada, north Mumbai, for the signing of the loan papers. My daughter was burning with a 103-degree fever after her BCG vaccination and I had sat in the bank manager's cabin keeping my head down as defence against his barbed remarks, my child crying pitifully for her feed, which I could not offer her there in the cabin, stammering from the strain of it all, having to give her into the arms of the gentleman who was the previous owner—where she proceeded to cry like her heart was broken—long enough to sign the endless cheques and papers and forms.

On the way back, I took a taxi which was hot and smoky and reeked of petrol. No respite here as well, for the driver kept looking in the rear view mirror to try and get a peak at the action while I tried to feed my baby. She kept sobbing through the ordeal and could not even fall asleep because of hunger and the fever. I later realised that her arm was swollen and that must have been hurting too.

I called my daughter's father on the way back. I needed to talk to someone and no one in my family was very sympathetic just then, even though they were supportive. He picked the phone up after a long, long time and after many attempts, and was absolutely not interested in anything I had to say. 'How can I help it?' he said. 'The bank manager didn't like your face, obviously.' I knew then what he was trying to say.

After that I went solo with a vengeance, this time not calling for, nor expecting any support from anyone. Once this deal was done I concentrated on only one thing—getting the flat ready to move into as quickly as possible. And since then, I have built my life with my baby from scratch and the process is ongoing.

I have no job but am busier now than I was when I was working—building a place in the world where I can find the peace and comfort to raise my child properly. I know that in this day and age, money is the key to independence and opportunity. To have enough financial stability in order to give the best opportunities to my child, I decided to rent out this flat—this home that I had fought so hard to make for us and which has cost me so much more than money—and move to my father's house in Nasik which is lying empty and uncared for since the day it was bought.

It was to be a new beginning, almost from scratch again—new school for the baby, new home for us, new friends, new bhajiwala, new everything. But as it turns out, this is not to be either.

And so here I am, busy planning, organising, arranging, and putting things into place ... again and again ... till we have a home and a life we won't have to move out from.

·*Mona Ambegaonkar*

# Sisters-In-Arms

She had run away from home to marry him. She was only eighteen. Her mother, widowed at the age of twenty-three, had raised her and her sister single-handedly on her late father's pension with great difficulty. She had thought that marriage to this man would mean the freedom she never had because of growing up under severe financial constraints. She was wrong.

He had encouraged her to work, as hard as she could, and to also look after the house. She had thought of him, with pleasure, as being liberal and supportive. Soon she was perpetually tired. Running to work, running back home to fulfil familial obligations, meeting social commitments, paying the bills, cooking, cleaning, being a 'good wife' every day, day after day!

On the face of it they were a modern, hip and happy couple. She went to work; he managed 'their' money. She made the house pretty, he encouraged her. They went to parties smiling and looking well-to-do, like a perfect couple; she paid the bills thinking it was an investment into a solid marriage.

They bought an apartment finally. She earned and invested the money; he registered it in his name. The marital album tarnished slowly as realisation dawned that he had no intention of going to work ever and that she was his money-cow and when she protested, he silenced her with a gift of 2.5 gm gold earrings and by playing on years of carefully nurtured emotional and mental dependence. She felt guilty; maybe she had misjudged him—after all true love does not need gold or diamonds to keep it alive, right?

Soon the mental abuse was intolerable and all physical intimacy was lost. She continued in the marriage until the exhaustion got to her—deep in her bones—and she walked out in order to protect the vestiges of life and sanity that still survived in her.

She thought she would get back all that she had put into the marriage once the divorce got through. Big mistake. She is still fighting for divorce and he is still living in the apartment she paid for and it's been twelve years now.

She had the good sense to move on and build her life again. She went back to work after a period but this time she was working and earning for herself. She found a man to love and she has a six-year-old son with him. It's a live-in relationship and works better than her marriage ever did.

Her time is spent raising her son, looking after her home with her companion and earning a living. However, the money she makes is spent on the unending lawsuits she is embroiled in with her husband. Her companion pays the bills because no matter how much she earns, eventually, the lawyer takes it all.

Firstly there is the divorce; secondly she wants her flat and her money that he had been 'managing' all these years; thirdly she is fending off his attempt to gain legal custody of her son; lastly her companion has also been dragged into a lawsuit which accuses her of not only adultery but also polyandry. Her case has finally come up for hearing in the courts and the court sent them to a mediator who asked the man in question why he continued to hang on to a marriage that was long dead. His reply was that he wished her well and therefore hung on hoping she would come back and take up from where they had left off. She looked at him incredulously.

The mediator then asked why he was trying to hold on to a person who didn't want to be with him. Did he honestly think she would come back to him especially since she had already moved on and had a functioning family with another man? He replied that he wanted her companion to transfer his apartment to her name. 'So that you could demand that as well in the divorce settlement?' she asked. He replied that he was worried about her and wanted her to be secure in life. She said, 'In that case, give me back my money and my flat.' He changed the topic and asked for his legal rights as a father to her son. The mediator terminated all further sessions as being unnecessary and ultimately fruitless and has forwarded the case back to the courts.

She has a custodial battle on her hands for her own son because, under the Hindu Marriage Act, the legally-wedded husband of a woman can actually take custody of a child she has had with another man! It is an archaic legal provision that allows 'infertile' men to 'have' children without having to go through the adoption procedure. What is mind-boggling is that the law of the land recognises the biological father as the parent of the child but its biological mother is merely a guardian. So now she has to prove that she actually did give birth to her biological son!

She has been diagnosed with a chronic stomach ailment which her doctor says is psychosomatic. She also has a perpetual pain in the neck, literally. But she smiles and she takes her child out to birthday parties and she works on her live-in relationship and she connects with friends and family and carries on as if all is well.

While she waits for her case to be called in the courtroom

each day, the stories she has encountered on the way are even more unbelievable.

There is a woman once married to a commander who flies for Air India. He fell in love with and married an air hostess, without her knowledge. When she found out, he gave her the 'chance' to 'improve' herself and assured her that he would give up the other woman if she 'came up to mark'. She, poor fool, set about the task and tried to 'come up to mark' within the given time limit set by him. Meanwhile, he gave her a lakh of rupees and got her to sign papers which supposedly 'sealed their pact' but were in fact divorce papers. He kicked her out of their flat, along with their two children, a month later. The lakh of rupees that he had paid her served to be the full extent of the divorce settlement. It is now twenty years since she has been fighting a case for alimony and child support.

Another woman has won her case for financial support from her ex-husband who incidentally used to beat her, but is yet to see a penny of it almost twelve years later. However, she has not lost hope and continues to fight to have the court's orders implemented even though, as the cops have told her on many occasions, being beaten by a man is not a good enough reason to either ask him for divorce or alimony!

The upside of these stories is that all the women have become stronger than they ever thought possible. All three meet at the court house and share their tiffins and jokes and have become friends and comrades-in-arms. They are all sure that justice will be theirs some day, and till that happens, there is a shared meal, stories of courage and resilience, and lots of laughter to keep them going.

*Mona Ambegaonkar*

# Warm Winter

Amrita was knitting a sweater for her granddaughter, another one of her intricate designs. She had, over the past forty years, knitted hundreds of sweaters, so many that she had lost count of them now. Knitting as a hobby was something she picked up from her mother. It was a family tradition percolating down many generations. As she was knitting, her mind flew back to life, twenty years ago.

Amrita and her husband, Ketan, were then nurturing a young family of four children. The eldest was named Kapil, named after Kapil Dev of the Indian cricket team as Ketan was a great fan of the legendary all-rounder. They had two daughters, Anushka and Arpita. The youngest was a son called Kartik.

Ketan was then deputed to Russia for training in designing power plants. He was to stay in Russia for about two years and decided to take his family along. The idea was to give the children exposure to a foreign culture. The only issue was that Ketan suffered from a chronic lung infection and it looked like the equatorial climate of India agreed with him better. Russia, being a cold country, was to prove a nightmare for him and his family.

Over time, they settled down. However, as Ketan spent more time out in the open and was constantly exposed to the elements, his chronic infection started getting worse. He would drive long distances in search for the medication prescribed for his condition but the drugs did not agree with him and turned out to be more damaging than beneficial. Unknown to Amrita and Ketan, the drugs had started affecting his lungs. Like an oil lamp slowly running out of oil, Ketan was running out of life too. Then one day it happened. His lungs collapsed and he died at work.

Ketan had battled and lost to the relentless Russian winter, but for Amrita and her kids, it was the start of an even longer winter. She saw her whole world crumbling around her. She was totally lost and distraught, and had nobody close with whom she could share her anguish. She began her long journey back to India under a pall of gloom.

She figured that the best way her children could get the best education was if she became a teacher at a reputed school. With some preparation and determination on her side, she managed to secure a trainee teacher's job in one of the best schools in the district. As an employee, she managed to get all her four children admitted in the same school.

She had to juggle the needs of four kids of diverse ages, cooking, running the house, taking care of day-to-day chores and work at school. Her resources were getting stretched but she really had no option but to go on. There were bills to pay and a family to care for. Ketan had foresight and had saved good money and some of it was coming in handy now. But Amrita was worried about how far and for how long that money would last.

Her eldest son Kapil was getting ready to go to college. She encouraged him to study hard and make a mark in the competitive exams. She went out of her way to spend money on books and tuitions to aid his success. Kapil managed to do well and get admission to a good college in another city, where he would study science. His leaving the nest for a better future brought happiness but also broke her heart.

Anushka had been a smart kid from her early days. She got admission in one of the best colleges in the state in medicine and Amrita was happy to see her succeed. Being the eldest girl child, Anushka had put in a lot of effort to make Amrita's life easier at home. But now, she too was gone.

Now Amrita had even more expenses to take care of with lesser help at home. Her hair started turning prematurely grey. Work, home, kids and all the responsibilities were taking a toll on her. She now started knitting sweaters and selling them to shops to bring in extra money.

Arpita was an artistic child and she never liked the academic drudgery. Amrita tried to encourage her artistic talents and enrolled her in a dancing school on the condition that she would have to continue doing well in academics too.

After a few years, Kapil got a good job, Anushka performed well in her academics and Arpita flourished at her dancing. She also managed to raise Kartik with all the love she could muster as the sole parent in the house. When Kapil found his job, the family relaxed a bit. Things were finally starting to fall into place. Soon, Anushka also found a good job in one of the state-run hospitals. Over the next few years, Arpita turned out to be a wonderful dancer, winning multiple awards and recognitions, and doing well in academics too. She was now ready to join college and got admission into a computer graduation course.

Soon it was time for Kapil to settle down and after many deliberations and discussions, the marriage was fixed. Amrita saw Anushka find a life partner on her own. Arpita went on to become a software engineer in a reputed company. Kartik finished his engineering and then went on to do an MBA and join a sports company as a marketing executive.

Amrita's life had come full circle. She had a smile on her face as she almost completed knitting her sweater. Like her knitting, she had managed to create a beautiful life for herself and her kids. She felt for the first time that the long winter of her life was over, and now it was time to look forward to spring and summer and the seasons of abundance and celebration. It was time for some well-earned warmth and some well-knitted joy.

*Aditya Prasad*

# To Be Whole Again

28 October 2009.

Bhagirathi Neotia Hospital, Kolkata.

I faintly remember being wheeled out of the operation theatre. Someone was trying to talk to me. I opened my eyes for a few seconds only to close them again. I felt nauseous. All that I wanted at that moment was my husband, Darshan.

A few minutes later, the nurses wheeled me to my room, which I was sharing with four other women. One of them had delivered twins that day. Another was going to deliver and the third one was pregnant, but had started premature bleeding. I was the only one here without a child to deliver.

I remember being helped onto my bed, feeling vulnerable even in my semi-conscious state, naked. I wanted to tell someone to cover me. I tried to open my eyes, but could not. The nurses finally covered me with a blanket and left.

I felt a hand on my forehead. I opened my eyes to see Darshan. I gave him the biggest smile ever. He smiled back at me and told me that everything was okay. I merely nodded. After what seemed like minutes, I asked him what had happened.

His eyes bore deep into mine. For a moment, I thought that he would tell me something really bad. For a moment, I felt that he would try and hide something from me. His silence was scaring me. And then, all of a sudden, he smiled. He told me, 'Everything is fine.'

I gave him a questioning look. I needed answers. Why was no one giving me any?

'What did Dr Rohit say?' I asked. Even Darshan knew that it was time for the truth now.

He looked at me, held my hand and said, 'Your right ovary is stuck to your uterus. Your right tube is blocked. So, basically, your "right side" is now your wrong side. But Dr Rohit has said that your left ovary and tube are perfectly fine. So, you will not have a problem conceiving.'

Shock and silence enveloped me when I heard this. I didn't know whether I was relieved to have finally found out the cause of our failed attempts to conceive or sad that, of all the women in the world, God had chosen me to go through this.

After a few minutes, Darshan left the hospital and promised to come back during the visiting hours. I was left alone with my thoughts. Surprisingly, I did not cry. A part of me found it difficult to accept the reality and a part of me was extremely positive that now nothing would stop us from being parents. That a miracle was just a heartbeat away now.

I took this quiet time to reflect back on the past ten months of my life, when I had visited Genome, a fertility clinic, for the first time. I remembered my fear. I remembered my first trans-vaginal scan. I remembered the pain, when the probe was inserted into my body. I remembered being literally naked before a man who was a stranger, my doctor. I remembered going through my first fallopian-tube test and wincing in pain. I remembered all the injections that I took. I remembered my first IUI, which failed, and the numerous ones after that. I remembered holding onto Darshan and howling and crying all through the night on the first day of my period. I remembered the nervousness while we waited for the results of the blood tests. I remembered sitting amidst the numerous women, of all ages, nursing the hope of being a mother some day. I remembered my husband's love, support and understanding which gave me the will to go on. I remembered my doctor's confidence and the will and courage he gave me to fight the pain and sustain my hope. I remembered the care which the nurses showered on me. I remembered how this place had transformed me from a scared little woman into a confident and positive fighter. And most of all, I remembered the lessons that had helped me understand and value the tiny miracle called 'life' which so many take for granted but for which I was willing to fight till the end. No matter what happened, no matter how many times I fell apart, I gathered myself and was ready for the fight once again.

28 October 2009—the day I went through a laparoscopy, a strong realisation struck me—somewhere, God was giving me the strength to fight through these times. He was there and I was safe. And somewhere, deep down, I realised that the point of falling apart is to become whole again.

And that I was willing to fall apart again and again just for that one moment when I would be whole again.

*Bali D. Sanghvi*

# Aal is Well

Recently, when mulling over a thorny patch in my life, thinking how capricious life can get, I felt a familiar tingling sensation in my nose and dived for the tissues before exploding into sneezes. The sharp sounds of a broom being wielded energetically on the road outside made me wish for the hundredth time that Goda bai, the lady behind the broom, was less enthusiastic about her work. As a perennial sufferer of allergic rhinitis, dusts and pollens are my sworn enemies. As soon as the thought formed, however, I guiltily expunged it, quickly thanking the Almighty for giving Goda bai the wherewithal to perform her tasks. Memories of her past made my personal thorny patch appear much smaller and less sharp, as if Rancho Aamir had put in a guest appearance and was saying 'Aal is well dadu, aal is well'.

Goda bai worked as a labourer in a rural hospital in Marathwada, where I worked and lived. On the rare occasions I saw her, she reminded me of those dark brown, short dolls with fuzzy unkempt hair and flat noses which are really cute, because all dolls are cute. I left the place after an initial stint and returned after several years. One night as we were watching television, Sunita bai, one of our domestic staff, came in dramatically flaying her arms and demanding that we do 'something'. She shrilly demanded that Goda bai be removed from her veranda where she had found her ensconced on going home from work. The visit was not being viewed as neighbourly courtesy since the visitor had recently clawed and bitten her own husband and daughter. Some of Sunita's neighbours (she had organised a lobby group) materialised out of the gloom. Could the boss kindly do the needful and have Goda bai 'put away'? The implications of those words are chilling to the initiated. The need was, however, circumvented by the offender vanishing into the night. Everyone was relieved and dispersed to their homes.

The next day Sunita bai threw light on Goda bai's transformation into public nuisance number one. Goda bai's life had been quite routine, up to a point. Her husband was an unemployed alcoholic and gambler. She earned the family bread doing hard physical labour. This did not give her an elevated status, as it would have her husband. In fact she was regularly beaten for failing to supply money to fund his habits. So far her story runs parallel to most others in her neighbourhood. One fine day, she diverged. She decided she had had enough and left home, not to go to her parental house, for her parents were long dead, or to any other shelter, for there was none, but to the great outdoors, to unlit, silent, village streets. She lived and ate with the other homeless, who in this village are pigs and stray dogs, obviously preferring them to her so-called home. When children ran after her throwing stones and calling her 'yedi'—Marathi for mad—she took serious exception and chased them away, stone for stone, further adding substance to the title of 'madwoman'.

After a while, the people at the hospital heard of her predicament and decided to step in. She was referred to a mental hospital in Pune. She stayed there for a month. Her husband had her discharged on request. He promised to keep her on medication and bring her back for follow-up. True to character, when the medicines finished he did not take her back for more.

Since Goda bai was considered unfit for work, she was started on pension. Her husband being mindful of her mental condition had refined his tactics. Now, instead of raining blows on her when he wanted money, he merely sat on her chest till, at the point of suffocation, she put her thumb impression on the withdrawal form. Probably, to his way of thinking, adopting this method was a considerate spousal thing to do. One day he suggested that she withdraw her provident fund for their son's marriage. The boy worked in Mumbai as a painter, and had received a marriage proposal from a girl's family. The husband said he would make all the wedding arrangements; she only needed to get the money out. Finally, here was one instance where she was happy to comply with his demand. Soon the fund was handed over to him. She started planning for the wedding. However, nothing happened for a long time, so she asked her husband what the delay was due to. The truth was hard to take—he had arranged the wedding elsewhere so that the girl's family would remain ignorant of her mental illness, and not create any awkwardness at the last minute. As a matter of fact, the wedding had already taken place and the newly-married couple had left for Mumbai, without even her blessings, as though she were non-existent or dead.

Goda bai was enraged and showed it. Betrayal the second time around, after a brief period of faith, hurts even more than the first time. She attacked her husband and daughter, and got a heavy stick to destroy everything in the house which smacked of deceit and betrayal—in fact everything did. She then left home for her second long tenure as a 'madwoman'. Kind people who knew her would give her food and clothing. In return she would make a broom out of dried twigs and sweep their compound clean. She would sleep in deserted covered places in winter and that was how she landed up on Sunita's veranda five years later.

Her story was so inhumanly exploitative that it was all I could do to not have her husband and daughter 'put away'. Since that would give only temporary relief, we decided in favour of a more permanent solution viz., to offer treatment for her illness, even though it was a moot point whether she would respond, since she had been unwell for so long. However, nothing ventured, nothing gained, and in her case, even small gains would be useful. So we made the offer through the kind people whom she trusted, and she agreed to meet us. She listened to what we had to say. Then she shut her eyes, bent her head, and joined her hands. Her lips moved soundlessly as we watched spellbound. Was this lady actually praying? Could anyone believe in God after living through hell? It was as though she were consulting a relative before making an important decision. After a while, she opened her eyes and agreed to take treatment. She, however, had a precondition—she would not go to the government-run place since they had been cruel to her during her last admission. If we could treat her ourselves, she was agreeable. We couldn't, but instead we offered to take her to an acceptable place. She was admitted into care at a private facility, where we committed to underwrite the costs.

Having us champion her cause made her relatives, including the renegade husband, regard her with respect. Her daughter took an active role in looking after her, leaving her own household to accompany her for up to six weeks at a time in the mental hospital. By the time she left the hospital, she had forgiven her family. This was the sustainable part of the whole venture—she got her family support back.

After she was discharged, she was given small chores to do around our rural hospital campus as occupational therapy. She was given a nourishing diet and was taken for regular follow-ups. Her response to treatment was so rapid that even the psychiatrist was amazed.

The good times did not end here. Her pension which had been building up was available to her as a lump sum. Furthermore, since her good fairy was in overdrive, the bank made a mistake in the calculation of her monthly pension, and she got paid several times her due. She became a heroine to her people. After one year of this run of good luck, the bank discovered its mistake and stopped the payout completely till such time as they could recover the excess. But by then she had been rehabilitated in society. Ever resourceful, she turned her attention to a plot of land she had obtained under the Bhoodaan movement and got busy cleaning and cultivating it. This was the other sustainable change that occurred—she had something which would always be a source of supplementary income.

She stopped medication after two years of treatment, though she had been advised to continue it lifelong, since the medicines made her feel very weak. The decision to undergo therapy was hers, so we allowed her to stop, but requested that she agree to restart if it became necessary. She agreed, and is still doing well two yeas after cessation of treatment. Her husband passed away during this time, which in my opinion played a vital role in sustaining the improvement to her mental health! Her son has materialized on the scene and visits or financially helps her off and on. She continues to potter around the campus, feeling protected.

When I compared her response to treatment with that of some others, I found that she beat them hollow. How did this happen? To my mind, just as the cruelty inflicted on her by her family made her feel like a stray animal, so also the affirmation she received from us gave her inner strength and equanimity ('Aal is well Dadu, Aal is well') and acted as bonus therapy. In addition, her abiding faith in God, which remained constant despite everything, protected her through her worst crises, and accelerated the healing process.

A couple of lessons can be gleaned from this. The first is that though Goda bai's case is an extreme example, almost all of us are guilty of exploiting those we love in some way or another, belittling them in many small or big ways, sometimes scarring them for life. Many people find it easier to be kind to others than to their own families. A little affirmation from us towards our spouses, children, siblings and parents would go a long way in making them feel secure and able to meet life's challenges confidently. It would also reduce the underlying despair which exists in many homes, and prevent the sort of crises which make news headlines.

Secondly, when we are faced with situations which call for involvement and action on behalf of someone else, but the task seems too gargantuan to take on and the likely outcome is uncertain, we need to remember that taking the first step is often all that is required. The energy within us which prompts us to respond to the need of others is also active in other people, and if we all do our bit in a timely manner, seemingly impossible things are achieved. This has been proved true many times. The more often we get involved, the easier it gets each time.

Rancho Aamir should have coined another mantra as well, 'Aal can be well dadu, aal can be well—just take the first step'.

*Renu Dyalchand*

# More Chicken Soup?

Share your heart with the rest of the world. If you have a story, poem or article (your own or someone else's) that you feel belongs in a future volume of Chicken Soup for the Indian Soul, please email us at cs.indiansoul@westland-tata.com or send it to:

Westland Ltd
S-35A, 3rd Floor
Green Park Main Market
New Delhi 110 016

We will make sure that you and the author are credited for the contribution. Thank you!

# Contributors

**Yusuf Arakkal** is one of the leading lights of contemporary art. He has won a sweep of international, national and state awards and is today at home anywhere in the world. He writes, paints and lives in a world full of light and laughter. He can be reached at yusufarakkal1@gmail.com.

**Shweta Bagai** honed her writing skills during the seven years she spent as an international development consultant for the World Bank, many companies and NGOs in the US, Africa and India. She maintains a blog where she explores the conflicts, the dualisms and the spaces in between the lives of traditional vs. progressive Indian women such as herself. She loves words, the sea, the skies, and a few things in between. She can be contacted at shweta.bagai@gmail.com.

**Raksha Bharadia** is the editor of the bestselling *Chicken Soup for the Indian Soul, Chicken Soup for the Indian Teenage Soul* and *Chicken Soup for the Indian Armed Forces Soul.* She is author of *Me: A Handbook for Life* and *Roots and Wings.*

**Aamrapali Bhogle** is the founder-proprietor of a Mumbai-based architecture and interior design firm. An active volunteer at many social service non-profits, this home-maker enjoys spirituality through photography, sculpture and deep silence. She can be reached at aamrapalibhogle@gmail.com.

**Anupama Bijur** is a Bangalore-based writer and journalist who has, in her own words, written on 'everything but war'. When she is not writing or at her day-time job as the Bangalore bureau chief for Magna Publishing Co Ltd, a publishing house with nine lifestyle magazines, she can be found in coffee shops, checking out bags or running a weekend gourmet 'soup kitchen' for the many fans of her cooking. She can be contacted at anupamabijur@gmail.com.

What makes women happy and sad? How do women tackle situations, crises, and life in general? These are some of life's questions of perennial interest to **Sonali Brahma**. She vouches for the strength of women's minds and, through her stories, seeks to pay a tribute to this quality and to inspire others. She loves to write and read, lend an ear to people in need, and be a good mother to her son. She also writes advertising copy and teaches creative writing to young student managers at B-schools. Reach her at copycaat@gmail.com and www.sonalibrahma.com.

**Harneet Brar** comes from an Army background with both her grandfathers and father having served the Indian Army with pride. Educated in various schools in different parts of India, she completed her post-graduation from Punjab University. She served for eight years in the CISF before taking to school teaching. She is married, has two daughters and her hobby is to get her hands on all the good books she can possibly read in one lifetime! She can be reached at harneetbrarasla@gmail.com.

**Dr Shoma A. Chatterjee** is a freelance journalist, film critic and author of sixteen published titles comprising seven books on Indian cinema, five on gender issues, three short story collections and one book on urban history. She holds two Masters' degrees—one in Economics and one in Education besides a Doctorate in History. She has travelled widely to make presentations on gender, cinema and literature. She lives in Kolkata with her husband.

**Saswati Chaudhuri** has been writing since childhood. Poetry and writing are her lifeline even though she has taken up art as a profession. She also did a short-term professional writing course from IGNOU in 2004. Since then, she has been writing articles on art for magazines, book reviews, web interviews of senior artists, poems and short stories for Bengali and English magazines. Her series of art books (practical and theory) for children was published in 2004, and is still being used in schools. She can be reached at saswatichaudhuri5@gmail.com.

**Rishi Chhibber** lives in San Jose, California with his wife and two children. He is a software engineer by education and profession. When not working, he enjoys spending time with his kids, and when they go to sleep, he sketches, reads, writes, and photographs—in that order. He can be reached at rishi_c@hotmail.com.

**Anu Chopra** is a writer based in Ahmedabad. She has published a book of short stories called *Scattered Thoughts* and loves reading, especially women-centric Indian fiction. She can be contacted at anuchopra77@gmail.com.

**Vibha Chowdhary** studied at Modern High School, Kolkata, and subsequently majored in Political Science from Loreto College, Kolkata. She is married and has two children—her family is her biggest pride and joy. In 2004, she moved to London from Ahmedabad to help her husband set up a paper recycling business and now juggles schedules between the UK and India, managing the company's accounts and finances. An avid photographer, her Nikon D60 is her constant companion.

**Yasmine Claire** lives in Bangalore with her husband, several cats and two dogs. She hopes that one day trees will replace malls. Till then, she is busy re-interpreting fairy tales, reading, teaching and letting her garden run as wild as it pleases. She can be reached at claireyasmine@gmail.com.

**Mahesh Dattani** is a playwright, stage director and film maker currently living in Mumbai. In 1998, he was awarded the Sahitya Akademi award for his collection of plays. He is also a columnist for *The Week* magazine. He can be reached at mahesh.dattani@gmail.com.

**Shashi Deshpande** is the author of ten novels, four books for children and a book of essays. She also has to her credit several volumes of short stories and translations from Kannada and Marathi into English. Three of her novels have received awards, including the Sahitya Akademi award for *That Long Silence*. Shashi Deshpande is married, has two sons and lives in Bangalore with her pathologist husband. She can be reached at shashideshpande04@gmail.com.

**Jaya Kaushish Dhawan** lives in New Delhi, India. She holds a Bachelor's degree from Jesus and Mary College, New Delhi, and a Master's Degree in Broadcast Journalism from Boston University, US. She has worked with various filmmakers and companies in the US and India, helping create documentaries, docu-dramas, lifestyle shows and Bollywood programming. Jaya is now planning to make a documentary on her own. She can be contacted at jaya.dhawan@gmail.com.

**Anjuli Dhiman** is a company secretary by qualification and currently works as assistant general manager with SEBI. She moved to Mumbai from Dehradun and loves to write. She is working on a book and hopes that she will be able to complete it soon. She can be contacted at desdemona.d@gmail.com.

**Khursheed Dinshaw** is a Pune-based freelance writer with more than 526 published articles in major Indian newspapers and magazines. An avid traveller, she writes on lifestyle, travel, health, food, trends, people and culture. She has also undertaken editing for publications and can be reached at khursheeddinshaw@hotmail.com.

**Darshana Doshi** is a freelance writer from Mumbai. She has written for *Times of India*, *Mid-Day*, Rediff.com and IndianTelevision.com for about five years. She was editor of a film magazine, a humour magazine and a weekly newspaper run by private publishers. She is currently working on books and scripts and can be reached at darshanadoshi2007@yahoo.co.in.

Daydreamer. Writer. Chocoholic. Chick-flick lover. And above all, mother. **Baisali Chatterjee Dutt** is all those and more. She shares a common passion with her two little boys—climbing. They climb curtains and furniture; she climbs walls. She can be reached at baisali.cd@gmail.com.

After working at several clinical disciplines, **Renu Dyalchand** launched into public health work in the rural and urban slum sectors, and was privileged to observe people and lifestyles in many states of India. Community work introduced her to the socio-economic, cultural and political determinants of health and what it takes to make different people feel 'whole'. She likes reading, writing, observing nature, watching movies, eating good food, and spending time with her family.

**Kanan Gautam** started her career as a transmission executive with Akashvani Shimla in 1988. She has written poetry and short articles for national magazines and newspapers. After 1992, she has been concentrating fully on her children and teaching career. She loves dealing with young minds, listening to music, dabbling in crafts, cooking for her family and painting her heart out. She can be reached at kanangautam@gmail.com.

**Aarthi Gunnupuri** used to be an advertising copywriter and briefly worked in television. She is now a freelance writer and the only thing she's currently pursuing is her love for writing. She can be contacted at aarthi.gunnupuri@gmail.com.

**Rani Rao Innes** trains English language teachers from about fifteen European countries and trains corporate clients and government officers in communication and soft skills. She travels extensively and helps train teachers of a school for underprivileged children. She has also been associated with theatre for over thirty years, first as production manager of TIPS in Tokyo and later as a director of Canterbury Players for twelve years. She also founded Spandana, a Bangalore-based theatre group, thirty years ago. She can be reached at raninnes@aol.com.

**Seetal Iyer** is an RJ and group programme director with a radio outfit. She enjoys interpreting the world with a quirky point-of-view, mentoring new talent, seeing the best in everything and everyone, smelling roses and coffee, making friends across the air waves and living life light. She lives in Bangalore and can be contacted at seetali@gmail.com.

**Resmi Jaimon** is an international freelance writer, blogger and copywriter with published clips in sixty-nine print and online publications on varied topics including travel, trade, technology, career, business, lifestyle, food etc. for publications in India and abroad. Spiritually inclined, she lives with her husband in Kochi, Kerala. She blogs at http://resmi-jaimon.blogspot.com and http://indian-chronicle.blogspot.com. Her website is www.resmijaimon.com and email, resmi.writer@gmail.com.

After studying Philosophy, **C.F. John** was initiated in Art under Jyothi Sahi at Silvepura, Bangalore. John has also been organising site/theme-specific art events using installations, dance and photography, and has had over thirty-five major group shows in India and abroad. He has won three national awards and two international awards and been selected by BBC Radio-3 as one among twelve artists internationally whose individual approaches have led to innovations in their field. Get in touch at cfjohn23@gmail.com.

**Roma Kapadia** is a freelance lifestyle journalist, is extremely passionate about her work, an avid reader, loves to cook and likes living life with a sense of aesthetics. She believes in the power of one and is always up to exploring varied avenues and challenges. She can be contacted at roma.kapadia@hotmail.com.

**Lavanya Karthik** lives in Mumbai with her husband and daughter, where she writes, draws and daydreams of a world that is cleaner, greener and more appreciative of her negligible singing skills. She trained as an architect and consulted on environmental management for over a decade, before finding her true calling—making fun of her friends and family through her comics and verse.

**Radhika Meganathan** is the author of twelve picture books for children, with twenty more under production. Her articles and feature stories have been published in more than fifty publications around the world. She is the author of the award-winning Golden Mythology Series for kids by Seasons Books and is the copyeditor of *Ramayana*, a graphic novel published by Chandamama Publications. She currently lives in London, attending screenwriting classes at

City Lit University. Her website is www.radhikameganathan.com and she blogs at http://writerintransit.blogspot.com.

**Lalitha Menon** is a corporate trainer, a Science graduate and has a diploma in International Tourism Management, another diploma in Front Office Management and the IRDA 100-hours course from LIC of India. She has also taught in South Africa and was a manager in a highly reputed clinical laboratory in Kerala. She can be contacted at lalithamenon632@gmail.com. She blogs at http://makeadifference-makeadifference.blogspot.com.

**Valsala Menon** currently works as an editor for Ability Foundation's magazine *Success and Ability* in Chennai. She is also a freelance journalist, contributing to leading dailies like the *New Indian Express* and *Times of India*. She is passionate about writing and is currently working on a novel. She can be reached at valsala.menon@yahoo.com.

**Parvathy Mohan** is an IT engineer who has wandered very far from her home turf in search of adventures. She writes in search of her true self, is optimistic, thoughtful and observant, and believes that everyone has a tale to tell. She can be reached at thrayambakaa@gmail.com.

**Sreeti Mondol** runs a company called *Memories of a Butterfly (MOAB)—Design in Beads*. She creates resplendent bead curtains for her happy clients. She can be contacted at sreeti@gmail.com.

**Madhavi Mone** is a homemaker who enjoys reading books on philosophy.

**Pooja Nair** is a happy-go-lucky girl who likes to see the sunnier side of things. Writing is her hobby as well as passion. One of her short stories has been published in a collection titled *Inner Voices*. She writes regularly for Indian weeklies and e-zines. She moonlighted as a film reporter some years back and has also dabbled in copy-writing. Currently, she is working as a lead technical writer for an IT company in Pune. She can be reached at istroller2010@gmail.com.

**Shalini Nambiar**, director, Excelsior American School, Gurgaon, is one of those people who takes life as a challenge and meets it with a lot of zeal and enthusiasm. An educationist to the core, she says, 'If I am able to make a difference to the life of a child, that would be my biggest achievement and would give me immense satisfaction at the end of the day'. Shalini totally devotes herself to her profession which is also her passion.

**Averil Nunes** is a student who is currently researching truth, meaning, love, faith and beauty in the laboratory of life. Maybe one day she'll figure it all out, and write and illustrate a book about her experiments. In the meantime, you can exchange a word or two with her at averil.nunes@gmail.com.

**Sanghmitra Paal** graduated in History and Economics from Delhi University and did her post-graduation in Journalism from Bombay University. She has worked for *Freepress Journal* and *Industrial Times* (Mumbai) and has been writing for major English language dailies and magazines on diverse issues. Recently, she edited a book on the rise of Islamic culture along the Silk Route. She is currently waiting a publication breakthrough for her first novel based on the Indo-China war of 1962. She lives in Bangalore with her husband and daughter. She can be reached at sangmitra.paal@gmail.com.

**Hemant Patil** is a Pune-based lifestyle and architectural photographer. He has worked with leading advertising agencies and business houses across the country and also captured the moods of a few leading industrial scions of India on film. His work has received wide recognition and acclaim and has featured in leading interior design magazines. Having extensively travelled across India and abroad, Hemant has recorded his journeys with photographs. For more details, visit www.hemantpatil.com.

**Carol Pereira** is currently an independent PR consultant and communications professional. Having been a business journalist for over ten years, with marquee brands, she has found her calling to build her own set-up from scratch. She currently provides integrated communications, with personal service and attention-to-detail in social media PR, internal content, digital marketing and creative services for emerging brands across multiple sectors. She can be reached at carol.pepereira78@gmail.com.

**Harini Prakash** resides in Mumbai with her husband and two children. She works for the Indian government, and during her spare time, writes a blog on food called Tongue Ticklers and another one with random musings called Trivial Thoughts. She enjoys writing, reading, photography and spending time with her family. She can be contacted at sunshinemomsblog@gmail.com.

**Shruthi Venkatesh Prakash** is a qualified dentist but it is her love for music that has given her a truly satisfying career in radio. She is currently the PD of a regional satellite radio station. She continues being an RJ and writes occasionally. She loves travelling, reading and cooking. Her long term wish is to start an eye-care facility along with her husband that aims at delivering cost-effective and affordable eye-care to economically weaker patients. She can be contacted at shruthi.prakash@gmail.com.

**Kala Raju** lives with her two sons and husband in Mumbai. Her hobbies include oil painting, reading and dancing. During her stay in Dubai, she painted an oil canvas for the Ministry of Education. Making friends comes naturally to her and she loves to be surrounded by friends and family. She is currently building her online real-estate and construction business. Passionate about life, she believes in living life to the fullest. She can be reached at kalaraju1970@gmail.com.

**Nirmala Ravindran** is a writer and theatre director. She lives in Bangalore and writes on art and culture for *India Today*. She has directed six plays in the last twelve years, two of which have been children's plays. She also conducts theatre and arts appreciation workshops for both children and adults. She can be reached at nimi.ravindran@gmail.com.

**Soni Razdan** is a well known actress living in Mumbai. She studied acting at the Guildhall School of Music and Drama in London in the Seventies, after which she returned to India to pursue her acting career there, which continues till date. She appeared in the path-breaking TV series *Buniyaad*, as well as the cult cinema classic *Saraansh*, among many other films. She directed her first film, *Nazar*, in 2005 and is in the middle of writing several scripts that she will be directing in the future.

**Sonia Sant**'s life journey so far has been inspired by strong and determined women—her mother, maternal and paternal grandmothers. She is an engineer, a wife and mother and believes that her success would not have been possible without her husband's support and the unconditional support of friends. She can be contacted at santsoni@gmail.com.

**Naini Setalvad** is a nutritionist, health and obesity consultant, columnist for *DNA*, *Life Positive*, *Upper Crust*, *Cooking More*, *Savvy* and *Times of India*. She is also a nutrition consultant for Marico, Piramal Pharma, Mother Earth, International Prune Council, California Pistachios and more. She can be contacted at healthforyou@nainisetalvad.com.

**Aditi Shah** lives in Mumbai and works with a wealth management company, handling operations—accounts and administration. She dabbles in pottery, sketching and painting, though finding time to pursue her passions is a struggle! She can be contacted at aditishah75@gmail.com.

**Parul Sharma** is a writer who lives in Mumbai with her family. *Bringing Up Vasu—That First Year* is her first book. She loves rock music, animals, travel and books, but is unsure of the order. Her aim is to look for wit and wisdom in everyday things and sometimes she even succeeds. To distract herself, Parul writes a blog at http://orangeicecandy.blogspot.com. She likes hearing from people and can be reached at parulsharma1503@gmail.com. At some point in her life, she would like to run an animal shelter.

**Vaishali Shroff** writes to keep her heart beating while juggling a job as an independent, marketing and business development consultant and managing family. She currently lives in Pune with her husband and son. Although she started with an anthology of short stories for children, she is currently writing scripts for children's movies. She paints, plays the guitar, dabbles in poetry, Haiku and enjoys making sense of the world through various creative pursuits. She can be contacted at vaishali.shroff@gmail.com.

**Navtej Sibia** is a water-colour artist and teacher. She writes poetry in Hindi, loves a good joke, watching films and spending time with family and friends. She can be contacted at teji6668@yahoo.com.

**Puneet Srivastava** is currently based in Mumbai and writes on business management, entrepreneurship and excellence. He can be contacted at puneet500@gmail.com.

**Dominique Torreto** has finished her Bachelor's degree in Pharmacy and is currently working with an automobile magazine. In her spare time, she likes spending time with her family and pets. She loves photography and is very fond of automobiles as well.

**Suparna Thombare** works as a journalist for a national newspaper in Mumbai. She has dabbled with city news, feature stories and currently writes stories on music and entertainment. Born and brought up in Pune, she graduated in English Literature from Fergusson College, Pune, before she moved to Mumbai to study journalism at the Xavier Institute of Communications in 2003. She has also been working on her first collection of poetry to be published next year. She can be contacted at suparnaa@gmail.com.

# Permissions